THE HOUSE THAT RYERSON BUILT

Essays in Education to Mark Ontario's Bicentennial

Edited by
Hugh Oliver, Mark Holmes, & Ian Winchester

OISE Press/The Ontario Institute for Studies in Education

Ministry of Education, Ontario
Information Centre, 13th Floor,
Mowat Block, Queen's Park,
Toronto, Ont.   M7A 1L2

The Ontario Institute for Studies in Education has three prime functions: to conduct programs of graduate study in education, to undertake research in education, and to assist in the implementation of the findings of educational studies. The Institute is a college chartered by an Act of the Ontario Legislature in 1965. It is affiliated with the University of Toronto for graduate studies purposes.

The publications program of the Institute has been established to make available information and materials arising from studies in education, to foster the spirit of critical inquiry, and to provide a forum for the exchange of ideas about education. The opinions expressed should be viewed as those of the contributors.

© The Ontario Institute for Studies in Education 1984
252 Bloor Street West, Toronto, Ontario M5S 1V6

All rights reserved. No part of this publication may be reproduced in any form without permission from the publisher, except for brief passages quoted for review purposes.

Canadian Cataloguing in Publication Data

Main entry under title:
The House that Ryerson built

ISBN 0-7744-0281-4

1. Education — Ontario — History — Addresses, essays, lectures. I. Oliver, Hugh, 1929-
II. Holmes, Mark, 1935-   III. Winchester, Ian, 1940-   IV. Ontario Institute for Studies in Education.

LA418.06H68 1984   370'.9713   C84-099053-7

ISBN 0-7744-0281-4   Printed and bound in Canada by T. H. Best Printing Company Limited
1 2 3 4 5 THB 88 78 68 58 48

*This book is dedicated to the memory of John Main,
who was Editor-in-Chief of OISE's Publication Division
from 1969 until his death in 1982
and who founded OISE Press in 1980.*

ACKNOWLEDGMENTS

Poems by Hugh Oliver
Cartoons by Catharine O'Neill

The Editors wish to thank those people who sent in personal anecdotes for inclusion in this book. Unfortunately, there was not room to print them all.

All possible care has been taken to trace ownership and obtain permission for each quotation included. If any errors or omissions have occurred, they will be corrected in subsequent editions, provided they are brought to the publisher's attention.

Note:
At the time the essays in this book were written, public funding for the Roman Catholic School system in Ontario extended only up to Grade 10. Since then, the Government of Ontario has announced plans to provide public funding for the Roman Catholic Separate School system up to and including Grade 13.

CONTENTS

Introduction — Clifford C. Pitt /1
Trends in the History of Ontario Education — Willard Brehaut /7
The Ontario School House — Jean Cochrane /19
Progressivism Versus Traditionalism — Mark Holmes /31
What to Teach — Walter Pitman /47
Education or Schooling? — Jim Parr /57
The Independent Schools — Harry Giles /65
Franco-Ontarian Education: From Persecuted Minority to Tolerated Nuisance — Stacy Churchill /75
The Schooling of Girls — Dormer Ellis /89
Special Education — Robert MacIntyre /103
The Emergence of a System of Continuing Education: 1945-1984
 — Alan Thomas /115
Unfinished Dreams: Education and the Oppressed
 — Paul Olson /129
Ontario and Its Universities — Robin Harris /145
The Gradual Emergence of Ontario's Community Colleges
 — Delmar McCormack Smyth /159
The Future of The House that Ryerson Built: Ontario Education in the 21st Century — Ian Winchester /179

INTRODUCTION

Education has exercised an engrossing hold on the hearts and purse strings of Ontarians, and in marking the passage of two hundred years from the Loyalist Canada of 1784 to the Ontario of 1984, it is certainly appropriate that we should celebrate something of the story of Ontario's education. This book, then, is a contribution to Ontario's bicentennial from The Ontario Institute for Studies in Education (OISE).

Since OISE is Canada's largest graduate school of education and is among the half-dozen most important educational research institutions in the world, it would have been a great temptation for its professors to have produced an eminently scholarly work which might well have had an important, albeit restricted, audience; in short, a contribution by researchers to other researchers in education. Instead, the attempt has been made to put together a book which will be of interest to educators at all levels and to a broad spectrum of the public.

Not quite half of the essays come from people outside OISE; the rest are from OISE professors. Authors had complete freedom to tackle the topic in their own way. Consequently, the pieces are quite variable in their treatment – some personal and some detached, some descriptive and some analytical. There is no attempt to offer a comprehensive chronicling of two hundred years of educational development. It was proposed, instead, that nine of the essays would each treat of a specific facet of our educational development whereas the remaining five essays would be more far-ranging.

* * *

Let me introduce the reader to the more general chapters first. *Trends in the History of Ontario Education*, spanning much of two centuries, identifies the major educational trends. Insofar as one man – Egerton Ryerson – was responsible for laying down the foundations of Ontario education out of which these trends have emerged, it is fitting that the present book comes full circle in the final chapter, *The Future of the House that Ryerson Built: Ontario Education in the 21st Century*.

Between these two essays, there are three others of a wide-ranging nature. *Progressivism Versus Traditionalism* deals with essential differences between the two movements in terms of philosophy, policy issues, curriculum content, and instructional methodology as they relate to education in this Province during the current century. *Education or Schooling?* raises some age-old questions, along with some new ones, in a markedly futuristic mode. Should education essentially extend the celebration of our being or train us for an occupation? Is the school system pricing itself out of the market place? Do the greatest possibilities for education lie outside the school system? In *What to Teach*, the author recalls Ontario education from the personal vantage point of an elementary school and collegiate student in the thirties and forties and of a secondary school teacher in the fifties. He concludes with the broadest of predictions: that for the forseeable future education will revolve less around economic productivity and more around the survival of the species, that the whole enterprise will be carried on in the shadow of Armageddon.

The more circumscribed essays present a comprehensive and authoritative overview of a single topic. In *The Independent Schools*, a headmaster of one such school gives a clear picture of their major groupings, the differing ethos of each, and the enrolments of particular schools. *The Schooling of Girls* provides detailed research findings about such problems as the restricted or unrealistic nature of girls' career choices and sexist inequalities in the teaching profession. In *Unfinished Dreams: Education and the Oppressed*, the author analyses "how oppression comes into being and ... how oppression is experienced." In the light of his analysis, he examines various aspects of the Ontario

School system and concludes that many changes have to be made before all our children can hope to achieve their potential. *Franco-Ontarian Education: From Persecuted Minority to Tolerated Nuisance* explores the injustices stemming from Regulation 17 (which was passed by the Ontario Legislature in 1912 and which forbade the use of French as a language of instruction beyond Grade 2) and recent legislation seeking to mitigate those injustices. *Special Education* provides a historical overview of such major issues as the move from residential to day-class programs and the fundamental medical/educational conflicts, and brings us to the present with the Provincial Government's current major initiative represented in the extraordinarily comprehensive Bill 82. *The Emergence of a System of Continuing Education, 1945-1984* examines not so much what is the effect of educational institutions on students but rather what is the mounting effect of students – part-time students, older students (many of them women) – upon the educational institutions. *The Gradual Emergence of Ontario's Community Colleges*, as the title suggests, focusses on the long series of developments leading up to the establishment of the colleges of applied arts and technology in the mid-sixties, together with the Government's intent as to their role and structure. Finally, in *Ontario and Its Universities*, the author deals with such matters as the move to a non-denominational provincial university, Government interference with the autonomy of the universities, and the current difficult dilemma for both the system and the Government: accountability versus accessibility.

* * *

By any criterion, education in Ontario has come a long way – at any rate over the more than 60 years during which I have been involved with it. I recall that we youngsters in a Toronto suburban elementary school lived in fear of an inspector from the Department of Education who always reduced at least two or three of our women teachers to tears before he left. As a defence against the threatening inspectoral visit, most teachers kept a few carefully prepared lessons in their repertoire – well-rehearsed with an anxious class ahead of time and ready to be trotted out at a moment's notice. In arithmetic class, we were introduced to rods and acres, a mystery to us urban youngsters. The reading lesson had little to do with comprehension: it was more of an oratorical contest with one pupil on his feet reading aloud while all the others, their eyes glued to their books in intense concentration, tried to follow word for word – despite the fact that in most unselected Grade 8 classes, some pupils' reading competence was at a Grade 4 level while others was at Grade 12; the trick was to be able to take over with alacrity from the reader who had been stopped in mid-sentence by a teacher intent on identifying the inattentive. We knew nothing of science in the elementary school. In the upper grades, British history and, to a lesser extent, Canadian history were learned rather well, as was geography of the world in general and of Canada in particular. I remember the rigid art classes where we drew flowers, year after year; scarcely ever did the art class (or the music class for that matter) tap our imaginations.

In the Entrance Class (today's Grade 8) where pupils were prepared for entrance to high school, it was common practice for some principals to persuade the slower youngsters not even to attempt the final entrance exams. Little wonder, because the results published in the local papers included not only the name of the school, but also that of the teacher and of each pupil. Then there was the elementary school cadet corps! Those days weren't all bad, of course, but the good depended very largely on our extraordinarily dedicated teachers, who took a very personal interest in our development.

Matters hadn't changed at the elementary level when I began my teaching career in that same school some seven years later. My Grade 5 class of nine-to-eleven-year-olds was often kept in until 4:30 or 5:00 o'clock as we prepared for the tyranny of county-wide examinations in every subject.

It was a case of drill, drill, drill! However, the situation was much worse in the Entrance Class when I taught at that level a few years later. Most of my professional peer group will remember the publications of The James Texts of Belleville, which were the teachers' best sellers of the day – very thick booklets of perhaps a dozen years' past entrance examination papers in every subject. Ambitious teachers aimed at finishing practically the whole prescribed course by Easter; then the rest of the school year was spent on the James Text papers, drilling youngsters on parroting model answers developed or delivered verbatim by the teacher.

If it was a difficult time for pupils, it was also a difficult time for many teachers. Those were the days when married men received a higher salary than single men for precisely the same job; when a man was almost invariably given preference over a woman; when only a handful of men – and many fewer women – attempted the long and arduous struggle to obtain an external B.A. degree, combining summer courses on a university campus with courses by correspondence in the winter. This was a time, too, when many had to carry on something of a juggling act as they taught all eight grades in the one-room rural school.

At the high school of my day, from the beginning of Grade 9 there was preparation for university entrance and not much else. The dropout rate through the grades was dramatic. We took five years of Latin; but we had only one year of art and no music, both of which are deeply enriching areas in my life today and which my time at school did nothing to foster. In Grade 13 Modern European History, we worked from a heavy tome – by Flenley, I think it was. Without any preliminary teaching or introduction whatsoever, the teacher spent days taking us through its several hundred pages, having us underline, at his dictation, sentence after sentence deemed important for examination purposes.

Compare all this with the experience of my grandson in a Toronto secondary school. In English, he had a marvellously creative time, and, to consider but one experience which turned out to be deeply moving for him, he was challenged to express his feelings on a theme central to his personal adolescent idealism in original poetry and in nine different verse forms ranging from the Shakespearean sonnet to the Japanese haiku. For a Grade 11 engineering project, he designed for paraplegics a mechanically operated dinnerplate which would revolve at a touch and which incorporated a fork that would move up and down and sideways. Learning the saxophone in the music program brought him in touch with classical music in the school symphony orchestra as well as with popular music in the school's stage band.

Don't tell me that education isn't enormously better today! And don't fail to credit the greatest achievement of all: the fact that our secondary schools have achieved such richness and sophistication at the same time as (in addition to that of serving university-bound-students) they have taken on the formidable responsibility of educating virtually *all* of our young people – a people, incidentally, become increasingly multicultural and multilingual. One consequence is that secondary schools now deal with almost the total range of abilities reflected in the normal curve, not simply the upper reaches of intellectual talent. Despite attendant problems as well as opportunities, this is a massive accomplishment which may properly give society in general and our teachers in particular very substantial satisfaction indeed.

This is not to say that Ontario's education system lacks for critics. On the contrary! Certainly there are things all of us would like to change. Nevertheless, we are typically silent when asked what other jurisdiction's educational system, considered *in toto*, we would prefer to our own. Would we rather have that of Britain or Russia or France? New York or California? I think not. When it comes to matters educational, Ontario *really is* where we'd rather be!

Clifford Pitt,
Former Director of OISE

MTL T13773

Egerton Ryerson, 1803-1882

In times when half of Canada was Upper
And pioneers ate pork and beans for supper,
When loyalists from Vermont to Valley Forge
Were seeking the asylum of King George,
The problems of survival in our nation
Left little thought for frills like education,
Except among the clergy and the rich,
The dominating principle of which
Allowed them to regard themselves as "betters"
Because they knew their numbers and their letters.

The British crown (oh may it ne'er forsake us)
Gave revenues from half-a-million acres
To fund this all-consuming need for knowledge
With grammar schools and possibly a college
Where sons of gentlefolk conjoined to seek
A smattering of Latin and of Greek,
Though teachers, being noted for defiance,
Would slip in bits of history and science.
The goal — to stabilize the status quo
And nurture rulers for this patch of snow.

'Twas then that Doctor (later Bishop) Strachan
Emerged from Aberdeen where he was bachan
To earn a reputation for his teaching
With practices both modern and far-reaching,
And also win acclaim among the great
As Anglican devout and advocate,
So to advance by favour (never knock it)
Whereby he had the Governor in his pocket.
Thus Knight, Bishop-to-be, and absent King
Controlled this far-flung board's partitioning,
And by the power that thrives as it suborns,
Conspired to keep in check opposing pawns.

Alas, no social order can we trust.
In Upper Canada, the upper crust
Found their provisions flagrantly abused
And ignorance, like geese, come home to roost,
For unenlightened by the lamp of learning
The vagrant youth were bellicosely turning
To lechery and crime and vulgar show
And other things that gentry think de trop.
Complaints were heard: "This modern youth are sick.
They'll ruin our whole body politic.

Our policies must forthwith be revised.
Learning they need to make them civilized;
For those who have the skills to read and write
Are less inclined to fornicate and fight."
And so, across the teacups on the lawn,
The common school for common folk was born.

The principle behind the common schools
Was to apply the paddle and the rules.
The teacher beat out lechery and sin
And tried to beat the three-R basics in,
Creating a curriculum de facto
For later generations to go "back to."
The pupils also learnt the fear of God
And paths of virtue which the saints had trod,
Instructed by such wise and learned teachers
As tramps, Americans, and ailing preachers
In heatless cabins where their brains might freeze —
And all of this for very moderate fees.
So education stumbled through the night.
God said "Let Ryerson be." And all was light.

TRENDS IN THE HISTORY OF ONTARIO EDUCATION

WILLARD BREHAUT

> By observation and enquiry, I am inclined to think that education of youth is too much neglected in this Province. In some parts they have masters, in others none; and indeed those who have masters had almost as well be without them. (Richard Cockrell, teacher, St. Catharines, 1795)

> The people of Ontario have good reason to be proud of their efforts put forth in the cause of education in the past. Indeed, in certain aspects Ontario has, from time to time, been in the forefront of educational progress. (Hall-Dennis Report, 1968)

On the bookshelf of time, one hundred and seventy-three years separate the sources of our introductory statements, the first from Richard Cockrell's booklet, *Thoughts on the Education of Youth*, and the second from *Living and Learning*, the Report of the Provincial Committee on Aims and Objectives of Education in the Schools of Ontario, commonly known as the Hall-Dennis Report. The first quotation appears to be an accurate assessment of educational conditions in at least some parts of the Province during its early years. The second would, in all likelihood, be accepted by latter-day observers and enquirers into the education of youth in Ontario. The striking difference between these statements provides a perspective for considering trends in the history of Ontario education.

Any brief account of the development of education in any Canadian province over a period of two hundred years is necessarily beset with the major problems of what to include and what to exclude. When Ontario (see Footnote) is the particular province to be "reviewed," the scope of the task is magnified by the variety of forces at work throughout this large and varied region and by Ontario's status for the greater part of the past two centuries as the most populous province in Canada. Within the limits of a historical sketch covering two hundred years, it would doubtless be possible to offer a strictly chronological account, a lengthy list of dates or milestones. But such a list would be of little interest to most readers.

The account that follows, then, is more akin to painting

Footnote: I have chosen to follow the example of G. P. de T. Glazebrook, who states in his preface to *Life in Ontario: A Social History* (University of Toronto Press, 1968):
By "Ontario" is meant the territory included within the present province. For that reason, and to avoid changing nomenclature applying to different boundaries, the word Ontario is used throughout, even though it may be technically an anachronism.

than to photography. Rather than attempt to describe developments in detail, I shall use broad strokes to draw attention to what appear to have been general trends over the years. In so doing, one runs the risk of over-generalization, of comparing the incomparable, and of neglecting to take note of certain events that do not readily fit into the overall pattern.

Among the most important of the historical trends in education in Ontario during the past two centuries have been the following:

1. From a religious to a secular orientation.
2. From parental or church initiative to broader public (provincial and local) support and control.
3. From voluntary to compulsory attendance.
4. From inequality of educational oppportunity towards equal educational opportunity.
5. From poorly qualified, male teachers in one room schools to professionally qualified teachers, mostly female, in large schools.
6. From small to larger administrative units.
7. From learning by rote memory within a narrowly restricted curriculum to learning by a variety of methods within a much broadened curriculum.
8. From harsh discipline towards humane discipline.
9. From a British orientation to an American orientation to a Canadian orientation.

Let us now examine each of these trends in turn.

Trend 1: From a religious to a secular orientation. Ontario, like other Canadian provinces, witnessed the beginnings of formal education through the initiative of one or more of the churches. The fact that the two outstanding leaders in Ontario education during the nineteenth century were also outstanding leaders of their denominations tended to ensure that education would have a strongly religious orientation. Both John Strachan, a convert to Anglicanism who became the president of the General Board of Education, and Egerton Ryerson, a convert to Methodism who became Superintendent of Education for the Province, were resolute in pursuing their objectives.

Under the auspices of the Anglican Church, some provision was made for the instruction of small numbers of children in the settlements, although this church and its adherents tended to emphasize the urgency of providing grammar schools for the preparation of potential leaders of the community.

Other religious groups, notably the Methodists, stressed the need for basic education for all children throughout the Province. Under the strong leadership of Egerton Ryerson, the Methodists promoted their religious and educational aims effectively, Ryerson serving as Superintendent of Education for thirty-two years (1844-1876) and guiding his newly created system through its most difficult period of development.

Firmly believing that the system of public education he had established was Christian but non-denominational, Ryerson opposed the attempt to extend the system of Roman Catholic separate schools which had been established. The struggle reached a climax with the Scott Act of 1863; this Act consolidated the separate school position in Ontario and was regarded by Ryerson as the limit beyond which the Government could not accede to Roman Catholic demands. (The struggle continued, however, and, despite reverses, Roman Catholics have been able to achieve most of their objectives, with the exception of obtaining public support for the costs of education beyond Grade 10.)

From time to time, other religious groups have attempted to obtain public funding for their schools and colleges. These attempts have been largely unsuccessful, and they will likely continue to be because Ontario is now home to a great variety of religions–the result of immigration from many areas of the world.

The marked change in recent years in public thinking about the place of religion in our society is noted in a comparison of the statement of aims of education offered in 1950 in the Hope Report and in 1968 in the Hall-Dennis Report. These landmark enquiries into education in Ontario stressed widely different fundamental aims:

> There are two virtues about which there can be no question—honesty and Christian love. . . .Honesty and love must be taught by precept and even more by example, as absolute rights, or eternal verities. . . .They may. . .be taught by the strongest means at the school's command—an absolute acceptance that they are right. If this be indoctrination we accept the stricture. (*Report* of the Royal Commission on Education in Ontario, 1950)

Eighteen years later, the Hall-Dennis Report made the following opening statement:

> The underlying aim of education is to further man's unending search for truth. Once he possesses the means to truth, all else is within his grasp. Wisdom and understanding, sensitivity, compassion, and responsibility, as well as intellectual honesty and personal integrity, will be his guides in adolescence and his companions in maturity.
> This is the message that must find its way into the minds and hearts of all Ontario children. This is the key to open all doors. . . .
> This above all is our task: to seek and to find the structure, the organization, the curriculum, and the teachers to make this aim a reality in our schools and in our time. (*Living and Learning*, 1968)

The difference between these two statements is considerable, but one should bear in mind that the first was prepared at the end of the Second World War, while the second was drafted in the economically buoyant sixties.

Although enrolments in the Roman Catholic separate schools and in some private, church-affiliated schools have risen more sharply than public school enrolments in recent years, this variation does not appear to mark a reversal of the general trend from religious to secular schooling.

Trend 2: From parental or church initiative to broader public (provincial and local) support and control. The earliest provision for education in Ontario resulted from individual parents' desires to provide their children with some basic training in the three Rs. Often this need may have been drawn to their attention by the local clergyman, who would have emphasized the importance—indeed the absolute necessity—of every person being able to read the Bible.

As groups of parents came together to hire a teacher (either one of themselves or an itinerant), the need for broader public support and control of this development became obvious, especially after 1816 when some limited provision was made for government assistance. As this support movement was extended, evidence of greater public control began to appear. Throughout Ontario's history, as in that of other jurisdictions, public support and public control have tended to go hand-in-hand.

With the grammar school, however, public support, dating back to the Act of 1807, preceded public control by many years. Not until the Act of 1853 did the secondary schools of the Province come under public control, and this control did not become effective until 1871. Part of this seeming neglect resulted from Ryerson's determination to improve the common (elementary) school system before turning his attention to the grammar schools, which catered to only a very small proportion of the total school population.

During the past century, there have been instances of revivals of church initiative in education with, in some cases, strong denominational and parental support for these undertakings. The fact that there has been an increase in the number of private schools, as well as of schools (both public and private) in which parents are playing an increasing role in administration, might even suggest that the trend line showing public support and control of education is becoming blurred. But despite such aberrations, the role of the public (provincial and local) remains dominant. Furthermore, despite constitutional barriers, there has been a marked increase in Federal intervention in education in all Canadian provinces – another strong indication of the trend to broader public support and control.

Trend 3: From voluntary to compulsory attendance. Before education became organized on a provincial basis, school attendance was voluntary, left up to the individual parent. In many communities throughout the Province, especially in the newly established school districts, problems of transportation and travel, as well as the need for all – children and adults – to work in the common cause of carving a living out of the wilderness, made the decision about attending school a relatively easy one.

During the years when parents had to pay tuition fees and there was only meagre public support for education, it was difficult, if not impossible, to require children to attend school for a certain number of days per year. When schools became free, however, the central authority was able to initiate legislation making attendance compulsory.

Compulsory attendance of children from 7 to 12 years of age for a period of 4 months in each year was included in the School Law Improvement Act of 1871, but the objectives of this legislation were not met. As a result, in 1891, *An Act Respecting Truancy and Compulsory School Attendance* was passed, requiring full-time attendance of children aged 8 to 14, with penalties for parents or guardians who did not comply with the law. In 1919, the Adolescent School Attendance Act was passed, calling for compulsory attendance to age 16. With minor changes, this law has remained in effect to the present.

Trend 4: From inequality of educational opportunity towards equal educational opportunity. Because education in early Ontario was looked upon as the responsibility of the parent and the church rather than the public (provincial or local), many children received little or no education. As stated above, the pioneer settlers faced the challenge of gaining a livelihood from an inhospitable environment, a task that commanded their wholehearted attention for many years. As a result, education was given low priority by most people, for their energies were turned in another direction.

Among the select few – members of the upper class who had themselves received an education superior to that of the general population and had risen to positions of power and influence – a strong demand arose for provision of education in the colony. Their concern, however, was not for education for the children of all but for the sons of the ruling group. Their priorities are apparent in the provisions of the Act of 1807 and the Act of 1816: the former set up grammar schools, and the latter (nine years after) provided for the establishment of common schools. In short, Government's early emphasis was on preparing leaders for the future life of the colony, not on establishing a democratic system of education.

The grammar schools were not under central control until 1853. Meanwhile, Ryerson attempted to set up a system of common schools, one providing equality of educational opportunity throughout the Province. Noting wide disparities between the rural and urban areas, he urged that the unit of educational administration be enlarged, but such a change was not to occur in his lifetime.

As previously noted, Ryerson's concern for the system of schools he had established for the children of all the people led him to oppose strongly any groups, Roman Catholic or otherwise, attempting to set up separate schools. Some of Ryerson's fiercest battles were fought against the leaders of the Roman Catholic separate schools, the Superintendent maintaining that any extension of public support for the schools of any religious or other select group would seriously weaken the public system.

A giant step towards equality of educational opportunity was taken in 1871 when elementary school fees were eliminated, but another half century elapsed before secondary schools became free. Each of these steps was accompanied by the introduction or extension of compulsory attendance laws.

Requiring that all children within a certain age range attend school made it necessary to broaden the curriculum to accommodate the breadth of talents and variety of interests. Because it was obvious that many children were neither able nor willing to follow the traditional academic program offered at the secondary school level, it became necessary to offer a variety of programs and courses to meet the needs of a vastly increased number. To this end, manual training, domestic science, and other courses were introduced, and later, technical and vocational schools were established.

"... to broaden the curriculum to accommodate the breadth of talents..."

Among the most important developments in vocational education was the introduction of Colleges of Applied Arts and Technology (CAATs) in the 1960s, offering a broad range of post-secondary courses and programs to those who, for one reason or another, were not university bound. The high enrolments in the CAATs and, in the main, the success of their graduates in the job market show that their contribution towards the provincial goal of equality of educational opportunity is significant.

Trend 5: From poorly qualified male teachers in one room schools to professionally qualified teachers, mostly female, in large schools. Most observers of early Ontario report that teaching was considered one of the meanest jobs available and was taken up, in the main, by persons unsuited to other kinds of work. In 1816, the only stated qualification of a teacher was that he be a British subject. Within various religious groups, however, teaching was regarded as an important missionary activity, and such teachers made great contributions to education in the Province from its beginnings. Among the outstanding teachers of Ontario's early years was John Strachan, a well-educated Scot who, soon after arriving in Canada, became an Anglican clergyman as well as the most respected teacher in the Province in his day. But there were few teachers of Strachan's calibre, and the records are replete with the woefully inadequate teachers who moved from community to community throughout the early years. One historian's comment that "(e)very kind of teacher could be found, good, bad and indifferent" seems a fair assessment.

It was this situation that caused Egerton Ryerson to give high priority to the establishment of a normal school to upgrade the low qualifications of the teachers in the common schools. To this end, he established in Toronto, in 1847, a normal school for the instruction of teachers, and he continued to emphasize the importance of this school throughout his tenure of the office of superintendent.

MTL T13802

John Strachan, 1778-1867

The success of the Toronto Normal School in raising both the academic and professional qualifications of teachers in Ontario was evident, and another normal school was opened in 1875 in Ottawa. Two years later, in 1877, a system of county model schools (see Footnote) was established in an attempt to meet the need for trained teachers. This new training program, more accessible but clearly inferior to that of the two normal schools in operation at this time, soon flooded the schools with teachers of the lowest certificate standing (and lowest salary), and the decision was finally made, in 1907, to end teacher training in county model schools and to set up additional normal schools.

Many years passed before Ontario teachers were able, through their professional associations, to gain significant improvements in their qualifications, salaries, and status. So long as teacher qualifications were influenced by variations in the teacher market, it was difficult for the practising teachers to standardize the qualifications required for entry into teaching. Eventually, with the passing of the Teaching Profession Act in 1944 and with the granting of automatic membership in the Ontario Teachers' Federation and one of its affiliates, Ontario teachers began to take on the appearance of an organized profession. The fairly constant upward movement of teacher qualifications (despite several periods when shortcuts to the classroom were authorized by the Minister of Education) finally resulted in the present requirement of an undergraduate degree and professional training for entrance to the teaching profession. In addition, the gradual move from the normal schools (through a stage when these institutions were called teachers' colleges) to the university faculties of education has helped to place teacher education on a footing similar, if not equal, to that of at least some other professions whose training is offered on the university campus.

In the earliest period of Ontario history, those offering their services as teachers were usually men. Even in villages and towns, teaching was considered to be an occupation calling for the physical and mental capacities of males rather than females. Gradually, this condition changed such that, by the time Ryerson retired in 1876, there were more female than male teachers in the elementary schools of the Province.

As with educational leaders in most jurisdictions, those in Ontario during the past two centuries have been almost exclusively men, although credit for the establishment of the first school in the Province is given to the Sisters from Quebec, who set up a school near what is now Windsor in 1786. In the main, however, women have been badly under-represented in the ranks of teachers at all levels except elementary school. This imbalance continues to the present day, although some progress has recently been made in bringing women teachers into positions of power and responsibility.

The pioneer Ontario teacher was often alone in

Footnote: Approximately fifty public schools throughout the Province were designated by the Department of Education as "model" schools in which candidates for the third-class teaching certificate might be trained in a brief course. Graduates of the county model school course were expected to upgrade their qualifications by taking the normal school course later, but few of them did.

attempting to cope with the responsibilities and problems of teaching in his isolated, one room school. Forced to accept the often wretched conditions of working in a community that did not hold the teacher in high regard, he showed high mobility – lateral, not vertical – staying in a community for but a short time before moving to a new and different set of problems.

Encouraged by Ryerson to meet regularly in Teacher Institutes, teachers gradually came to the conclusion that they could improve professionally through close association with their colleagues and through certain forums (such as the Ontario Educational Association, established in 1861) wherein both teachers and others interested in education could interact.

> **N**ow, in the United States, a system prevails unknown to, or unpractised by, any other nation. In all other countries morals and religion are made the basis of future instruction, and the first book put into the hands of children teaches them the domestic, social and religious virtues; but in the United States politics pervade the whole system of instruction. The school books from the very first elements are stuffed with praises of their own institutions and breathe hatred to everything English. To such a country our youth may go, strongly attached to their native land and all its establishments, but by hearing them continually depreciated and those of America praised, these attachments will, in many, be gradually weakened, and some may become fascinated with that liberty which has degenerated into licentiousness and imbibe, perhaps unconsciously, sentiments unfriendly to things of which Englishmen are proud.
>
> REV. DR. STRACHAN
> (FROM A REPORT TO THE LIEUTENANT-GOVERNOR, MARCH 1826)

Despite the cooperative benefits accruing to teachers who joined with non-teachers in the Ontario Educational Association, many felt the need for a more selective professional group. The first major teachers' association in Ontario – the Federation of Women Teachers' Associations of Ontario (FWTAO) – was established in 1918, followed by the Ontario Secondary School Teachers' Federation (OSSTF) in 1919, and the Ontario Public School Men Teachers' Federation (OPSMTF) in 1920. The major step of setting up the Ontario Teachers' Federation was taken in 1944, providing a more united voice for Ontario teachers in a province with several separate teachers' organizations.

Trend 6: From small to larger administrative units. The pioneer schools in Ontario were usually the result of local initiative and were intended to serve a small number of parents who cooperated in obtaining the services of a teacher. This pattern of development, whether the result of local initiative or of prodding by the initially ill-defined central authority, lasted for several generations, with a three-man board of trustees ("three fit and discreet men") responsible for the operation of the local one room school.

The traditional picture of the small board's pioneer school, whether in a settled community or on the frontier, depicts a room with little light, practically no amenities (sometimes lacking both pump and toilet), with pupils, huddled on backless benches around a pot-bellied stove, trying to learn under almost intolerable conditions. Usually, too, there is no evidence of any teaching equipment except a few books and one or more birch rods.

Despite Ryerson's efforts to promote enlarged school areas and the later move to larger administrative units in some other Canadian provinces and many parts of the United States, Ontario was slow to abandon the one room school model. Eventually, however, in the name of efficiency and equality of educational opportunity, the Provincial Government introduced larger administrative units and proceeded to eliminate the small schools. The latest step in this development was the introduction, in 1969, of the county as the administrative unit in education.

Trend 7: From learning by rote memory within a narrowly restricted curriculum to learning by a variety of methods within a much broadened curriculum. In most schools in early Ontario, memorization of often meaningless material was the standard method of "learning." The typical pioneer teacher did little teaching. Before "classing" of the children was made possible through the introduction of standard texts, the teacher was kept busy "assigning" (i.e., "from here down to here") and "hearing" lessons in whatever books were

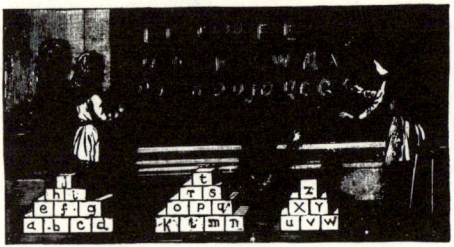

From Royal Canadian Primer, 1883
Published by The Canadian Publishing Company (Limited), in the office of the Minister of Agriculture

brought to the school by individual pupils and the teacher. Thus, "individualized instruction" was provided at an early date–but not of the type aimed at these days. Because the teacher spent so much time "hearing" individual lessons, there was little left for teaching individuals or classes.

The curriculum of the pioneer Ontario school was restricted largely to the basics of the three Rs, badly taught. A fourth R, religion, was often incorporated within reading, for the Bible and various religious tracts were among the most frequently encountered books in the school.

When standard texts were prescribed and class teaching thereby became possible, marked changes in teaching and learning methods evolved. The importance of these new methods and the need for teachers to be trained in their use were emphasized by Ryerson in his *Journal of Education* and in the normal school. A boon to this development was the establishment of the Educational Depository in 1851 to make available to schools, libraries, and mechanics' institutes such teaching aids as maps, globes, apparatus, "object lessons," and books.

Over the years, there has been an increase in the number of subjects taught, together with less rigidity in the prescription of textbooks. Although ultimate control of the curriculum rests with the Minister of Education through Circular 14 (setting forth the texts authorized for use in the various subjects), the overall trend has been towards an increase in flexibility.

Trend 8: From harsh discipline towards humane discipline. Reflecting the severity of life outside the school and the status of the child in society, pupils in the pioneer Ontario schools were often subjected to stern, even inhumane, discipline. Undoubtedly there were teachers who were gentle in their relations with children, but the profusion of accounts of the opposite type leads one to conclude that school days in early Ontario provided unhappy memories for many.

Contributing to this situation was the general attitude of a people who accepted the dictum that to spare the rod was to spoil the child, an attitude understandable in a society in which both men and women were dealt with severely for minor offences against the law. Also, inadequate preparation for teaching together with inadequate remuneration made positive teacher/pupil relations extremely difficult.

As trained teachers, better qualified both academically and profesionally, entered the schools, despotic rule in the classroom became less evident. Training in classroom organization and teaching methods helped the teacher to avoid many of the problems besetting the untrained teacher. In addition, Ryerson's *Journal of Education* brought to every school the more up-to-date ideas about school management as well as other aspects of education.

In later years, new thinking about the possibility of making schools into places where children could experience growth rather than repression began to emerge. Studies undertaken in psychology and sociology caused educators to question the earlier rigid school discipline. This changed attitude was well expressed by James L. Hughes, Inspector of Public Schools in Toronto from 1874 to 1914, in a poem entitled "Why He Is Bad.'" The concluding stanza offers a capsule statement of the Inspector-poet's message:

> Was it his fault that he was born
>   'Mid horrors here;
> With vileness shadowing his heart
>   And naught to cheer?
> Blame not the boy. Society
> Must bear the blame.
> We are responsible. To us
>   Belongs the shame.

(from *Life's Glories: How to Keep Them.* Toronto: Hambly, 1926)

By all accounts, it appears that teachers moved from a

dependence on harsh discipline, including corporal punishment, to a more humane attempt to understand the causes of children's misbehavior.

> One day one of the big boys, named Begley, was leaving school for good. He had it in for the teacher to even up for a hard whipping he got from him once. Now, the teacher had to go to the village for dinner, and during his absence Begley gathered up all the chewing-gum (nearly every boy and girl chewed gum, about the only luxury in those days. It was pine gum, and had great chewing powers). He then got a tin cup full and put it on the stove to melt. We were all sworn not to tell. Just before the master came back to the school, Begley poured the melted gum on his chair. Master entered, took his seat, and began to call the roll. Someone started to snicker, and that set the rest going. Master reached out to grab his rawhide whip, but when he jumped up the chair stuck to the seat of his pants. He was red-hot. I see his red face yet. He had to call a big boy to help him get the chair pulled away from his pants. Then he called the whole school to stand around the walls and questioned each one to find out who put the gum on his chair. He never found out. However, he suspected that two of the big boys knew about it, so he made them take the chair outside and scrape the gum off. What gum stuck to his pants remained there. Pants were discarded for a new pair next day.
>
> GAVIN HAMILTON GREEN
> (FROM *THE OLD LOG SCHOOL*, PUBLISHED 1939)

Trend 9: From a British orientation to an American orientation to a Canadian orientation. The strong British orientation that marked the beginning of Ontario resulted from the arrival of a large number of United Empire Loyalists who moved north after the revolt of Britain's Thirteen Colonies. This initial demonstration of loyalty to Britain was strongly reinforced by the War of 1812 and, to a lesser extent, by the 1837 Rebellion and, later, in the 1860s, by the threat implied in the American Civil War and by the achievement of Confederation.

This British orientation influenced education at all levels, causing the colonial authorities to try to duplicate the English grammar school in the new colony and to provide for education at the secondary level before any provision was made for education at the elementary – a task that was left, as in England, to the parents and the church. Furthermore, early legislation showed that those in authority were more concerned about the possibility of Ontario children being exposed to the republican propaganda found in the American school books than they were about the quality of work being done in the schools.

The architect of the Ontario educational system, however, was not strongly anti-American and was ready to adopt and adapt American ideas and practices. Although Egerton Ryerson travelled widely on both sides of the Atlantic in preparing his blueprint for Ontario education, he was greatly influenced by what he found in the states of New York and Massachusetts. Thus, during Ryerson's tenure, there was much less reluctance to accept the example of the American educational systems when changes were being introduced in Ontario. Increasingly, Ontario educators became associated with American educational organizations, and some (for example, James L. Hughes) came to be recognized as educational leaders on both sides of the border. That Canadian educators should be prepared to borrow from American educators is a reasonable expectation, given the similarities in historical development over the years. But although Ontario teachers and administrators, especially at the elementary school level, were ready to look south for inspiration and for their advanced degrees, the Province became known as more traditional and conservative than any of the provinces to the west.

Gradually, Ontario educators began to place less importance on imported ideas and practices and more stress on Canadian, particularly Ontarian, developments. In curriculum, for example, the development of book publishing companies in Toronto led to the production of school readers and other textbooks considered to be better suited to the needs of Ontario students and teachers. In addition, recurring demands from both the lay and professional public for greater emphasis on Canadian content in such subject areas as history and geography have been of long standing. The most significant of recent campaigns to this end was that undertaken in the 1960s by A.B. Hodgetts, a teacher of history in one of Ontario's independent schools, whose efforts led to the establishment of the Canada Studies Foundation and the creation of both new educational materials related to Canada and of new attitudes towards the teaching of Canadian studies.

This then concludes the list of those trends that I have chosen to consider. Others might have been noted, but only at the risk of duplicating, to some extent, the developments dealt with in later essays of this volume. Among these trends are the following: from little or no public expenditure on education to heavy public expenditure on education at all levels; and from a view of education being for children and youth to that of life-long learning. Still other trends might have been noted by different observers, depending upon the location of their observation towers. Regardless of their particular viewpoint, however, observers will agree that any trend lines noted are not smooth depictions of steady development from the time of Richard Cockrell to that of Hall-Dennis; rather they show "ups" and "downs," reflecting the effects of socio-economic, political, and ideological changes.

Within each of the trends noted is not only a past filled with debate and controversy but also a present showing still unattained objectives. For example, although great strides have been made towards equality of educational opportunity, this objective remains unattained – perhaps, some would say, unattainable. Similarly, the attainment of the objective of more humane discipline in the schools may have brought in its wake certain undesirable conditions associated with a permissive society, causing individuals and society to reassess their objectives.

Whatever trends are discerned, Ontario's first two centuries of educational development offer strong support for W.G. Fleming's choice of *Education: Ontario's Preoccupation* as the title of one of his last books. It would appear to be historically accurate and, as seems likely, prophetic as well.

WILLARD BREHAUT was on the staff of the University of Toronto's Department of Educational Research before joining OISE in 1965 as a founding member and as the first chairman of its Department of History and Philosophy. A former teacher in a one room school in Prince Edward Island and, later, a supervisor of schools for the P.E.I. Department of Education, he has taught educational courses at Prince of Wales College and Bishop's University as well as at the University of Toronto and OISE. He has published articles and monographs on Ontario and Canadian education, teacher education in Ontario and Prince Edward Island, and educational research in Canada and the United Kingdom.

This frosty morning let my flames rejoice
(My summer hibernation long since dead),
While drones the teacher's matronising voice,
Pouring her words inside each empty head.
Many a generation I've observed
Imprisoned at my feet and then set free;
And I grown wiser than the ones I've served
With all their wisdom rubbing off on me.
And yet of all their lessons that I've learned
One truth remains, one lesson I can trust —
The logs they feed me, after they have burned
Leave but a cold and paltry pile of dust.
And so to keep the chill beyond the door,
I needs must seek accord — a cord and more.

THE ONTARIO SCHOOL HOUSE

JEAN COCHRANE

One room schools are a part of the lore and legend of Ontario's life. There's an aura about them of laughter and hardship, and a fust of humanity that doesn't seem to attach to the memory of urban schools. That may be because, from the time the rural school system struggled into being in the 1840s until it was extinguished in 1964, it was something the whole community was involved in. It wasn't the separate preserve of students and teachers and a few parents and politicians. The community built the school, maintained it, hired the teachers, supplied the wood for the stove, attended church in it, and danced on the classroom floor on Saturday nights.

The system grew initially because it was the only way. You couldn't get the students to school, so you built the schools where the students already were. There are still a handful of small schools operating in Ontario's north for just that reason.

In the mainstream, these schools outlived their time, overtaken by society's demands for the kind of education needed to function in an increasingly complex world. Educators and parents say that in the hands of a good teacher, a one room school could be academically good, that it developed resourcefulness and independence in students. What it could never provide were the things that only size could justify and money buy — specialist teachers, libraries, laboratories, and gymnasiums.

The schools should probably have disappeared forty years before they did. They were preserved by the poverty of the Depression in the 1930s, by the demands of the Second World War, and by the determination of rural people to maintain that personal control of the schools their children attended.

There was a hodge-podge of private, church, and state schools in Upper Canada in the 18th and early 19th centuries, but apart from the sons of the gentry, only a few children received more than the barest minimum of schooling. However, the idea that there should be education for the masses was taking root. The Loyalists gave it impetus in British North America, as did some of the settlers from Scotland, because they were used to a system of small, local schools.

Organized, state-run education got seriously underway in Canada West during the 1840s. Egerton Ryerson was appointed the first Assistant Superintendent of Education in 1844 to begin a reign that would last until 1876. He embarked on a grand tour of England and Europe to survey current

Blenheim School, c. 1905

educational practices, and published a report in 1846. The report recommended what would now be described as an enriched curriculum that included history, civics, nature study, agriculture, music, hygiene, and physical training.

Ryerson introduced a standardized text – the Irish National Readers – which would serve until a native product became available twenty years later. More importantly, he espoused the cause of universal, tax-supported schooling at a time when a lot of people could see no reason to spend their money on educating other people's children.

Under this high profile Methodist, a non-sectarian system was established that would bend to accommodate separate Roman Catholic schools provided they met the provincial standards for all tax-supported schools. This was no mean accomplishment. Religion was a hotly debated, divisive issue, tangled with politics and social status, and its place in the schools was one of the liveliest areas of contention.

A School Act had been passed in 1843 that offered grants from the Government to be matched by townships to help pay for the construction of a school and the salary of a teacher. A Common School Act in 1846 followed Ryerson's report. It called for a strong central education organization, for regularized school sections, for school visitors to inspect schools, and for a normal school to train teachers.

That has a crisp and efficient sound. The reality emerges from old records as a selling job and a struggle. Backwoods settlers often had to be persuaded about the value of schooling. Strong young backs could be useful at home, and farmers, fishermen, and lumbermen didn't need much in the way of education. If they were convinced, they then had to find the time and resources to build a school when their homes might still be only rough cabins and cash was a scarce commodity. As for the curriculum, a backwoods teacher with no training and few teaching aids was doing well to cover the basics.

A citizen of Aldborough Township notes that the first school (erected in the 1840s) "was built of clay mixed with timber, and had a wide, open chimney at one end. The chimney was built of clay and sticks, as there were no bricks made here at that time, and it was a very common occurrence for the chimney to catch fire, which always caused a commotion in the school . . . .

"The teacher had a taste of the blessing of boarding round, having to spend a week in the home of each scholar as he went his rounds. Beds were not very plentiful, and lucky was it for the teacher if he did not have to sleep with at least three of his pupils."

Full time inspectors started on their rounds in the 1860s, cajoling, bullying, and reporting on what they saw. The following, unusually sunny account from Madoc in 1875 reflects conditions nearly 30 years after the Common School Act.

After "a day or two of travelling, I found one of the trustees of the school at Bark Lake waiting to convey me to my destination in his 'spring-board.'

"It is a Log Building. The roof is composed of basswood troughs. With the exception of the door, window sashes and the Teacher's desk, the whole owes its construction to the chopping and broad axe. Floor, Benches and Desks are made of planks hewn from logs.

"Sixteen pupils were in attendance. The Teacher is ambitious to have a reputation for success . . . . Possessed of a limited education, she has not, of course, the most approved methods. The School, however, does not compare unfavorably with other Schools in new and remote districts.

"Much of its success is due to the perseverance and intelligence of a few of the settlers. Mr. Whelan, the tavernkeeper, never loses a fitting opportunity for pressing the claims of the school upon his guests. By their personal donations and by the voluntary contributions of the Settlers, also by the liberal aid granted by the Education Department, the School has been kept open during the past two years, a suitable supply of Maps, Tablet Reading Lessons and Apparatus has been provided, and even Prizes have been distributed among the Scholars.

"Still another noticeable feature about the School. The Scholars were, at my visit, Protestant and Roman Catholic in about equal proportions. All, however, joined in singing religious songs, their Teacher accompanying them with the music of a concertina. The whole thing was very pleasing.

"Here I addressed a meeting of residents. The immediate result was that I was presented with a Petition, asking to be formed into a regular School Section. An assessment of taxable property will be made this season. The Trustees also promised to raise the walls of their School House some two feet and put on a better roof.

"My tour extended over fifteen days. I inspected fifteen schools and travelled over three hundred and twenty miles of Colonization Roads – bush, track and water."

What was true of those early days continued to be true throughout the history of the one room school. If a rural community was prosperous and interested in education, it provided a good building and the best teacher it could. Without money or conviction, the provision was often meagre, if not downright depressing. The three-man boards

> It was long after my early education in a one room country school that I recognized the significance of this renowned vanguard of our present educational system. The one room school was a close and integral part of the home and community in those early days. Schooling was a part of daily discussion. Everyone considered he/she had a part in all aspects, which included construction, maintenance, and operation. Every family participated in the spelling matches and the debates, the concerts, and the sports. Every parent knew what he/she had not learned and needed. Every trustee had a definite idea of what ought to be taught and made sure that it was. High moral values were paramount, and the teacher had to be beyond reproach. Discipline was strict, and justice was seldom delayed. Subjects were taught by example, with rigorous attention to work habits. All ages had to work together, play together, and get along together. The older pupils had to look after the younger, and this responsibility extended to sports and to the long walks to and from school.
>
> There was, I think, one big advantage to the one-room school: the learning process of all grades was exposed to all pupils. An apt student could satisfy his ego, and also please the teacher mightily, by using any spare time to observe the class ahead being taught and to benefit accordingly. A good student could advance at nearly double the ordinary speed.
>
> HAROLD CROWDER,
> SCHOOL TRUSTEE

of trustees that ran the schools were not anonymous politicians. They were the neighbours and friends of the people they had to tax, and it behooved them to keep costs down.

As the backwoods and pioneer days receded, so of course did the crudest conditions. But there were always pockets of rural poverty where money was short, and amenities such as electricity and running water were often a long time coming. A 1941 report stated that 37 percent of Ontario farm homes had electricity and only 10 percent had baths or showers. Recollections of school conditions turn on discomfort.

A woman, recalling her school days in Thornhill about 1915, said, "It was always cold and drafty in the winter. We wore drawers and long woolen stockings, and we kept our rubber boots on, though that was supposed to affect your eyesight."

Right to the end, most of the schools were heated by cantankerous, demanding wood stoves that threw sparks, smoked, and consumed wood with such a voracious appetite that they dominated the life of everyone around them.

A woman who taught in Elizabeth Township near Brockville said, "Farmers brought the wood in, sometimes in lieu of taxes. Every day, every child brought in a load of wood, the little ones kindling and the big ones logs. We filled the stove before we left, and someone was supposed to come in early to get it started."

After all that, it rarely heated the whole room.

"I have seen a pan of water under my desk freeze while the children next to the stove smoked. I rotated the kids, not on the basis of class, but on the basis of who sat next to the stove."

The stove was also a cook stove, used to heat cocoa, to bake potatoes, or to cook turnips and so ensure that the poorest child had something warm at lunch time. Sometimes it was cooperative soup. One child brought carrots, another the onion. They went into the pot in the morning, and by noon the aroma must have been maddening.

On winter afternoons when, without electricity, it got too dark for the children to see the blackboard or their desk work, many a teacher had them gather around the stove while she stood at the window and read aloud to them.

School boards were not left to their own devices where

the buildings and grounds were concerned. It was part of an inspector's job to keep an eye on the physical conditions, and he could threaten to withhold provincial funds if he was not satisfied with what he saw. There was also a barrage of instruction from the Province on how to build a school, how big the windows should be, and where the well and outhouses should be located to minimize the risk of contamination. Pranks apart, the memory of some of the outhouses still makes people shudder.

The water supply could also be a problem. Lucky schools had wells of their own. The rest used water hauled by the pailful from nearby farms. Water pails and dippers stood on a shelf in the corner, wash basins and slop pails near the entrance.

An 1886 Education Department guide offered tests for the well water. "It should be colorless or blueish if looked at through a depth of two or three feet; green waters are not generally hurtful; yellowish or brownish are to be looked upon with suspicion . . . .

"There should be no history of having caused diarrhea, typhoid, diphtheria or of having conveyed scarlatina, etc."

In the 1920s, public health nurses began to pay periodic visits to schools to examine, advise, and immunize. One who worked in the 1940s remembered neglected outhouses, scabies mites burrowed in winter clothing, and classrooms full of flies that she described as "great, groggy buzzing brutes."

At home as well as at school, good hygiene was difficult to achieve, and medical help was miles away. Over the years, inspectors' reports note small schools being closed because of epidemics of head lice or measles or one of the deadlier diseases. Teachers learned to recognize symptoms and to doctor children as best they could, but if the disease was contagious, it was probably too late by the time they saw the signs.

The standard of education in any of the schools was as much the luck of the draw as the physical surroundings. Rural schools had their share of good, effective teachers. However, rural boards could and did issue what were called letters of permission to allow low priced, under qualified teachers to work. Some got a bit of training in model schools where they watched another teacher conducting a class and then were assigned practice lessons. According to a teacher

"Every day, every child brought a load of wood. . . ."

Students learning First Aid during World War I

of the model school in Perth County, "A master from normal school would come to criticize them. They'd come four or five at once, and just stayed a week. It was a holiday for them in a way."

Even when teaching standards and conditions began to improve, the rural schools got the beginners. They also hired a preponderance of women. As early as the 1850s, it was noted that more women than men taught in rural schools because they could be paid less.

A 1947 report on the rural teacher stated: "The teacher is still very much the employee of the local board. They tell her, they rarely seek her advice. They know full well that she is John Brown's daughter, and from her not much can be expected."

But a great deal was. Whatever her qualifications as a teacher, she had to be a model of virtue. A teacher recalls the 1920s when "a lady teacher at Cochrane had gone with a gentleman friend for the day down line. They missed the train back, and she had to stay overnight with some of his friends. She was almost barred from teaching, and we had quite a time to get it settled."

She usually lived with a family not far from the school, and this kept privacy to a minimum. When cars became common, rural boards still tried to insist that the teacher live near the school. She often had to light the morning fire and keep the school clean. She could well be expected to play the piano for Sunday church service. She sometimes had to teach beyond Grade 8 students who wanted some high school training and couldn't get to a high school. During the 1920s, Ontario had nearly two hundred so-called continuation schools – rural schools that offered high school courses as well as Grades 1 to 8, though by 1940, only 30 percent of farm children went past Grade 8.

The pattern of a day in a one room school seldom varied. The teacher rang a bell and the children marched in, boys at one door and girls at the other. Opening exercises might include a Bible reading, the Lord's Prayer, and a pledge of allegiance to the British monarch, whose picture hung over the blackboard.

Then came the daily juggling act, keeping all the pupils busy and getting them through the curriculum, with all eight grades to think about. A young man teaching near Oakville

"... and a pledge of allegiance to the British Monarch...."

> I can remember in the late twenties, when my father was chairman of the three-man board for our local country school, the excitement abroad when they fired the teacher and advertised for a new one. Applications flooded in — 120 in all. As well as the daily letters arriving, prospective candidates also flocked to our door, pleading for the chance to fill the vacancy. So persistent were the applicants that in order for my father to get to church on time, he had to appear in the yard with a Bible in hand and ask that the zealous contenders come back another time to speak with him.
>
> MURIEL TETROE
> (FORMER SECONDARY SCHOOL PRINCIPAL)

gave up the unequal task and played his fiddle for the children to dance to – until the inspector came to call.

The open concept classrooms of the 1960s and the idea of allowing children to learn at their own pace was not new for graduates of one room schools. In that room, the teacher had one group doing desk work, another at the blackboard, and another reading or reciting lessons aloud. The bright children completed their own work, and then did what they called "listening ahead" to their elders; they moved up through grades and readers when the teacher thought they were ready.

As in any school, the better teachers did what they could to help any of their exceptional students, but even the best had little time and little training for dealing with the unusual. And in the isolated world of the one room school, they had almost no one to turn to for advice.

A teacher in Leamington began her career in 1933 in a school with 55 children – including 18 in Grade 1, four in Grade 8, and one high school girl who had to be taught algebra, Latin, and French. Three years later, in her second school, she arrived one Monday morning to find that 17 students had arrived over the weekend with their families from Yugoslavia.

"None of them spoke a word of English, and they ranged in age from six to 16. I didn't have enough seats, so we took boards and put them between the seats. Chairs were put around the teacher's desk and around the table in the teacher's room. The children learned their English from the other children at recess and lunch time."

Another teacher who worked north of Parry Sound in the 1930s recalled, "The school was in the bush, four miles from the railway. There was no hydro, no mail delivery, no cars. I had 17 pupils, only three spoke English. The others were Russian, Finnish, and Polish.

"The inspector came the second week and told me to help them live in Canada and to forget history, geography, and science. We set up a house in one corner of the room and a store in the other, using pictures, samples, and crudely made furniture. It was a memorable year."

A teacher who worked near Peterborough said, "I had a mental retardate and a child with speech problems in one school. If I had understood child growth and development, I might have been able to help them more."

Discipline could also be a worry, particularly if there were bored big boys in attendance for the few weeks when work on the farm allowed. Male teachers were challenged to fights. Notions of humor were fairly basic, knocking over desks with as much noise as possible, letting small animals loose in the classroom, putting fire crackers in the stove. Discipline, particularly in the early days, was in kind, running to dunce caps and the strap. The fortunate teachers who had community backing rarely had to resort to the strap. The kids knew that if they were in trouble at school, they were in trouble at home.

There were two major events in the year at a one room school. One came at the end, when the Grade 8 students had to be crammed past Ontario's high school entrance exams. Even the students who had no intention of going to high school wanted to pass that exam, and a teacher's job could depend on how many passed or failed. Teachers and students worked early and late, using old exam papers to stuff enough answers into young heads to get them through.

The other major event was the Christmas concert. Every child had to be in it. Mothers made costumes. Fathers rigged a stage with a curtain of bed sheets. On the night, every parent and aunt in the neighborhood came, with lanterns to light the school and bountiful helpings of food and coffee for afterward. Memories are bright with candlelight and fun, tempered by the practical touch of generations that could never afford to waste anything.

In Loring in 1929, "The Christmas concert was the great winter event. The whole community helped. Then shy, backward children came out of their shells, as excitement mounted. The school room had no ceiling, and the Christmas tree reached to the rafters. Later it appeared in the church, glowing in the beauty of pure candlelight as the German settlers kept up their traditional customs. Year after year, there was a sudden, marked improvement in language and reading after the Christmas concert."

Near Geraldton, "We depended on our Christmas concert to make money to buy supplies, a pencil sharpener, story books and maybe a new pail and dipper for drinking water. But I think my greatest thrill at Christmas was when I saw the excited faces of pupils and their little brothers and sisters come up to the tree to find a gift and candies from Santa because they had been good."

The work in the small schools was slower to reflect educational and social change than was work in urban schools, though some crusaders will always get through. Just after the turn of the century, when the learning-through-doing period brought with it kindergarten, manual training, and home economics, it was difficult for the one room school to respond. Manual training could be little more than working with a few hand tools in the corner of the classroom.

(Courtesy Canadian National Railways)

The Ontario Department of Education used railway cars to bring classroom instruction to children in remote parts of Ontario from 1926 to 1967

Home economics often became a matter of stitching patterns on scraps of fabric, though an enterprising teacher could turn that into a class quilting project.

The rural schools did see an agriculture and nature study campaign that was launched through the aid of tobacco millionaire Sir William Macdonald. He was a philanthropist who did a great deal for rural schooling and for education generally. One of the things he did, beginning in 1904, was to finance teacher training and pay for supplies so that children could be taught to handle their own small plots in school gardens. The goals were mixed. The gardens were a part of the new belief in the value of practical as well as academic work. They represented an attempt to upgrade farming skills that were scorned by most farmer fathers. They were also intended to help make farming and rural life seem interesting to young people and so counteract the move to towns that began emptying the countryside after the 1870s.

School books carried stories designed to illustrate how exciting life on the farm could be. A lesson in a 1924 reader recommended for use in rural schools in Ontario began:

"If Dick here wants to play war, let us begin right here on this farm.

"Dick thought it would be great fun, and Nora and Milton agreed to join on one condition – that Nora should not

27

OA S14672

Rural School Gardens, North Gower

be called upon to do any of the actual fighting."

The enemy were rats and mice, weeds, and unwanted bugs.

Ontario supported the school-garden project for years, and encouraged the development of school fairs and school sections in the annual community fairs. The Province suppplied seeds in the newest strains and prizes for competitions in all kinds of farm and home skills.

A 1909 report stated: "The work is accomplishing what was intended. We hope to have our people realize that the soil is God's best gift to man, and that the position of husbandman is after all of very great importance to the state."

That may have been all in your point of view. Not only did rural depopulation continue unabated but also there was often dark suspicion of favoritism in the awarding of prizes and a fairly widespread conviction that the school section at the fall fair was only there to ensure that parents attended.

The move to close some one room schools in favor of consolidated schools began almost as soon as roads were good enough to make it possible. Even three or four room schools in accessible areas had obvious advantages in providing human and material resources. Besides, it had become too costly to operate dozens of small schools with just a few children in each. The Ontario Government offered to finance consolidated schools, and Macdonald set up several as models. But the rural community resisted for many, many years.

In Aldborough Township, a small school was demolished in a wind storm in 1919, and the minutes record an Inspector Taylor's vain attempt to have it replaced with a consolidated school.

"He spoke at some length on the question of consolidated schools which he considered the best place for educating the children.

"He emphasized the fact that the attendance at all the surrounding rural schools was very small.

"He also stated that the Government paid 40 percent of cost of erecting a suitable building, 40 percent of transportation charges, and also donated $2,000 to each of the first ten consolidated schools in Ontario."

A poll on consolidation was held a few days later. The community rejected it.

Parents were concerned that the trip to and from school would make a long day for the children, especially the little ones. Rural communities were also concerned about the taxes involved, convinced their mil rates would rise. But their main objection was that they felt this was the beginning of the end of local autonomy and local control.

Kenneth Armstrong was one of the officials who presided over the change when it finally came. He described how it worked in Trafalgar Township, north of Oakville, in

> On the evening of 6 October 1963, when the late Hon. Leslie Frost, Q.C., former Premier of Ontario, officially opened North Cavan Central School, it was the culmination of many meetings and months of planning. Those attending that evening were able to tour a fine one-story building which had six bright cheery classrooms, a large playroom with stage, and washrooms supplied with water from a drilled well that pumped water high above the required gallonage per minute. The school, situated close to the county road on a seven-acre playground, was one of the first in the Province to be heated by electricity.
>
> Six country schools were brought together to form the new school, and the staff comprised five of those teachers and one replacement. My application for principal had been accepted; so with an excellent staff and with the friendly help and guidance of Mr. Clifford Holmes, Inspector of Public Schools, we launched our program for Education in an entirely new environment.
>
> GRACE LOWES,
> FORMER ELEMENTARY SCHOOL PRINCIPAL

1952. They began with the older children, he said, "selling" the new schools on the basis of their gymnasiums and work shops. They reassured parents by making the buses run like clockwork.

Armstrong and his colleagues all across the Province worked with rural teachers; getting them together before they began work in the new schools, helping them to adjust.

"It wasn't that the teachers were obstinate or mule headed. They had come to fit a mould that was suitable to the job they had been doing. They had been isolated from one another.

"Then, they were used to knowing their kids, all their short-comings and long-comings, as it were. Suddenly, they had a room full of kids, all at the same grade level, that they didn't know. In September, a few of them threw up their hands and said they didn't know how they were going to do it.

"Some made the change, some didn't. Some were happy, and some were unhappy."

Closing all the schools was a formidable undertaking. In 1960, they were being centralized at the rate of 150 to 200 a year, but in numbers they still represented half of all elementary schools in Ontario, with 10 percent of the teachers and nearly 10 percent of the pupils. By 1964 they were gone, mourned, in a world grown colder, by farm families who had lost a part of their lives.

There are still half-a-dozen one room schools and a few two or four room dotted across northern Ontario. They're referred to as isolate schools. The Ministry of Education recruits teachers to work in them and gives the schools a budget, because they can't raise enough taxes locally to support themselves.

Isolate or not, they're in touch with the world these days. They keep in radio contact with the nearest city. They have video machines, and in the not-too-distant future, they'll get information directly from satellites. That's faster than by colonization road, bush, track, and water.

JEAN COCHRANE is author of *The One Room School in Canada* and of several curriculum books published by Fitzhenry and Whiteside. She is a former reporter and freelance contributor to several Canadian magazines. She is Director of Communication with the Ontario Council of St. John Ambulance.

A student indulgent and slack
Was struck by a pendulum. Thwack!
"Hell-Mennis!" he cried.
"Soft options have died;
Those mind-boggling basics are back."

PROGRESSIVISM VERSUS TRADITIONALISM

MARK HOLMES

Ask most experienced teachers about educational change, and they will soon tell you that today's orthodoxy is yesterday's aberration. Were not the "basics" rather passé in the optimistic "life adjustment" times following World War II? Were they necessary to compete with Russian technology in the post-Sputnik sixties? Were they overlooked in the heady Hall-Dennis times of the early seventies? But now they are required again in the gritty eighties.

There can be little doubt that such perceptions reflect real changes in the daily lives of children, even if the changes, for better or worse, are less dramatic than they seem to their most vigorous defenders and detractors. But is there an educational pendulum swinging between two clearly defined philosophies? Or is education characterized by a continuous growth – malignant or benign – as it is touched by the forces of progressivism?

Although progressive education has a 200-year history stretching back into Europe, the source of its Canadian influence is American. Lawrence Cremin, in a history of the American school focussing sympathetically on the progressive movement, identifies three key categories of progressive change: "The broadening of program and function of the school"; the introduction of new "pedagogical principles";

and "tailoring instruction more and more to the different kinds and classes of children" (*The Transformation of the School*, 1961). Although those three categories clearly do not encompass all the changes that Ontario (and North American) education have experienced in the last 50 years, they provide a useful starting point.

Cremin's first category – the broadening of program and function of the school – becomes one of four dimensions with which I deal in this essay. Generally, the progressive, as Cremin suggests, wants an elaborate, unstructured program with much free choice for students. By contrast, the traditionalist wants sequence, structure, compulsory subjects, and fewer of those subjects that do not contribute to the education of the so-called "educated citizen." Yet, in at least one area, the traditionalist is likely to want more variation, more choice – that is in vocational and technical training. The difference then is not simply a matter of more or less choice, more or less variety, but of what constitutes the stuff of education. The progressive wants content that is intrinsically interesting, relevant to the daily lives of citizens, interdisciplinary, and individually "liberating." The traditionalist wants content that is related to the fundamental disciplines and that will lead either to profounder education and wisdom or, at least, to practical application in the workplace. But, as I indicate shortly, arguments about educational content tend to become proxies for differences about educational methods and purposes.

Cremin's second and third categories of progressivism (introducing new pedagogical principles and tailoring instruction) combine to become my second dimension – instructional methodology. There are three major differences between progressivists and traditionalists within this dimension, and all three are crucial to an understanding of the educational debate. The first is the obvious difference between progressive and traditional methodology. Progressives berate traditional schools for their "regulated" hours, controlled movement, "countless restrictions," and "impos-

---

It was some time in 1954. Fully immersed in the local curriculum movement in Ottawa, I was asked to speak to the school trustees at the Easter gathering of the Ontario Educational Association on the topic of "The Role of the School Trustee in Curriculum Revision." Manfully I recited my lines, and the perfunctory applause at the end was evidence that I had not bowled them over but I had at least assisted in filling up a bit of free time.

The chairman then called for questions from the floor. After a long silence which might have been caused by boredom, or hopefully, rumination on my striking speech, a gaunt figure rose from the back seat and queried: "Mr. Pullen, what do you think of frills?"

What I didn't know was that the new minister, Dr. Dunlop, had given an old boy's talk the night before which had hit the morning papers. In it he had extolled the values of the one-room school and deplored the modern emphasis on "frills" in education.

Clutching the microphone for support, I blurted out: "I have children in high school and if art, music, and household science are frills, I cannot accept it. Our young people should have the opportunity to take these subjects."

That ended the question period, but the afternoon paper came out with headlines, "Pullen Contradicts Minister." I became an overnight celebrity, and during the next few weeks received about ten invitations to talk — not on Curriculum Change but Frills in Education.

HARRY PULLEN,
FORMER SUPERINTENDENT OF SECONDARY SCHOOLS

ed, involuntary, and structured" learning experiences in which the pupil is expected to "mimic, regurgitate, and duplicate the pearls of wisdom to which he is exposed" (*Living and Learning*). Progressives, so they assert, want methods which help children "to cope with their everyday problems," avoid physical punishment and rewards, have children actively involved in joint projects and play, abolish "failure," and, for the purposes of instruction, focus on small groups of individuals rather than large groups. By contrast, traditionalists – backed by research showing that progressive methodology leads to low levels of academic achievement and thus to the lowering of standards – argue that instruction should be sequential, structured, and demanding; the pace should be that which pupils can be pushed to achieve, not that which they want to achieve; and educational techniques should be adopted on the basis of positive empirical findings rather than elegant hunches.

The second difference, one mentioned by Cremin, is the belief of progressives that instruction should be tailored to the "needs" of the particular child: "Every effort must be made to fit the learning opportunities to the potential, tempo, and level of each child" (*Living and Learning*). By contrast, the traditionalists, while recognizing the obvious differences between the mentally retarded and the genius, are more likely to press for the same instruction for, if not all, at least the vast majority. Instruction, they argue, should be differentiated for young children only where empirical research shows it is necessary, and for adolescents only where their different interests and ability take them in different directions toward different goals.

The third difference is crucial yet is often overlooked. To progressives, instructional methodology is an article of central belief. *Living and Learning* is essentially about pedagogy, as is *To Herald a Child* (LaPierre). Traditionalists are more reactive than proactive in this regard – they do not care for progressive methods, and particularly they object to methods being promulgated without their being tested, and to their being pursued even when empirical research finds them disadvantageous.

These differences being noted, there is obviously more to the educational debate than content and methodology. As the reader might suggest, are there not major differences of philosophy and public policy? Don't educators differ about access to university, about the organization of secondary education, and about fundamental goals and directions? Although philosophical differences – which represent my third dimension – underlie the debate between progressives and traditionalists, it is not evident that there is a single, unitary, coherent statement about the purposes of life, the meaning of knowledge and wisdom, and education's relation to those concepts that would gain consensual support from the adherents of either group.

Progressive educational philosophy, as I have suggested, rests heavily on the nature of the educational process. The journey is more important than the destination. The medium is the message. Rousseau is generally seen as the father of progressive education. His book *Emile*, first

". . . *the child is innocent, good, and free but is confined and dulled by adult restrictions*. . . ."

published in 1762, outlines an ideal education based on the acquisition through the physical senses of knowledge as ideas. "God makes all things good; man meddles with them and they become evil." Self-love is always good. The notion that the child is innocent, good, and free but is confined and dulled by adult restrictions remains a pervasive myth in modern times. Such ideas about education are combined by modern progressives with liberal, rational utilitarianism – developed by Hume, Locke, Bentham, John Stuart Mill, and Bertrand Russell. To the idea of the child as innocent are added two further beliefs: first, "inalienable" human rights; and second, the use of an objective, value-free, problem-solving mode of inquiry (adopted from the physical sciences) as the appropriate means of attacking human (including educational) problems. Now, within such an eclectic background, there is ample space for differences of opinion. One can be a rational empiricist without adhering to Rousseau's ideas about unfettered growth. One can believe in fundamental human rights without bowing to logical rationality. Insofar as there is a collective wisdom among such disparate ideas, it is that the school should recognize the unique individuality of each child, should accord the child fundamental rights and liberties, and should approach all problems – moral, religious, intellectual – with an open mind in the spirit of free inquiry.

This brings us to a paradox. Doesn't progressivism (my Satan) sing all the best tunes? Is there anybody who does not ascribe to some variant of the systems of thought described above? Even a major, contemporary supporter of traditionalism, Alasdair MacIntyre, agrees that utilitarianism is the preeminent philosophy of modern times. The paradox is that the public, although confused, is not notably supportive of progressive ideas in education. The public tends to dislike the relativist approach to moral education (known as values clarification) on the very ground that it assumes there are no fundamental virtues, there is no basic truth, no overall good. The public tends to believe that school programs should focus more on study in the disciplines or on usable job skills (although that belief is probably attributable more to interest in jobs and money than to the value of learning), teach more about what people have in common and less about their ethnic, racial, and religious differences, and be more uniform and rigorous rather than differentiated and individualized.

The traditionalist philosophy that helps uphold some of those paradoxical public beliefs is probably less coherent than that underlying the powerful and dominant progressive school of thought. Traditionalist philosophy has its origins in Greco-Roman classical times and in the Judaeo-Christian heritage. Its most dominant characteristic is a belief that precedes all other educational considerations. Plato called it the "good"; Aristotle saw it as the good life characterized by virtuous behaviour; and Christians and Jews have called it God and His teachings. Although the chasms dividing the variety of beliefs held by those following these traditions are even wider than those within the modernist school (one of whose aspects is educational progressivism), there is some consensus among them about the centrality of fundamental virtues –truth, courage, generosity, compassion, and justice. The effect of this consensus is even more pronounced than may, at first sight, appear. A mediator might think that belief in virtue need be no barrier to compromise with progressives. In practice, will not progressives agree that most of the central virtues are useful if not fundamentally right? They are unlikely to advocate untruthfulness and cowardice. But that is to miss the point of the traditionalists' view, for such a mediator would obviously be a modernist. Virtue is not, for traditionalists, a commodity that happens to be useful to schools in the maintenance of order and discipline (although order and discipline are prerequisites for purposeful instruction). Virtue, for the traditionalists, is both the means and goal of education; and whereas to the progressives the means become the end, to the traditionalists the end becomes the means.

If the differences among traditionalists and among progressives make it difficult to make clear philosophical statements that characterize an overall consensus on either side, it is even more difficult to analyze the differences in major issues of public policy – my fourth dimension – in those same terms. Two major issues facing the Ontario educational system today are accessibility to post-secondary education and equality of educational opportunity. Progressives have, in the main, been in favor of expanding educational accessibility. They have also been willing to pay lip service to equality of educational opportunity – at any rate, equality of results as distinct from equal choice of access. Thus there have been some suggestions for ensuring that both sexes and different ethnic groups are guaranteed places in competitive programs commensurate with the proportion of each group in the population at large. Traditionalists, by contrast, have been more equivocal on the issue of accessibility and less on the issue of quotas. Although they too favor broad access to education, their concern is that the lowering of entry standards together with mass university education will promote mediocrity. As for equality of opportunity, they believe that all should have a fair chance of entry – and that means some single system of external tests and examinations for all – and that quota systems institutionalize unfairness, fail to accommodate the different interests and aspirations of different groups, and lower standards. Thus, in broad terms, there are differences, but it would be rash to identify too closely what I have called progressive views on policy issues and the more clearly defined progressive views on methodology and content within the public school system.

So far, then, I have discussed four different dimensions of the progressive/traditional split: curriculum content; instructional methodology; philosophy; and policy issues. The most clearcut distinction emerged for instructional methodology, and differences in philosophy and policy issues were rather more confused. However, I am not for one

---

COUNTY OF WATERLOO

PROMOTION EXAMINATION

June 23rd, 24th, 25th and 26th, 1931

GEOGRAPHY

Form III, Jr. to Form III, Sr

TIME—ONE HOUR AND A HALF

Values	
1	1. (a) Who lived in our country before the white man came here?
2	(b) What tools did they use?
2	(c) What tools do they use now?
2	(d) What did they bring to the trading posts?
3	(e) What did they exchange them for?
1	2. (a) What shape is North America?
1	(b) What continent is similar in shape?
3	(c) Name 3 highlands of North America?
6	(d) Name 3 of the largest provinces in Canada with their capitals.
4	3. (a) Name two Atlantic Ports and two Pacific Ports of North America.
5	(b) Name five products which are shipped from any one of these ports.
10	4. What country furnishes:— Your sugar? Your tea? Your coffee? Your rice? Your raisins? Your oranges? Your rubber? Your coal? Your flour? Your cotton?
8 × 2	5. State why each of the following is important:— Fraser River, Quebec City, Ottawa, Algonquin Park, Halifax, St. John, The Great Clay Belt, Niagara Peninsula.
2 + 2	6. (a) What is meant by the (1) equator, (2) axis of the earth?
4	(b) What causes day and night?
2	(c) What shape is our earth?
2	Give two reasons why you believe it to be this shape
2	7. (a) What is "raw material"?
10	(b) What is the raw material from which each of the following, respectively, is made:—Leather, cheese, lumber, lime, brick, cider, sauer-kraut, linen, paper, yarn?
2	8. (a) What is a canal?
2	(b) For what two purposes are canals usually made?
3 × 2	(c) Locate these canals and tell why each was built:— Soo, Murray, Welland.
5 × 2	9. On the accompanying map of the Saskatchewan and Nelson River System, name five of the lakes and rivers.
100	

(Property of Madeline Lavender)

moment suggesting that there are not likely to be deep philosophical differences between a given progressive and a given traditionalist. Not in the least. Simply those differences are matched by differences within the two opposing camps.

I turn now to the Ontario school to see how and to what extent these four dimensions relate to progressive change in Ontario education. But before a relationship can be established, it is necessary to determine just when progressive change occurred. There is general agreement that Ryerson developed, in the late 19th century, a strong, traditionalist, centralized school system in Ontario, a system that resisted major change until well into the 20th century. Ryerson's reforms can rightly be seen as denoting major progress in Ontario education, but they were not "progressive" in the sense applied in this essay. And here it is important to distinguish between the terms "progress" and "progressivism": if "progress" merely means to be in favor of improvement, then, by definition, we are all progressive.

According to W.G. Fleming, in his history of Ontario education, the progressive ideas of Comenius and Froebel were beginning to seep in by the early 20th century with the introduction of art, music, "constructive work," nature study, and physical culture; but the first real progressive thrust came in 1937 with the adoption of a revised curriculum reflecting progressive ideas at the elementary level. At this time, British influence on Ontario was still strong, and the changes reflected early progressive, Deweyan ideas introduced in British elementary schools. The changes were almost entirely in methodology. The school was to stimulate the pupil "through his own interests" and to help him "satisfy his own needs." Promotion was to be by age rather than achievement, and emphasis on examinations was to be reduced. However, plans and implementation are horses of a different color, and the thrust had little overall impact.

The next major progressive thrust noted by chroniclers on Ontario education came with the Hope Commission in 1950. Hugh A. Stevenson, like Fleming, a historian sympathetic to progressive ideas, writes: "Outright advocacy of progressive education was often euphemized or muffled by educational jargon. But there is no doubt that learning by doing, client-centred schools, activity programs, and respect for the child's individuality and developmental growth toward independent adulthood were accepted as tenets of the curriculum" (*So Little for the Mind? Reaction and Reform in the Modern Curriculum*). Nevertheless, according to Stevenson, these favorable changes were still opposed by recalcitrants: "Deep-rooted authoritarian practices, the simplicity of a narrow curriculum and the rather sparse training of new teachers often resulted in the perpetuation of traditional methods, strict discipline, recitation, rote learning, great reverence for the subject and little respect for the student." He goes on to state that the narrow secondary curriculum was not challenged until the sixties, not by his and others' accounts a period of progressive strength. Beneath the rhetoric, it is clear that Stevenson (a voice of the progressive, mainstream, educational establishment) sees the major dimension of the dispute as being one of methodology.

The early sixties saw an interlude during which there was no major progressive thrust, although progressive forces in the Province, particularly in the Department of Education, were gaining strength. The examination system endured, although it was modified by the addition of objective components. New curriculum innovations were made by the Ontario Curriculum Institute, but the basic subject matter remained, and even geography and history resisted the North American trend to merge them in "civics" or "social studies." The major turning point in Ontario education, in terms of a chronicle of progressivism, was the publication of the provincial report on aims and objectives, *Living and Learning*, in 1968. It is this publication (commonly known as the Hall-Dennis report) that marks the beginning of Ontario's progressive era. Fleming notes enthusiastically that by 1968 the "Department (now Ministry) of Education was unequivocally in progressive hands." Progressivism quickly became the philosophy of the educational establishment; and likewise of the Ontario Institute for Studies in Education (OISE), which had been established in 1965 and in which a substantial proportion of the staff were young American educators eager to convert an essentially conservative province to a new, modernistic, secular, humanistic, less restrictive education of progressivism; ironically, the main dissent from within OISE came not from traditionalists wanting to maintain traditional standards but from Marxists wanting a more thoroughgoing egalitarian revolution. The climate had moderated by the mid-seventies, but OISE is still seen by the public as being in the progressive camp.

A visiting English professor, writing on the Canadian curriculum, noted that, even a decade after the publication of *Living and Learning*, progressive "rhetoric still imbues Ministry of Education directives and is still current among the establishment figures in the Ontario Teachers' Federation" (Robin Barrow, *The Canadian Curriculum: Personal View*). Indeed, about the same time, the teachers' associations representing elementary teachers funded a report, *To Herald a Child* (published in 1980), by an extreme progressive, Laurier LaPierre, which predictably made recommendations even more radical than those of Hall-Dennis, arguing that the state should intervene much more strongly to override the traditional responsibilities of parents and to impose inalienable children's rights, both inside and outside the school.

Despite the continuing progressive power within the educational establishment – the Ministry, teachers' associations, school board administrations, and schools of education – a turning point can be seen around 1975 when public dissatisfaction with the progressive reforms began to surface. In a case study of education in Guelph, published in 1977, Hall and Carlton described the feelings of abandonment prevalent among teachers, particularly at the elementary level, who felt that they had been led into an extreme progressive posture, only to be abandoned by the establishment leaders, who ran for cover the moment public anger began to swell. "Radical discontinuity in policy-making at higher levels, concerning goals, pedagogy, and the value of core curricula and external examinations has resulted in

---

A memory that stays with me from my years in education involves not just an area of education but a close association with a person — a man whose influence on all aspects of education in Ontario and Canada over three decades is now legend. Sad to say, aside from educators and a sprinkling of politicians, he will not be remembered, short of a few lines in the record books read by few of the millions who will continue to benefit from his influence.

Bob Jackson lived and loved education. Our early meetings and discussions about the future of education, and more especially educational research, worked its way through a maze of faculty organizations, school boards, research groups, politicians, civil servants, and benign vested interests. I'm sure, through all of this, Dr. Bob had clearly in his mind the kind of institution needed for Ontario at that particular time in the pursuit of the goal of educational excellence.

I well recall the day we decided on the name for the new Institution — a name suggested by another great educator, Dr. "Butch" Morgan. When it was finally agreed upon, Bob was quick to say, "Those initials spell out O.I.S.E. Quite likely, the first letters of the words will come into everyday use." He stood up, smiled, and jokingly said, "We will likely be referred to simply as OY-SEE." His assembled learned friends said, "Never." But, Dr. Bob was right again.

THE HONOURABLE WILLIAM G. DAVIS,
PREMIER OF ONTARIO

abrupt shifts and reversals which have left the teachers confused or even resentful" (*Basic Skills at School and Work*). Hall and Carlton conclude that there is a perplexing overall contradiction between "recent aims" of greater student "interest" and "involvement" and the outcomes of greater "apathy" and "unwillingness to work." Since that time, the public perception, carefully tended by Ministry releases, has been that there has been a slow move back to the centre, with more regulated, centralized curricula, more compulsory courses in the secondary school, and the intimation of more disciplined schools to come.

At this point, I shall address two questions. First, what is the character of the changes that have accompanied the perceived swings toward progressivism in the late thirties, the fifties, and, more particularly, the late sixties and early seventies? Second, is there really a pendulum swinging between the forces of traditionalism and progressivism or are the changes taking place more like the waves in an incoming tide – sudden rushes followed by periods of temporary withdrawal and consolidation?

The first two progressive surges (those of the thirties and fifties) have much in common: both were focussed on the elementary school; both concerned methodology far more than curriculum content, fundamental philosophy, or public policy; and for several reasons, neither had much effect. The most obvious reason was the resistance of inspectors, administrators, and teachers, who rarely shared the progressive zeal of their leaders. Underlying the resistance, there may well have been a philosophical thread. Reformers of the thirties and fifties were careful to tread around the pinnacles of Christianity and the Judaeo-Christian heritage. Such sidestepping inevitably weakened the force of the reformers, for the religious intensity of modernism stems precisely from its refusal to accept automatically traditional virtues, beliefs, and values, its endorsement of a liberating secular humanism, and its replacement of ends by means. How important that thread was is difficult to determine. What is not difficult to determine is that the nature of the envisaged reforms had to do with the *process* of education: less restriction to a specific text; promotion by age rather than by competence; and learning by informal "experience" rather than by formal instruction.

As suggested previously, the Hall-Dennis reforms were those that had the most deep-rooted and persistent effects. They too appear to have been directed more at the elementary grades than at the secondary grades. Prescriptions for the secondary school were vague, and the actual secondary reforms that were implemented reflect only in part the spirit of progressivism. Thus, the secondary school reforms eliminated the separate tracks of the Robarts plan, and they downgraded technical and vocational education, effects consistent with the Hall-Dennis emphasis on individualistic, aesthetic, and expressionist education. But they established the technocratic, time-oriented, computerized scheduling system that has arguably made schools more "factory like" rather than the freer, educational drop-in centres implied by Hall-Dennis. The reforms also included the abolition of external examinations, as Hall-Dennis wished. The result was not, however, any loss of interest by students in marks. The competition to enter post-secondary programs became more heated as the public became more aware of the financial and social consequences of success. One result of the abolition of external examinations was the lowering of standards (but not necessarily of levels of achievement), witnessed by the more than doubling of the proportion of students receiving honors averages in Grade 13. Another result was increased parental concern about the differences in standards among schools, with the bizarre phenomenon that, in terms of access to further education, it became advantageous for an aspiring student to attend a school with low standards. The high school program after Hall-Dennis was supposed to proliferate, but apart from the much abused *Man and Society* and a few local, experimental courses, the basic program of study for academically oriented secondary students has not changed greatly. There has, however, been some change of methodology and content. Except in mathematics and science, courses generally have become non-sequential. Physical, economic, and regional geography may be taken indiscriminately, and students may or may not take courses in the history of modern Europe and of classical Greece and Rome. In English, sequence in literature and language is so lacking that the grade levels become indistinguishable, and it is difficult to determine, either by examining the student or by reading the curriculum (let alone by observing the classes), what different academic outcomes are required from different courses.

At the elementary level, the effects have been more profound. While schools with open architecture proved generally a short-lived fad, informal instructional techniques have taken a firm hold on Ontario schools, particularly in what are known as "language arts" and "social and environmental studies." The continuing hold of these methodologies, originally imported from the United States, is the more remarkable in that recent American research on the effective use of instructional time has not been generally supportive of informal techniques. Indeed, the massive movement toward "effective schools" in the United States today is predicated on clear objectives, direct instruction, and logical sequencing. By contrast, there is renewed vigor in Ontario to teach reading by allowing children to read what they want, to teach writing by allowing children to write what they want, and to teach social studies and science through individual or group activities based on studying what they want. Indeed, the Ministry of Education's first goal is to help "each student develop a responsiveness to the dynamic process of learning" (*Issues and Directions*, 1980). That, needless to say, is a classic progressive statement. The philosophy of the Ministry becomes even clearer when one finds in the statement of goals no mention of such traditional aims as the development of virtue, good character, and manners, learning in the disciplines of knowledge, or even the development of competence in the country's second language. Competence is out. Process is in. Ministry reviews focus on classroom methodology rather than on levels of achievement; and although there are indications Ontario may be moving, after the rest of Canada, to some use of standardized testing, student evaluation is still carried out chiefly by personal observation – a trend very different from the American move to re-establish order and standards.

I suggested earlier that it would be difficult to formulate two clear competing philosophies of education. That difficulty probably explains in part why educators today generally eschew a label of either "progressive" or "traditional." Nevertheless, as the progressive thrust of the thirties and fifties may well have failed because they ran against an iceberg of traditionalism whose tip was Christian doctrine, so the success of the progressive thrust of the late sixties may be attributable to the erosion of traditional beliefs and the strengthening of the religion of modernism – the belief that there are no fundamental truths; that all values are relative and the product of specific situations; and that how we educate is more important that what we want young people to become. Yet, there remains the paradox that the Ontario public is still quite traditional in its beliefs about education, even if it does not adhere to any coherent system of beliefs. The key to the paradox lies in the observation of the (progressive) historians that the failure of the earlier progressive thrusts could be attributed to the conservatism of educators – not the conservatism of the people. So, perhaps the success of progressivism, despite public resistance, can be attributed to the progressivism of so many educators. Their reluctance to label themselves can be understood partly in the context of public opinion. Beyond that, progressivism has become so much a part of the general discourse of education that many educators do not recognize particular ideas as being progressive.

To turn to my fourth dimension, the realm of public educational policy cannot be distinguished entirely from the

A traditional view of a traditional class

dimensions of curriculum content and instructional methodology with which I have been primarily concerned. Those two dimensions may be seen as being aspects of public policy. In the broadest sense, that is obviously the case, and *Living and Learning* was a public policy document largely concerned with methodology. Yet, for the most part, questions of content and methodology are thrashed out in the back rooms of the Ministry, in school boards, and in committees. Only rarely do they merit major focussed discussion by the Legislature or media, however important they may be to the daily lives of teachers and pupils. That point is particularly true of methodology, which, I suggest, is the core belief of progressivism.

But public educational policy obviously encompasses much beyond those two specific issues. Progressives might be expected to support such liberal causes as individual freedom, educational expansion, equality of educational opportunity, modernization, and decentralization. Traditionalists might be expected to promote such conservative policies as traditional standards of excellence, firm discipline, the inculcation of virtues, centralization, standardization, and an emphasis on tradition.

Yet there are obvious problems with simple "liberal" and "conservative" labels. For example, equality of educational opportunity is now defended by conservatives and is attacked by left-wing liberals (who would like to introduce quota systems to ensure "balance" in restricted university programs in terms of sex and of ethnic and social background). Beyond such problems of definition, the reality in the Ontario context is that a Progressive Conservative Government has been in power during virtually the entire period of the progressive thrust. If one, as a rough guide, uses the two lists above, the Conservative Government's record conforms more closely to the liberal list, particularly over the last three decades. Clearly, party political labels do not explain changes in educational policy; but are there important educational policy issues whose resolution explains the perceived swing of the pendulum (leaving aside issues of pedagogical content and methodology)?

Even by the pragmatic standards of political parties, the Conservative Government's endorsement of progressive ideas has been remarkable. Periodically, it has moved so far to the left that, in the late seventies, the Liberal Party, under

A traditional view of a progressive class

two leaders, Robert Nixon and Stuart Smith, actually used conservative positions (with respect to more rigorous standards and more directive curricula) as part of its election platform in order to capitalize on voter discontent. At the same time, as public opinion swung away from progressivism, the New Democratic Party was forced to stay unnaturally quiet on the question of education, presumably in the knowledge that the Conservative Government was already to the left of the people. To be more progressive would be to alienate itself entirely from popular support outside its base in Toronto. In 1984, as Government cutbacks in educational spending become more rigorous and as teachers, a potentially powerful lobby for the N.D.P. (as has been shown in British Columbia), chafe at the effects of salary controls, that situation may be changing. Even so, it seems likely that any N.D.P. platform in the next few years will stress educational spending rather than progressive policies.

Ontario, unlike the United States and Great Britain where educational policy changes reflect the changes of government, has seen both the progressive swings and retrenchment carried out under the same regime – in one case, by the same Minister of Education. One of the greatest policy changes in Ontario educational history came about not as a result of the progressive thrust of the fifties, not as a result of the progressive thrust of the late sixties, but in the relatively conservative interim. It was in the late fifties and early sixties that the high school became the place for the custody and, perhaps, the education of the mass of youth rather than a place of specialized training for a minority. At about the same time, the greatest expansion of the university system in Ontario's history took place – with the founding of new universities and the growth of the old. However, in some universities, the education was traditional rather than progressive. The University of Waterloo, for example, forged its way over the next decade into the front rank of Canadian universities in some specific fields (chemistry, computer studies, mathematics, engineering), but it did so in a most unprogressive way. It emphasized high standards and rigorous excellence, and even introduced competitive examinations (for the award of scholarships).

Further evidence that the educational expansion of the sixties was not entirely progressive is provided by the establishment during that same period of the colleges. Ontario is virtually unique in North America in having a comprehensive network of post-secondary colleges that are vocational in nature and entirely separate from the university system. Whether or not the decision to segregate the two post-secondary systems was wise, only time will tell; it was certainly not progressive. One only has to contrast the situation with that of Quebec. In that Province, the change of the secondary school program, the introduction of progressive methodology in the elementary school, and the establishment of the college system were all part and parcel of the same thrust. Not only are the colleges integrated in the entire system but also attendance at college for two years is prerequisite for entrance to university. Similarly, the new University of Quebec is seen as an institution reaching out to the grass roots of the Province, and its goal is the "animation" of the public – very different from the goals set by Waterloo, or Guelph and Carleton for that matter.

In the Ontario school system, a major policy initiative outside the discussion of content and process has been the passing of Bill 82, a bill giving every child the right to an appropriate education. This bill, passed long after the progressivism of the early seventies had gone, illustrates the continuing grip of progressives in a time of supposed retrenchment, aided, without doubt, by a strong-minded Minister of Education of medical, client-centred, individualistic bent. Although the legislation will have some humane effect in extending special educational provisions to a few children hitherto deprived, its main effect will be to create a more specialized, distinctive pedagogy, thereby reinforcing the progressive thrust toward the emphasis of individual differences. This latest progressive advance, running against an anti- progressive tide of public opinion, illustrates two things: the continuing progressive hold on educational power, and the extent to which progressive ideas have come to dominate the educational dialogue. The opposition to Bill 82 was based on such problems as cost and increased bureaucracy. The lack of a coherent traditionalist opposition to a liberal bill from a Conservative Government went unnoticed. The bill extends further the idea that education is no longer to be a social activity embedded in the community, where young people are brought up to be good members of society and incur obligations to that society; instead it is to be an individualized prescription whereby individuals obtain their rights – just as they get their prescription from their doctor to treat their particular medical ailment.

Most teachers, as I suggested at the beginning, perceive a swing to and fro between progressivism and traditionalism. There can be no doubt that there have been times when progressive ideas have been touted from the rooftops, and other times when they have been kept hidden between plain, brown wrappers. Yet the overview I have offered does not suggest any lack of overall movement. The schools of today are very different from those of 1934, certainly more different than those of 1934 were from those of 1884. It is more accurate, then, to see the growth of progressivism as being persistent, if not continuous. There is no pendulum, but a succession of surges. Each surge is stronger than the previous one, and any retrenchment is less than complete. Progressivism, however, must be fairly narrowly defined. The progressive surges observed by historians in the thirties, the fifties, and the late sixties are concerned above all with instructional methodology in the Province's schools. They are not concerned with broad public policy and scarcely with the colleges and universities, whose rhythms have not been entirely in harmony with those of the schools. That is not to assert there is no underlying philosophy and no clash between the forces of modernism and those of traditionalism.

We have not seen a clash between two coherent, consensual philosophies of education, but the schools have been one of the battlefields where modernism has gradually eroded traditional beliefs and customs. To that extent, the philosophical clash is of preeminent importance.

That brings us to the question whether the growth is benign or malignant. Before addressing that question directly, it is important to re-emphasize the distinction between progress and progressivism. There can be no question that schools, colleges, and universities are better than they were 50 years ago, or 200 years ago. That improvement is partly a question of quantity. More people are being educated in a variety of ways. To traditionalists, that itself is good. Education is desirable simply because it promotes knowledge and wisdom; it gives more people more glimpses of ultimate truth, and it provides more people with the opportunity to become better at the various activities they undertake. As for the quality of the educational experiences, it is probably fair to say, with many more limitations, that there has also been some overall improvement. A few ineffective teaching techniques have been eliminated, and the climate of some schools has improved. Some new ideas have proved effective (although many more, often in continued use, have proved counterproductive), and yes, there has been progress in education.

There has been progress, but progressivism does not appear to have been associated, on the whole, with educational improvement. It has generally proved unpopular with the public, who see it as promoting unpleasant behavior, bad manners, poor work habits, and low levels of achievement. Research evidence, too, tends to suggest that, where there is a difference, achievement is enhanced more by "effective school" techniques (such as raising expectations, rigorous teaching, and a sequence of objectives) than by progressive techniques. Perhaps one of the most unfortunate manifestations of progressivism is the totalitarian way in which its methodology is being introduced in the schools today. Teachers have traditionally not had the freedom to choose what they want to teach but they have had the freedom of determining how to teach it. Now, educational methods are being prescribed even more closely than educational objectives. Sadder still, the teachers' professionalism is being impugned not by government directly but by their colleagues working on curriculum committees.

The historical verdict on Ontario's affair with progressivism will probably be based not on its effects on reading, writing, and mathematical skills, important as they are; not on the loss of teachers' professionalism, important as it is; but on its part in the larger fight for children's minds. On the one hand, there are the beliefs in the objectivity of scientific inquiry, in the relativism of all moral and spiritual values, in education as an individual contract for personal development

---

One of my first administrative tasks as a new vice-principal (in 1960) was to help my principal convince the Department of Education that one small part of the very rigid system then in vogue should be relaxed for a student who had a valid alternative to the required pattern for a SSGD. We failed.

My last task as a principal (1978) was to try and convince the Department (then the Ministry) to allow me to retain a prerequisite for a Grade 13 subject in order to strengthen and give validity to the decidedly un-rigid credit system then in vogue. I failed.

Conclusion: The only valid stance to have taken in the interests of a reasonable consistency was one of continuous opposition to the Department's vacillating positions.

T. R. DUNFORD,
FORMER SECONDARY SCHOOL PRINCIPAL

between pupil or parent and the state, and in the means of learning as the purpose of learning. On the other hand, there are beliefs in fundamental values on which all education must be based and in that genuine freedom which can only be achieved from a foundation of knowledge, wisdom, and virtue. Ontario's flirtation with progressivism must be seen in the larger context of the conflict between traditionalism and modernism. Looked at over a time span of 60 years, modern secular humanism appears to have won a spectacular victory. But 16 years of real progressivism, from 1968, is a mere hiccup even in Ontario's short history. If we look outside Ontario, east to Europe, south to the United States, and west to the Rockies, we see that the forces of progressivism are less ascendant than they are here. Ontarians of different ideological persuasion will watch the unfolding Titanic struggle, both in the larger society and in the microcosm that is education. There will be few disinterested observers.

MARK HOLMES, who was born in England and grew up in the Isle of Man, was educated at the Universities of Cambridge, New Brunswick, and Chicago. He was a teacher and a principal (of both elementary and high schools) in Saint John, New Brunswick, and became a curriculum superintendent and director of education in Quebec. He joined OISE in 1975 as an administrator responsible for the Institute's field activities, and he is presently a professor in the Department of Educational Administration. He has written, spoken, and carried out research on a variety of educational policy issues, including student evaluation and effective schooling.

His class expectant, Doctor Preach
Deliberating what to teach
Decided on arithmetic,
But figures made his students sick.
They neither could subtract nor add,
Their mastery of tables — bad.
They couldn't even read or write;
Their manners too, quite impolite.
Said Doctor Preach, "Ah woe is me!
Perhaps I'll teach them history."
But nothing he could do or say
Would make the present go away.
They would not memorize the dates
Of kings and queens and heads of states.
He switched to physics, then to French,
But failed their apathy to quench.
"Ah woe is me," the Doctor said,
"I'll have a go at Moral Ed;
How virtue is its own reward."
But soon his restive class grew bored,
Hostile, inciteful, and perverse,
Displaying manners even worse
Than they'd been guilty of before.
Said Doctor Preach, "I'll teach them law!"
And laying round him with his cane
Instructed them in feeling pain.

Moral

Students like quadrupeds, I think,
Will seldom feel compelled to drink;
And though their minds you may expose
To what the tree of knowledge grows,
Imploring them with strictures stern,
Yet you will never "make" them learn.

WHAT TO TEACH

WALTER PITMAN

". . . a respect for the British monarchy and government institutions, an appreciation for punctuality and cleanliness. . . ."

An examination of curriculum and instructional practice in the schools of Ontario can be approached from a number of directions. Obviously curriculum outlines and teachers' manuals represent a source of documentation not to be lightly ignored. As well, there have been countless reports on education, and each one has been a reaction to societal pressures of the day and deserves our attention and study. I have chosen, instead, the experiential approach. I have confronted the world of curriculum and teaching methods in Ontario both as a student and as a teacher and administrator. In an age glorifying nostalgia, heritage, and memories of happier times, it may be instructive.

During the thirties, I attended a "public school" which looked like any of dozens of other red brick schools, and in the mid-forties I moved on to a large collegiate institute in Toronto.

Much of what we experience as curriculum comes as a result of the school system's perception of its mission and of its judgment of its clientele. The elementary school's job in pre-war Ontario was clearcut – it was to ensure the learning of the 3 Rs, along with a healthy dose of Christian ethic, a respect for the British monarchy and government institutions, an appreciation for punctuality and cleanliness, and, in

47

my case, a capacity to sit still with my hands behind my back. There was some recognition of the reality of the Canadian nation (but little emphasis), and in the war years, an enthusiasm for endless marching around a schoolyard in a scarlet wool tunic. All this I had experienced before I was 14 years of age.

The school system of Ontario, even in the thirties, was coasting largely on the impetus created by that giant of an initiator, Egerton Ryerson, who had determined that the "Americanization" of the British colony through neglect of curriculum planning was not to continue and that the creation of a provincial system of schools was the only way to ensure a population that was loyal, Christian, and literate. Ryerson's wish served well the largely agricultural society of the newly created Province of Ontario. Those who spent a few years in the free and compulsory elementary schools of the Province could contribute as farmers or tradesmen to the community in which they would live for the rest of their lives.

By the early years of the 20th century, there was recognition that an industrial society had developed in the United Kingdom, Germany, and the United States, and that future economic well-being would depend on manning the machines in a factory – as opposed to following a plough or selling over a counter. A Royal Commission on Industrial Training and Education released its report in 1913 and made this point.

By the time I reached the higher grades of elementary school, the system's recognition of working with the hands had determined that while girls learned something of sewing and cooking, boys should partake of manual training. I recall being taught how to assemble certain tools, how to join wood in various ways, and how to sandpaper the wood until it was as smooth as silk.

In the light of wartime needs, one exercise was that of building solid model planes to be used, we were assured, in the training of aircraft observers who would warn the authorities in the event of air attack. We can be thankful that

---

In our school, in 1944, scrap drives to help Britain were a patriotic effort undertaken with greater zeal than working in the Victory Garden. The search for iron and steel objects in our industrial area was an adventure. I recall one such scrap drive when our spirit and patriotism overrode our good judgment.

St. Joseph Elementary School was located in "Ford City" beside the C.N.R. tracks. Tie plates, railroad spikes, brake shoes, pry bars, and a variety of heavy signs, all steel and all neatly piled along the tracks, found their way to the school and into the bin in which our contributions were stored.

Soon, however, the Railway Police also found their way to the school. After endorsing our patriotic efforts and explaining to us the difference between "scrap steel" and "track maintenance parts," they helped us to identify their materials. We dutifully removed these from the storage bin and loaded them onto the yellow railway truck.

What had seemed to be building towards the most successful scrap drive of all time became instead a very embarrassing lesson.

M. LaMARRE, PRINCIPAL,
WILLIAM HANDS SECONDARY SCHOOL, WINDSOR

---

enemy aircraft technology never developed sufficiently long-distance planes to threaten our shores as the products of our efforts would have given little preparatory advantage to even the most perceptive observer.

The arts were seen as recreational, a kind of reward for keeping collectively quiet and having accomplished something in the real curriculum – reading, writing, and arithmetic. Or we might be allowed to draw and paint on Friday afternoons when it was assumed that students were in an unproductive state of mind. However, some schools managed to develop a strong choral musical tradition, and I was fortunate to be attending one of them. The Kiwanis Festival was the central event of the year.

Only a handful of my friends accompanied me after graduation from "public school" to the neighborhood collegiate – most dropped out to go to work; some went off to a nearby technical school. (In larger cities, these technical schools had arisen in the wake of the new interest in industrial education.) The purpose of the secondary school curriculum was unquestionably that of preparing a fraction of students who were able to survive the early grades to pass the provincial examinations and thus move on with distinction to the university. High school was far too much a "culling" process, designed to ensure that the school, its principal, and its teachers were never embarrassed by unacceptably low examination results published for all to see in the local newspaper. These examinations were written in the school, papers were not linked by name to students (thus assuring anonymity at the point of marking), and were scored by the cream of experienced teachers in the shadow of provincial parliament buildings. The teaching methods were geared to achieve the best results, and as marking schemes gave marks to "facts," the accumulation of factual information was paramount. This was achieved through textbooks and, in the classroom, through teaching in a style that was casually and inaccurately called the "Socratic method." In the hands of some teachers, this method of instruction could achieve heights of intellectual triumph as an entire class was brought through an analytic process quite beyond the capacity of any one of the participating students. In most classrooms, however, it was too often a quizzing of the brighter students to elicit unconnected facts found the previous night in the assigned pages of the textbook.

The curriculum was focussed on a narrow band of liberal arts, mathematics, language (French, German, Classics), and the sciences. The English literature courses were centred on Shakespearean drama and Dickensian prose.

"... *in a style that was casually and inaccurately called the Socratic method.*"

Neither I nor my fellow students had an inkling that there were Canadian authors writing novels and living within a few blocks of the building in which we found ourselves. Languages were essentially for examining the literature and culture of a foreign country and expressing one's view in turgid prose. Ironically, those who graduated during this hey-day in the teaching of French in Ontario's high schools found it impossible to converse in even the simplest terms with Quebec citizens across the Ottawa River. The sciences, which had not seemed particularly important in the mid-19th century, had, by the thirties and forties, gained full recognition in Ontario schools, and their teaching was accompanied with less hysteria than that which followed upon the Russian "Sputnik" success of the fifties.

The pressure to ensure that every student knew something of technical employment meant that first-year students in my collegiate were tramped a half-mile one afternoon a week to the nearby technical school where we learned the parts of a car, how to change a tire, and, in the wood-working shop, about how to operate drills and lathes. This was insufficient to provide any skill or, indeed, appreciation of skill, but it apparently satisfied some bureaucrat that a link between the head and the hand had been forged.

". . . a link between the head and the hand had been forged."

The arts received a little more recognition at the secondary level. One could pursue an arts option – painting and drawing or music. Indeed, both of these were compulsory in first-year, and the music teacher, faced with over 300 students a week, took refuge in music appreciation and whatever information about music notation that could be self-scored on tests. Yet, ironically, no course in my experience was to give me greater pleasure in mature life than that pathetic, inadequate, institutionalized effort to expose students to the mystery of music. In sheer desperation, the teacher played classical records continuously and thereby exposed a doorway to the entire classical repetoire, which has been my delight ever since.

The school system had, by the thirties and forties, determined that physical well-being was important – the "strong-mind-in-a-healthy-body" philosophy had triumphed. Emphasis turned on team sports and exercises. I learned, in the most mindless detail, the rules for Canadian football and basketball. One test was designed to discover how many baskets I, just a little over five feet tall, could sink in two minutes. In this process, I gained little understanding of the need for life-long fitness or of the recreational means for achieving some modicum of physical well-being.

Perhaps the major influence for change since my days of schooling in Ontario was the passing of the Vocational Training Act by the Federal Government in 1961. This legislation poured hundreds of millions of dollars into provincial educational systems, and Ontario took the greatest advantage of this largesse. Vocational wings – housing chiefly wood-working, machine, and automotive repair shops – were added to countless high schools and the level of activity in vocational education escalated dramatically.

This commitment powered a major shift in the curriculum of the secondary school. Now, the basics – history, geography, languages, maths, and the sciences – were balanced by an expectation that students would "learn to earn" either in the shop or office while going to school. But

Vocational training burgeoned following the Federal Government's Vocational Training Act passed in 1961

the change was accomplished without much analysis of the real needs of a technological society – and there is good reason to suggest that the Federal intervention put immense resources into vocational education at too low a level to give Canada any competitive edge. The developing technological society would demand highly trained, sophisticated graduates at the post-secondary level; but I found when, in the seventies, I became President of Ryerson Polytechnical Institute (the only such institution in Ontario) that Canada was content to import its technologists and technicians from the United Kingdom and Europe. The present extraordinary efforts at both federal and provincial levels to encourage both public educational institutions and the private sector to increase its commitment to the manpower needs of a technological society indicate the results of this short-sightedness.

Reflective articles about education tend to emphasize the changes in our school system, but analysing those things which remain stable and immovable are equally revealing. In spite of massive technological change, the fact remains that students are assumed only to learn between 9:00 a.m. and 3:30 p.m. on five days a week. Only in the past year has it seemed advisable to revise the view that students in Ontario needed 13 years of continuous instruction before advancing to university – with other provinces accomplishing this in 12 years. Students are presumed to receive the best instruction in groups of 30 – though some deviation has been forced by the inclusion of subjects where health and safety standards or accessibility to specialized equipment have imposed smaller groupings. There have been significant additions to the

---

My first week of teaching school was nearly over. There I stood at the blackboard, writing "Bell Work" as the Grade 3/4 class dutifully filed in.

I turned to say, "And now class," when I stopped short. I was looking down the barrel of a 45 colt revolver. A young ragamuffin was gripping the weapon with both hands, pretending to be shooting people in the room. One of those people was me. I heard the click, click, as he pulled the trigger.

Normal School had not prepared me for this. When he gave me the revolver, I opened the chamber. To my amazement there were two bullets left in it. We had inadvertently been involved in Russian roulette.

When the principal called the police, we learned that there had been a hold-up the night before; the revolver had been discarded during the get-away chase.

A very important impromptu lesson on firearms began that morning.

GORDON PENROSE,
AUTHOR

curriculum, particularly in the vocational areas, and certain subjects, like the Classics, have almost disappeared. Nevertheless, the core curriculum has held tough. Indeed, one could suggest that the effect of the "back to basics" emphasis of the late seventies and eighties has been a resurgence of traditional courses. That is not to say that these courses in maths, the sciences, history, geography, and languages have not been revised over past decades. But the fact is that schooling tends to be one of the more uncritical activities in which a society engages, probably because of the egotistical compulsion that those who follow us will have endured the same "rites of initiation" to maturity and responsibility. Then, it is hoped, they will not change too much of what we find comfortable.

Although some elementary schools have experimented in ungraded classrooms and although secondary schools have emphasized instruction through individual projects, team teaching, and educational television, the central reality of schooling in Ontario continues to be the textbook, the blackboard, and the teacher standing at the front of a classroom. Whether the computer with its extraordinary capacity to individualize instruction and with its relevance to the job market can make a dramatic impact on how things are taught has yet to be judged. I suspect the chances are good for any number of reasons.

It is my observation that not only have the day-to-day practices and curriculum directives held together solidly over many decades but also the unwritten curriculum has not changed substantially. Education is still in the context of a competitive model – students continue to compete with each other regardless of any number of personal factors which make the competition irrelevant and also frustrating beyond measure to the "losers." The curriculum is designed too often for male success; thus, women find themselves at risk in certain subjects and, as a result, they find themselves less welcome in certain occupations. (At Ryerson, we tried to encourage women to invade the engineering technology programs but without much success.) All we know about left and right functions of the brain has been little recognized in either how we teach or what is taught. Nor is all the learning theory of how people learn throughout their lives given much credence. The curriculum still portrays classroom learning as pre-eminent – at a time when young people learn so much from electronic media that even the myth is now completely empty. The preoccupation with paper qualifications continues to influence young people to believe that there is an "ending" to education and that there is something intellectually valid about a graduation certificate – as opposed to a transcript which is never completed and is enhanced by additions of life-long accomplishment. There is still the fact of compulsory attendance attached to learning in a way that other aspects of Canadian life (for example, military service and voting) have managed to avoid. With compulsory attendance comes the curriculum of external discipline, the constant necessity to compel young people to carry out functions of the personal activity of learning at times which may be inappropriate from every point of view – psychological, economic, and physiological. As well, compulsory attendance at particular ages connects with the major influence on curriculum change – both change in levels of possible attainment and change in variety of subject matter; I am referring to the incredible growth in the school population from the late forties to the mid-seventies, as the "Big Generation" worked its way through the system. Indeed, the problem of scale is one that is little understood in education, but the expansion of schooling was the major contrast in my experience as a student and as a teacher. Finally, equality of educational opportunity is still an ideal – the poor, native people, the disabled, and the disadvantaged still receive fewer services in the state school system.

I met the Ontario curriculum again in the 1950s as a history teacher in a very large suburban secondary school. The great controversy was by then the legitimacy of social studies – in place of geography and history initially, but in the minds of enthusiasts threatening to encompass the entire liberal arts scene. The other cause of disruption on professional development days was the advisability of accepting the "new math." Neither, by present standards, seems earth shattering. Indeed, in those days of assured mobility (both lateral and upward), of expansion, and of unlimited resources, the morale of the system was incredibly high. These were the vintage years. By the early seventies, I had become associated with a new Ontario university – Trent – and some of the resources available in the sixties quickly disappeared. At the post-secondary level, it ended an era of massive construction of facilities, generous research grants, plenteous assistants and secretarial staff, and a sense of mission accepted unquestioningly by provincial authorities. In the elementary and secondary schools, the decade was to see a drastic change, with teachers and trustees often at odds with each other or in confrontation with the Ministry.

I find it hard to believe that all the ill-will which was so much a part of the system in the seventies did not influence the unwritten curriculum. Probably young people learned more about conflict and breakdown and less about compromise and accommodation; and if so, these lessons will be influential in determining the quality of industrial relations throughout this century.

There are many inadequacies as one views the curriculum development of the seventies and eighties, and confusion over the nature and extent of vocational education is certainly one of them. But perhaps most unfortunate in total terms has been the unwillingness to accommodate to the reality that education can no longer be seen as something which happens to children. Since 1980, there has been more institutionally organized learning directed to adults; yet the work of Roby Kidd and the Canadian Association for Adult Education from the 1930s had made more progress in society at large than in the sheltered halls of formal academe. Schools still seem caught in the perception that there is a body of knowledge and a collection of skills that each adolescent has to grasp before the tentacles of compulsory education relax their grip. As a result, there is little effective cooperation in developing opportunities for the part-time student and the adult learner between those associated with evening classes, college and university extension, or the educational activities of the private or voluntary sector and those in the established schooling system. Rather, there is continuous criticism of the inadequacies of the secondary school graduate as an employable individual – and an equal anger on the part of administrators and teachers that all of society's unsolved and unsolvable problems are being dumped on the school. Now, as I work outside the schooling system (elementary, secondary, and post-secondary), I am struck by the impervious commitment to the questionable styles of teaching and learning.

Looking to the future, the continuing pressure of unacceptable levels of youth employment will surely have the effect of creating a co-operative phase in the mid-teens' educational experience. No one will ever again see keeping young people longer in school as a solution to that problem. Instead, it is more likely that part-time work/school programs will involve business, industry, and the service sector, along with the secondary school. The concurrent effect will be a recognition of the need to develop mechanisms for community involvement in the curriculum building process. Teaching methods will be influenced as well – because expectations of productivity in the community will certainly generate pressure for more thoughtful instructional modes in the classroom. The computer, with its capacity to provide both individualized instructional programs and relevant evaluation mechanisms, will be influential – though to what extent, as already stated, cannot yet be determined.

However, the major shift for the long-term future must be that of a commitment to the arts. But although nearly all Canadian provincial ministers have made warm statements to this effect, neither new resources nor the latest changes in the

Students at Parkdale Collegiate Institute in 1970

secondary school curriculum indicate any immediate focus.

In arguing the case for the arts (a position I find comfortable both as an enthusiast and as an "articrat" with the OAC), I suggest that the curriculum should reflect not only the school's perception of its role and the needs of its clientele (and here the challenge to find alternative employment to traditional jobs will obviously be critical) but also the imperatives of an external world. There is little doubt that the world is confronted by cultural conflict – the Middle East, the Far East, Central and South America, all point to confrontations that are not essentially political or economic. Even the threat of a U.S./U.S.S.R. nuclear showdown, foreseen as the inevitable outcome of world-wide power entanglements, mutual distrust, and the mindless escalation of military technology, is essentially a cultural conflict. This means that we must find more lateral, more interdisciplinary ways of reaching across the abyss. And there is no doubt that the arts represent the most valid way of achieving mutual respect and understanding. We do have the planetary resource of a literature, of painting and sculpture, and of music and drama that is our common heritage – both East and West.

Such an emphasis will radically change the curriculum, for the arts defy the influence of compulsion, of external discipline, and of sexism; on the contrary, they celebrate the harmony of multiculturalism, of sexual equality, and of left and right brain accomplishments. Furthermore, the arts can involve the participation of every discipline, for they are totally cross-disciplinary.

Whereas 1984 is being celebrated as the year of

> One of the most imaginative arrangements for developing student interest in drama was made by Jean Stewart Coupe, the Head of the English Department at Etobicoke Collegiate Institute until her retirement in 1964.
>
> Mrs. Coupe made a deal with The Canadian Players (most of whom enjoyed Stratford Theatre fame) that when they began their annual cross-country tour, they would give their first performance in Etobicoke Collegiate auditorium on a school afternoon for students of Grades 11 to 13. These students had, by that time, studied the play to be presented; consequently they enjoyed The Players' production immensely — their interest was heightened and their understanding increased.
>
> The Canadian Players regarded the event as an opportunity to fine-tune the production. The English Department received a share of the modest admission charge and used these funds to purchase good quality art for the school, acquiring over the years quite a valuable collection.
>
> J. EUGENE DURRANT,
> FORMER ASSISTANT SUPERINTENDENT,
> ETOBICOKE BOARD OF EDUCATION

Ontario's bicentenary, so it has been endlessly trumpeted as the year of George Orwell's predicted disaster-society. The main fear is that the technology that man has created will, in fact, erode his humanity and, ultimately, end his presence on this planet. The arts, with their commitment to individuality and, most of all, creativity, are the single best defence against this very real threat.

Finally, the curriculum of the future and how it is conveyed will revolve less around economic productivity and the exploitation of human and natural resources and more around the survival of the species. The 1980s will be a decade of transition and a good deal of directionless flailing, but the imaginative presence of the liberal arts, the visual arts, and the performing arts as a core ingredient of every human being's lifelong educational development can scarcely be denied.

Thus, for the foreseeable future, education will be carried on in the shadow of Armageddon. As Jonathon Schell has pointed out in the *New Yorker* (2 January 1984), there is indeed a new predicament for mankind to confront, a new choice for mankind to make – "to choose human survival." Recognition of the extent of the international arms arsenal, along with recognition of how close to midnight we are, will impose new learning imperatives; as Schell points out, this threat represents "not so much each person's life . . . as the meaning of our lives." And in seeking to avoid this disaster, we must look to what is taught and how well it is taught. Could there be any greater challenge for the teachers? Scarcely!

WALTER PITMAN studied history at the University of Toronto and subsequently became a high school teacher. He was M.P. for the constituency of Peterborough from 1960 to 1962 and was M.P.P. for the same constituency from 1967 to 1971; as an M.P.P., he became education critic for the N.D.P. in the Ontario Legislature and ultimately deputy leader of the Ontario N.D.P. He joined Trent University in 1965 and was appointed dean of arts and science in 1972. Three years later, he became president of Ryerson Polytechnical Institute for a five-year term, and he is presently executive director of the Ontario Arts Council.

"Tis a terrible crisis for Cam and for Isis;
Fat butchers are learning dissection;
And looking-glass makers become sabbath-breakers
To study the rules of reflection;
Sin Φ and sin Θ — no sin can be sweeter,
Are taught to the poor of both sexes,
And weavers and spinners jump up from their dinners
To flirt with their y's and their x's.

       Winthrop Mackworth Praed (1825)

The present day student, more pampered, more prudent,
Prefers an electronic tutor;
And so, while he dozes, acquires through osmosis
His wisdom straight off a computer.

       Modern Addendum

EDUCATION OR SCHOOLING?

JIM PARR

"To almost every Englishman up to the age of three or four and twenty, classical learning has been the great object of existence; and no man is very apt to suspect, or very much pleased to hear, that what he has done for so long a time was not worth doing."

The Reverend Sydney Smith (of whom George III said, "He is a very clever fellow but he will never be a bishop") made this observation about 150 years ago in an essay whose title tells all: *Too Much Latin and Greek*.

"A young Englishman," Smith continues, "goes to school at six or seven years old; and he remains in a course of education till 23 or 24 years of age. In all that time, his sole and exclusive occupation is learning Latin and Greek, he has scarcely a notion that there is any other kind of excellence...."

* * *

As Smith wrote this, he seems to have had in mind the companions whom he enjoyed around the dinner table at Holland House rather than his humbler parishioners in Combe Florey. But his point that Latin and Greek were no longer in tune with the times flowed from his belief that the classical spirit of the Renaissance had been lost to grammatical pedantry and a recitation of minutiae. Smith's essay reminds us that educational reform associated with England's industrialization was in the air.

The generally accepted beginning of the industrial revolution is a century earlier; but the great production boom in factory goods, which caused immense social change in Britain and many parts of Europe, happened about the middle of the 19th century. Fifty years later, the United States began to lead world production, and most of the Western world became a consumer society.

Smith, along with the other Edinburgh Reviewers, recognized the educational skills that the new commerce would need. In his essay, he called for economics and chemistry, and for mathematics and experimental philosophy; and he justified their placement in a university curriculum as he asked, "What other measure is there of dignity in intellectual labour, but usefulness and difficulty? And what ought the term University to mean, but a place where every science is taught which is liberal, and at the same time useful to mankind?"

The universities responded with a sluggish acceptance of the sorts of subject to which Smith referred. But in doing so, they tended to embrace the practicality of the earlier medieval curriculum which trained young men to become doctors and priests and lawyers. Now, however, the call was for people who might give substance to a great commerce based upon mid-19th century industrial production.

Gradually, practical subjects became respectable – even though they were associated with lower class achievements and remained so for a long while. "It is strange," remarked Eric Ashby, "to hear a man as enlightened as Lyon Playfair, even as late as 1875 saying that 'the stronghold of literature should be built in the upper classes of society while the stronghold of science should be in the nation's middle class' " (*Technology and the Academics*).

As the universities trimmed their curricula to a shape that a later age might have applauded as "relevant," the school system made its adjustments too. Relevant curricula appeared initially in those European countries that were first industrialized. The North American continent followed.

Fairly obviously, Latin and Greek were inappropriate for a society whose character was to be determined by a shift from self-sufficient subsistence to consumer-dictated affluence. And whereas the manipulation of the new machinery could be taught on the factory floor, the ability to read instructions, write letters, tally accounts, and to recognize those parts of the world involved in mid-19th century trade had to be taught in the schools.

The gearing of educational systems to social needs is nothing unusual. Indeed, what other purpose should an educational system serve? If the concern is for a promulgation of religious ideals, then the churches will see that their schools make it so. If a country embarks on mass manufacture, then those schools which are supported by public moneys will be enabling.

The need to design a curriculum that fits an industrial society is obvious enough. But the educational system teaches a couple of other "lessons" that are not so immediately apparent. The first is what Toffler calls the "covert curriculum."

"It consisted – and still does in most industrial nations –

". . . *Latin and Greek were no longer in tune with the times.* . . ."

of three courses: one in punctuality, one in obedience, and one in rote, repetitive work. Factory labor demanded workers who showed up on time, especially assembly-line hands. It demanded workers who would take orders from a management hierarchy without questioning. And it demanded men and women prepared to slave away at machines or in offices, performing brutally repetitive operations."

Toffler does not deny the humanizing effect of mass public education. But having acknowledged this, he writes: "Nevertheless, Second Wave schools machined generation after generation of young people into a pliable, regimented work force of the type required by electro-mechanical technology and the assembly line" (*The Third Wave*).

The second contribution of the educational system to a consumer society is more subtle but no less influential. It has to do with the coupling between schooling and earning a living. There is an accepted notion that if you "do well" at school, you will "get a better job." The better job means that you will earn more money; and if you earn more, you will buy more. Because you are able to buy more, not only will you gain that sort of pleasure and prestige associated with the power to purchase but also you will fuel the engine of the economy.

Children start school with the idea that if they do well, they will be able to buy a bigger house, a cottage, and more than one car for the family. Doing well means, no less, enjoying the wherewithal to subscribe to the symphony, make a decent contribution to charity, and grumble about heavy taxation.

A substantial part of the tax dollar goes in two supportive directions: into health care programs (which, in fact, do less to care for health than to cure sicknesses intrinsic to a consumer society), and into educational systems.

Because more schooling is generally equated with a better education, and this, in turn, presents the prospect of a better job, the business of teaching has itself become a prime service industry in a commercial world. Hence the teaching profession, like all professions, has taken upon itself the responsibility of protecting the public (and incidentally protecting itself) from the unqualified.

The school system has worked well in the industrialized world, but it may be pricing itself out of the educational marketplace. Furthermore, the marketplace is changing: the old economic levers are no longer predictably effective; inflation is reduced only at the cost of unemployment; and employment, as we have known it for the last century, is losing its central position in determining our lifestyle.

A meaningful indicator of massive change is to be found in the world's steel output, for steel is a barometer of traditional industrialization: following a slackening after the Second World War, it has levelled off; and today, world production is much the same as it was a dozen years ago. Few people predict any permanent recovery.

I can recall a time in Grade 5 when we put on the play *The Wizard of Oz*. Unfortunately, I didn't get the lead. I was one of the winged monkeys. We went up on the stage and kidnapped the Tin Man, the Scarecrow, the Cowardly Lion, Dorothy, and her dog Toto. We threw hay over them and took them out of the auditorium.

Our costume was very embarrassing to wear. We had brown knit stockings and a brown shirt that came to the waist. We had thick brown cardboard wings that were tied to our shoulders. Hanging from our wings was a tail that came past our knees. We caked our face with brown make-up.

The first time we went on stage everyone laughed at us. All our faces turned red. One girl started to cry. Next time on stage, a funny thing happened. The leader of the monkeys got her tail in the toilet, and there was water dripping everywhere. When we went on the stage behind her, I slipped and fell, and all the other monkeys fell as well. That taught me never to walk around in stocking feet on a wet floor ever again.

DIMITRA KAPPOS, STUDENT,
CLARKE ROAD SECONDARY SCHOOL, LONDON

Meanwhile, the progressive industries of a new age use armies of robots (in Japan) or erect congenial workplaces for creative entrepreneurship (in California's Silicon Valley). In Canada, as in other parts of the world, the conflict between what Toffler has called second and third wave societies is poignantly illustrated by a level of unemployment which, in the younger age groups, is treble the average.

There are other signs of massive change – change which does not follow that old curve of reliably predictable growth. Major political parties in democratic countries are no longer instruments of reform; rather, they present vehicles by which activist groups may effect reform. (In the United States, more money is said to be donated to the collectivity of small action groups than to the two major political parties.) Divorce breaks and re-forms families; fads and cults cut new shapes in society to an extent that is hardly comprehensible to a yo-yo and hula-hoop generation. And the fear of nuclear disaster is so traumatic that most people avoid the thought of it.

Not every signal is so discordant. Among all the nastiness, there are actions of heroic gentleness; the arts flourish not only around the old aficionados but in new forms among an urban peasantry of the streets; and while the word "love" continues to be used carelessly, it is used more generously and with less inhibition.

Meanwhile, the educational system – the schools, colleges, and universities – have made some adjustments to their curricula, and they continue that important debate whether an education should extend the celebration of our being or train us for an occupation. That it might do both appears to be elusive.

If the function of the schools (at all levels of the enterprise) is to train for occupations, then the schools must have some notion what those occupations may be – and even adjust to the idea that an occupation may be no occupation at all in the traditional sense. The question whether a person should be trained for unemployment is not a facetious one.

But if, by exercising our minds and stimulating our spirits, the function of curricula is to celebrate our being, then we must take a new tack; for the educational system over the last century and a half has been an integral part of an industrial strategy and limited largely to prescriptions for pre-employment years. (En passant, those protesting students of the 1960s were not altogether wrong in their perceptions, however inexcusable were some of their actions.)

The educational system has, as I have tried to assert, been effective in the subjects it has taught, in the context it has provided, and in the ambitions it has motivated for people of a consumer society. But any suggestion that the system might be less materialistically oriented has not met with approbation; or, if there was any, it was short-lived. (In Ontario, the Hall-Dennis Report and the Report of the Commission on Post-Secondary Education come to mind.)

Shortly, I will conclude by suggesting that the best possibilities for education lie outside the schools. But first, I want to recommend what the schools might do. This is presumptuous; but the alternative – that of making no suggestions at all – is susceptible to even harsher criticism.

If we recognize that our society is already being carried by the third wave of change, then there are important things to be learned. I am not speaking here of a working knowledge of computers, or a modest comprehension of information theory, or a conversational understanding of biofeedback, although all of these are important and fun. Rather, I am pointing to much more basic stuff – that which allows us to avoid being conned and may help us to be honest and to stay alive; in short, the subject matter that has to do with logic and ethics.

These are subjects that, even though they are not traditional, are susceptible to treatment in the classroom in traditional ways. In other words, they have not been extensively taught during the past century and a half, but they contain elements of older curricula.

> **M**y own involvement in the birth of educational television in Ontario surprised me, as it must have everyone else. I had become interested in the application of television to education in the late fifties and early sixties while a member of the Ontario Teachers' Federation Board of Governors, and I had conducted some summer courses at Ryerson Institute on their behalf. That was the extent of my experience.
>
> During a curriculum meeting early in 1966 at the then Department of Education, I received a note to see the Deputy Minister. At the time, I was a secondary school superintendent in Port Arthur and had never seen a real live Deputy Minister. I thought I was about to be ticked off either for breaking a provincial regulation or for some other venial sin.
>
> However, Zack Phimister — a most formidable figure, especially to someone from the North West — told me without any preamble that the *Minister* (not he) had decided to have educational television in Ontario and that they — he and the Minister — had agreed that the person to head the enterprise must come from Ontario and be a teacher with experience in both administration and television. Further, he noted that they had only identified three people with these qualifications and that the others had turned the position down. Therefore, he asked me to accept, with 24 hours to make up my mind.
>
> I accepted.
>
> T. RANALD IDE,
> FORMER CHAIRMAN, TVONTARIO

It is hard to understand that while children are encouraged to analyse the grammar in newspaper editorials, they are not led to analyse with equal rigor the strategies of the advertising that makes the editorials financially viable.

Children are subjected to the novel and the play – although not always successfully – in order to appreciate human interactions, social contexts, and so on. But the television screen, which occupies more time of the average child than does the classroom, is not seriously included in these studies. Indeed, if the lack of concern for television literacy is to be projected into all the newer aspects of electronic culture, then the classroom will become a museum, of interest only to educational historians.

A third subject amenable to classroom treatment has to do with war. This is one of many topics that raises moral questions; but because it involves more than the lives of individuals, more than the life of a generation, indeed is crucial to the survival of our planet, I put it at the head of the list of moral questions. It seems to me that if a study of the past is worthy of two or three hours each week, then the question whether there will be a future is deserving of more than a passing comment.

The educational system of schools, colleges, and universities responds rather than leads in its teaching. It carries such a heavy obligation because it is expected to produce young people who are trained for what is seen to be current. What is *actually* current tends to be ahead of where schools, colleges, and universities are allowed to be – except, of course, in university research, which is seldom a component of undergraduate teaching. Hence there is an inevitability to the Sabre-Tooth Curriculum syndrome.

Yet there is no excuse for not enjoying the spectrum of current learning opportunities. These are presented by the television screen; by the actions of the police; by striking workers; by arguments between labor and management; by the peregrinations and promises of politicians; by seeing things grow in the garden; by lively conversations; by bursting into song; or by being thoughtful. You might want to add to the list: designing a dress, painting a landscape, writing a poem . . . the scope is almost limitless. Even to contribute to the list is to learn.

The educational system has captured – can only capture – a small part of this rich fare, whereas its professionals have led us to believe that only their menu constitutes the proper diet.

In his book *The Disabling Professions*, John McKnight makes the insightful observation that it is the professions themselves rather than the people whom they serve that suffer from need. "We *need* to solve your problems. We *need* to tell you what they are. We *need* to deal with them in our terms. We *need* to have you respect our satisfaction with our own work." McKnight's inversion was recently echoed in an industrial idiom when a television commentator, reviewing some economic crisis, remarked, "The orders do not fill the manufacturers' needs."

> The new curriculum guidelines for Human Growth and Development had just been introduced to the elementary schools, and the part on Human Sexuality was proving particularly controversial. It happened that, at that time, our school had chosen a full length feature film to show the students. We were somewhat taken aback, however, when we received a phone call from an irate mother who was threatening to keep her children home if the school persisted in showing "dirty movies." The film: *Born Free*.
>
> LAURIE GORDON, TEACHER
> FAIRFIELD ELEMENTARY SCHOOL, AMHERSTVIEW

In this context, growing numbers of people that the educational profession serves are seeking ways for their children to learn without school – though whether their judgment is based on their children's school experiences or on their own is a moot point. It is, of course, unreasonable to expect that school can provide for the whole child. Nevertheless, the classroom must shift into a new perspective that recognizes a panorama of learning experiences extending beyond the needs of industry and trade.

Part of the new scene has to do with adult education. Continuing education may be, as Ohliger once suggested, a guarantee of continuing ineptitude. But I believe he was referring – and somewhat provocatively – to that sort of continuing education which is required by the courts as they seek a guarantee of responsibility or by an employer as he wishes to justify a promotion. The sort of continuing education I have in mind is that which springs from the aspirations of the individual who seeks it. While this may coincide with classroom subjects, it is no less likely to lie outside them.

The learning experiences that adults want are of two kinds. First, there are training programs: the retreading and the introduction to new rungs on the ladder of commercial success; these experiences are generally institutionalized. Second, there are opportunities – usually less formalized – in which one learns for the pleasure of it. Here the resources are almost without limit.

The process of learning, wherever it happens, causes change. That is why, whether there is a little of it or a lot, learning is a dangerous thing. For change moves us into the unknown. But no learning at all is even more dangerous, for it denies the world of the mind; and hence it denies our evolution. There is not even an unknown.

Learning is shifting from its old practice of training youth to prop up commerce to a new practice of fulfilling all people. It is seeking to encourage that joyful Chestertonian capacity for finding interest in all things, and all things interesting. Through learning, we may yet unlock laughter and again praise the human spirit.

JIM PARR is the author of a book of verse, a history of metals, a book about committees, and some metallurgical texts. He has taught at the Universities of Liverpool, British Columbia, and Alberta, and he was dean of engineering at the University of Windsor before becoming deputy minister of Colleges and Universities in Ontario. Since 1979, he has been chairman and chief executive officer of TVOntario. He sits on the OISE boards of governors.

Floreat the private school
Floreat, florebit.
Play the game and work to rule.
Aetas non delebit.

Gaudeamus work and play.
School could not be sweeter,
While the public go their way
Semper in excreta.

THE INDEPENDENT SCHOOLS

HARRY GILES

The independent schools in Canada are at once the representatives of choice and freedom and a form of economic privilege for the children of those who can either afford the fees or who give up homes and vacations to ensure the kind of education – religious, bilingual, drug free, or academic – which the state system (offering job security to the incompetent and influenced by the political meddling of elected activists) denies. The Universal Declaration of Human Rights states that "parents have a prior right to choose the kind of education that shall be given to their children." Many parents feel it to be unreasonable that state monopolies exist which deny children religious, ethical, or enriched education. Consequently, some of them argue that they or their children's independent schools should be supported financially by the public purse. Be that as it may, when some near the poverty line take the bread out of their mouths to pay for an education which the state in theory provides free, one recognizes that free public education does not always meet perceived needs.

The independent schools in Ontario fall into various groups: the Conference of Independent Schools (a division of the Canadian Association of Independent Schools); the Ontario Association of Alternative and Independent Schools; and various other independent schools that are generally affiliated on the basis of religious or instructional methodology. In total, there are presently some 550 independent schools in Ontario, representing a dramatic growth over recent years. Religious affiliations aside, the independent schools tend to differ from those in the public system in a variety of ways. Most of them are small, and this leads to close contact between teachers and students. It is a dictum that economies of scale can be achieved only in high schools of at least 1500 students. But most independent schools would argue that as soon as a school has more than 500 students, it has ceased to be a human institution, for at that point the principal no longer knows, or can know, the names of all the students.

In most independent schools, there is also a greater emphasis on extra-curricular activities. Public service and social responsibility are expected. However, not all independent schools are the same: some are influenced more by social considerations, others by academic achievement. It is fair to say that in their variety, they represent a microcosm of our society.

The Conference of Independent Schools (C.I.S.) is an association of twenty-three non-profit schools, each with an independent board which hires the Head. To be admitted to the group, the school must be approved by an academic selection committee. Some of these schools admit students as young as three and all of them educate students to university entrance. Five are boarding, nine are day schools, and nine admit both day students and boarders; between them they encompass boys' schools, girls' schools, and co-educational schools. (A few boys' schools now admit girls in the higher grades.) The total enrolment in these schools is over 10,000 students.

Most of the Heads in C.I.S. are products of the system, and to raise the high fees to keep their schools afloat, one Headmistress defined the minimum prerequisite skills as including "the education of a college president, the executive ability of a financier, the humility of a deacon, the adaptability of a chameleon, the hope of an optimist, the wisdom of a serpent, the courage of a hero, the gentleness of a dove, the patience of Job, the grace of God, and the persistence of the devil." For the history of the independent schools in Canada is one of a continual struggle to survive, and it is a struggle which has been often lost.

At least half of the C.I.S. schools originally had a religious affiliation, and although all of them are now ostensibly non-denominational, most of them retain a religious orientation. Most of them, too, place a strong emphasis on the house and the prefect systems, on sports, games and outdoor education, and on emotional support both for the child who has learning problems and for the child who is gifted. The schools believe that the creation of a clean mind and the inbuilding of decency, social responsibility, and

MTL T12269

Upper Canada College — Déjeuner in the prayer hall on the occasion of cornerstone laying of King's College, on April 23, 1842

> Splendid incomes are given to the masters of the new (Upper Canada) College, culled at Oxford by the Vice-Chancellor, and dwellings furnished to the professors (we may say) by the sweat of the brow of the Canadian labourer. All these advantages and others not now necessary to be mentioned, are insufficient to gratify the rapacious appetite of the "Established Church" managers, who, in order to accumulate wealth and live in opulence, charge the children of His Majesty's subjects ten times as high fees as are required by the less amply endowed Seminary at Quebec. They have another reason for so doing. The College (already a monopoly) becomes almost an exclusive school for the families of the Government officers, and the few who, through their means, have, in York, already attained a pecuniary independence out of the public treasury. The College never was intended for the people, nor did the Executive endow it thus amply that all classes might apply to the fountain of knowledge.
>
> WILLIAM LYON MACKENZIE
> (FROM *SKETCHES*, PUBLISHED IN 1833)

integrity rank highly. As was stated fifty years ago by an outspoken Montreal headmistress: "The building of character is the whole aim of any school worthy of its name." Her views are echoed by her present-day peers.

The values of the schools are not those of the rich but rather those of the middle class: integrity, fair play, service, and responsibility. Far from seeking to develop elitist, aristocratic values, the independent schools are committed to preventing them. Mottos of the schools include: "Not for Ourselves Alone," "Knowledge is Strength," "Simplicity, Sincerity, Service," "Serve ye Bravely," "A Healthy Mind in a Sound Body," and "Truth, Virtue, and Loveliness." These are usually delivered in Latin, French, and even Gaelic, and although such exhortations may have little real impact on the students, the Heads use them and other precepts regularly on Prize Days.

Most of the boarding schools in Ontario are members of C.I.S., and almost all C.I.S. schools have scholarships for the truly needy and bursaries for many who, without them, could not attend. Some parents send their children to be richly educated in an academic sense or to ensure entry for them into the highly competitive professional schools; some are seeking a clean and decent environment for their children in a time of collapsed values and ethics; still others simply want their children to rub shoulders with those who are better off and who will make good contacts for the future. Most schools reserve the right to expel students immediately if their conduct is found to be unacceptable by the Head. They do this to protect the interests of the majority of the students, who represent a perception, and often a reality, of the best that young people can be. The independent school, because it is not subject to politics in the same way as the public system, has been a well-spring of curricular and other innovations, many of which have later, if in a watered-down form, found a place in the public system. Perhaps the most striking of these innovations derives from a relatively new school, The Toronto French School (opened in 1962), which created French immersion programs for Anglophones in both the public and private systems.

To achieve its ends, The Toronto French School had to publish many of its own texts, create its own programs, experiment with spelling, writing, grammar, and mathematics, and train teachers for itself and others. Its needs opened the way for it to enter programmed learning and the computer field very early. Likewise, it was in at the early stages of experimental mathematics teaching, and through its contacts with French, Belgian, and English researchers, the school pioneered the introduction of the Papy and Dienes math in Canada, leading to a whole revolution in secondary school teaching in mathematics.

Lakefield College School near Peterborough has been intimately involved in the development of Outward Bound, outdoor education, and the Round Square movement—involving schools in Canada, the United States, Australia, the United Kingdom, and Germany. Such programs have helped many unsettled youngsters "find themselves" while gaining a sound academic education. A similar Outward Bound orientation characterizes Rosseau Lake School and Appleby College, and the commitment of C.I.S. schools in general to the fostering of leadership (as typified by the Duke of Edinburgh's Award) epitomizes the concern with the child which is so much a part of C.I.S. education.

". . . *created French immersion programs for Anglophones.* . . ."

Many of the C.I.S. schools have international ties, and as a result, they are able to maintain the highest international standards. Thus, Ashbury College, Bishop Strachan School, Pickering College, Hillfield-Strathallan College, The Toronto French School, Trafalgar Castle School, Trinity College School, and Upper Canada College are members either of the Headmasters' Conference in the U.K. or of the National Association of Principals of Schools for Girls in the U.S., and through attendance at annual conferences and school visits, keep up-to-date on educational technology, pedagogical support texts, and new teaching methods. Also in this context of sharing experience, The Toronto French School has initiated teacher exchanges for members of the Canadian Association of Independent Schools with schools in the U.K. and one-term scholarships to colleges at Oxford and Cambridge.

The C.I.S. schools are international in another sense in that many of them are committed to the independent evaluation of their students by external exam. Thus, Ashbury, Elmwood, and Pickering offer the International Baccalaureate as well as the Ontario diploma, helping them to keep pace with the highest international standards in education. And The Toronto French School, a bilingual institution, prepares students not only for the Ontario model of Secondary School Diploma but also for the English General Certificate of Education (O and A levels), Scottish Highers, and the Baccalaureate of France.

Many C.I.S. schools have superb physical education programs. Upper Canada College, for example, has compulsory sports daily for every boy, as do Trinity College School, St. Andrew's, and Ridley College; St. Andrew's even has a polo team. The girls' schools emphasize artistic interests along with sport.

As the adjacent table shows, many of the C.I.S. schools were founded a long time ago and are comparatively large.

Another group, the Ontario Association of Alternative

C.I.S. Schools	Date founded	Grades	Total students
Upper Canada College	1829	3 - 13	950
Pickering College	1842	7 - 13	180
Albert College	1857	7 - 13	180
Trinity College School	1865	7 - 13	329
The Bishop Strachan School	1867	Jr. K - 13	702
Trafalgar Castle School	1874	7 - 13	170
Alma College	1877	9 - 13	162
Lakefield College School	1879	7 - 13	246
Ridley College	1889	6 - 13	515
Ashbury College	1891	5 - 13	430
St. Mildred's Lightbourn School	1891	K - 13	406
Havergal College	1894	Jr. K - 13	717
St. Andrew's College	1899	7 - 12	425
Hillfield-Strathallan College	1901	K - 13	838
St. Clement's School	1901	1 - 13	375
Branksome Hall	1903	K - 13	730
Appleby College	1911	4 - 13	391
Crescent School	1913	5 - 13	360
Elmwood School	1915	2 - 13	296
St. George's College	1961	4 - 13	397
The Toronto French School	1962	Nursery - 13	1240
Rosseau Lake School	1967	8 - 13	85
St. John's School (Elora)	1972	4 - 12	235

and Independent Schools, strongly advocates that its schools are as much entitled to public funding as those in the bureaucratically run public system. The Association, which is essentially an alliance of religious schools (Protestant,

Gymnastics at Havergal College in 1913

Jewish, Catholic, and others), bases its argument for public funding on the belief that young people should be educated in a moral and specifically religious environment.

The Association now has 125 schools with an enrolment of over 17,000 students. The schools include Calvinist, Mennonite, Jewish, Catholic, non-denominational, Waldorf, and Montessori schools; schools for children with learning disabilities, schools for gifted children, schools that employ French, German, Hebrew, or Armenian as either the first or second language of instruction, and schools concerned with Head Start programs; schools for children needing individualized instruction; schools for residential students who must live away from home, schools for foreign students coming to study in Canada, and schools specializing in music and the arts.

Most of these schools have international ties, stemming either from their religious affiliation or, like the Waldorf and Montessori schools, from their educational orientation. In many respects, the schools represent a mirror image of the cultural groups within our society.

The first Catholic elementary schools were established in Upper Canada in 1804 by the Right Reverend Alexander Macdonell, but it was not until the middle of the century, when free schools emerged, that a separate system of Catholic schools came into being. As the then leader of the Irish Catholics put it: "All that the Catholics wanted was that their children should be educated in the manner that their parents thought proper."

From the outset, Catholic elementary schools received some form of public funding, and in modern times their receipt of tax grants and assessments has been progressively extended up to Grade 10. After Grade 10, however, those who want a Catholic education for their children are obliged to send them to independent high schools.

The seventy Catholic high schools in Ontario are broadly spread through the Province and have an enrolment of over 30,000 students. (In some areas, such schools are part of the Separate school board and are independent only for Grades 11, 12, and 13.) They include such well-known schools as Brebeuf High School, De La Salle Oaklands, Loretto Abbey, St. Michael's Choir School, St. Michael's College, and Michael Power (in the Toronto area), Regiopolis-Notre Dame College (in Kingston), and The Pines (in Chatham).

In all the Catholic schools, the main concern has always been the building up and the handing on of the principles and traditions of the Catholic faith, together with a commitment to the love of learning and to academic excellence.

Likewise, the large Jewish community in Metropolitan Toronto is served by its own system of independent Jewish schools. Several of these schools offer immersion programs in Hebrew. They are generously supported by the Toronto Jewish Congress.

The elementary schools include Leo Baeck, United Synagogue, Associated Hebrew, Eitz Chaim, Beth Jacob, and Yeshiva Yesodei Hatorah; these offer a continuous program from either nursery or kindergarten to Grades 8 or 9. She'ariam, a Hebrew day school, offers special education. After Grade 9, some children proceed to B'nai Akiva, an orthodox high school which attracts Eitz Chaim and Associated children. (B'nai Akiva consists of two separate schools – one for boys and one for girls.) Most of the others either go on to the Community Hebrew Academy or to a high school for girls, Beth Jacob, which also functions as a private

---

In 1948, I was 10 years old and in Grade 5 at the first full-time Hebrew-English school in Toronto. Ours was the small, proud, pioneering class at the private Toronto Hebrew Day School situated in the downtown ghetto, and inevitably, given the era, we were ever vigilant for the slightest nuance of anti-Semitism.

Imagine, then, my outraged reaction when word spread through the community that "they" were cutting a sacred prayer from "The Jolson Story." My movie! My showbiz hero! My Asa Yolson! I did not, rest assured, take it lying down. I was going to be a freedom-fighter.

I inflamed my good pal Murray X (now an embarrassingly successful proctologist), and early one Tuesday morning, baseball bats firmly in hand, we hopped on the street car to City Hall, ready to force our spineless mayor to take up the cudgels on behalf of the Chosen People. We reached City Hall just before 9 a.m. — and panicked. Al Baby, forgive me. Forget the mayor. Race back to our little private enclave. Pray the principal would understand — maybe congratulate us! — for the patriotism and courage that made us 20 minutes late. In that authoritarian school? Gimme a break. Obviously a cynical fifth columnist, she strapped us raw. It could turn a kid into a real conservative.

Happy ending: the movie opened later that year at the new Eglinton theatre. My parents took me. It was my first night-time movie, and I wore long pants. And despite the failure of all those cowardly bigots to restore the prayer scene, it wasn't such a bad film. I've seen it 28 more times since that vivid and historic evening.

GERALD L. CAPLAN
FEDERAL SECRETARY OF THE NEW DEMOCRATIC PARTY OF CANADA

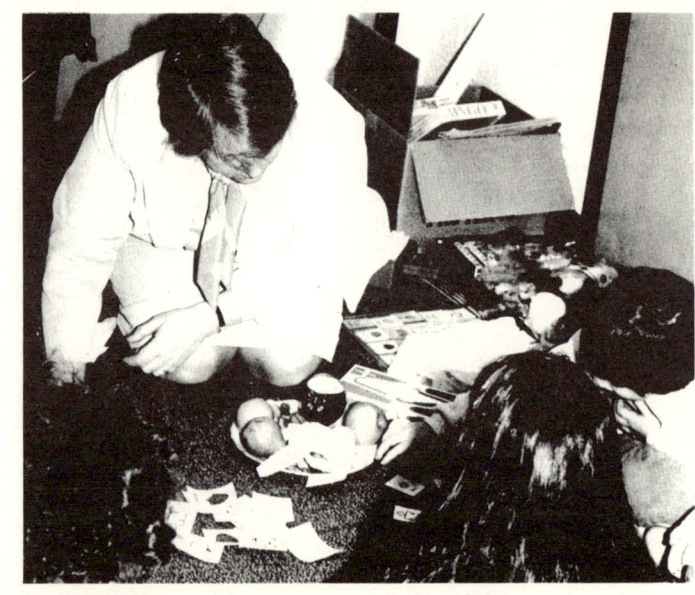

Children at the Leo Baeck Day School, North York, enjoying an innovative reading lesson

training centre for teachers of girls' schools.

The Jewish schools in Toronto have an enrolment of 7,211 students and, among them, cater to different branches of the Jewish faith. They see their contribution as that of educating the children in a caring way – a way which reinforces the children's culture, their language, and their Jewish heritage. Many of the schools are members of the Ontario Association of Alternative and Independent Schools discussed earlier.

Another significant, if smaller, group are the Montessori schools. Based on the principles of early childhood education laid down by Maria Montessori, the education offered by these schools stresses self-reliance and many sensorially based learning approaches which have had a significant effect on more traditional education. This system trains its own teachers in accordance with the doctrines of its founding pioneer. Most Montessori schools cater to young children at the kindergarten and primary levels.

The Confederation of Canadian Christian Schools has 16 member schools in Ontario, representing over 2,400 students. The Confederation, which is an association of Protestant evangelical schools, includes among its schools Niagara Christian College (which has complete boarding facilities for students in Grades 9 to 13) and the Paul B. Smith Academy in Toronto. Most of the schools are committed to a standardized curriculum, with a strong emphasis on evangelical doctrines. The Confederation has ties with a similar group of schools in the United States.

As the foregoing suggests, the independent schools cover a spectrum of educational needs. There are schools which provide education at the kindergarten level and others which do not. There are schools which operate only at the elementary level and others which operate only at the secondary. There are schools for special need groups. Some schools take only boys, some only girls; some are residential and some are not. Most secondary independent schools are inspected by the Ministry of Education, but a few are not.

It is in this sense that private education mirrors the public system. Where the independent schools differ tends to be in their commitment to specific religious or educational philosophies. What each of the independent schools would say about their school is that their greatest contribution is their graduates. Based upon the quality of these and the standards of decency which seem omnipresent in the graduates as a group, they have much of which they can be proud.

"... the education offered by these schools stresses self-reliance...."

HARRY GILES, a lifelong resident of Toronto, attended Malvern Collegiate, the University of Toronto, and Osgoode Hall Law School. A widower with three children, he is best known as the headmaster and founder of The Toronto French School, the premier immersion school in Canada. Begun in 1962 with six students in the Giles's home, TFS now has 1240 students and is the largest independent school in Canada. The programs and teacher training methods of TFS have been emulated in school districts across the country. For his contributions to the growth of bilingualism in Canada, Harry Giles was made a Member of the Order of Canada and was awarded the Silver Jubilee Medal.

No-one could possibly be contrarier than
Your plaintive Franco-Ontarian.
We Anglos, out of kindness, bend our rules,
Allow their children access to our schools
Only to find them making frightful moan,
Demanding education of their own.
Instead of decent English every day,
They want their offspring parlezing Français,
And argue it's essential to preserve
Their language and their culture. What a nerve!
Lord knows, we've all accepted with good grace
Their metric and bilingual round the place.
But no, they seek to exercise control —
Convert us into Frogs would seem their goal.
Have they forgot or count it not a damn
What happened on the Plains of Abraham?
They act as if the noble victor's palm
Had bypassed Wolfe and carried to Montcalm.
For what it's worth, I know what we should do:
We ought to send them packing to P.Q.

FRANCO-ONTARIAN EDUCATION: FROM PERSECUTED MINORITY TO TOLERATED NUISANCE

STACY CHURCHILL

One of the more demanding tasks facing Franco-Ontarian teachers is explaining to their students the reason why, in a province settled originally by the French more than three centuries ago, 1984 has been designated as the "Bicentennial Year." The difficulty is not in finding an explanation rooted in history. It is in trying to hide historical facts from the students in order to comply with the upbeat, positive tone of all the official announcements. Persecution, discrimination, and neglect of Franco-Ontarians by the provincial authorities and the majority of provincial residents is an integral part of the heritage that they are being asked to celebrate. Resisting when all the odds are against you, fighting against your own inner belief that your cause is lost, ignoring common sense and continuing to try: until about 20 years ago, that was the meaning of being a Franco-Ontarian. Today, the meaning is a little changed. It means trying to believe that the last 20 years make a difference and that your language and culture will some day be treated as if they had a rightful place in Ontario.

The pedagogical solutions to the teacher's problems are numerous. Historical relativism is useful; after all, to talk about the settlement of Ontario by the French is simply to ignore the other unhappy reality of our early days–that the

Amerindian population had already been here from time immemorial when the so-called "settlement" occurred. Maybe the brochures and circulars are right: choosing any one date was purely arbitrary, and the important thing is to celebrate what holds us together and to plan the future we can build. Tunnel vision also comes in handy: you can talk about the history of the Franco-Ontarian community from an internal perspective, discuss its customs and traditions like so much folklore, and ignore the relationship with the surrounding society. "Two solitudes" played to the tune of a quadrille! The ultimate weapon in the teacher's arsenal remains, however, the tried and true: going through the motions. Maintain discipline, say all the right things, and get through till the end of what appears to be the requisite number of lesson periods. In the elementary years, the basic enthusiasm of the children will overcome any possible difficulties and, from puberty on, you can count on disinterest to discourage debate.

A trifle too cynical for your taste? Then the chances are your grandparents never talked to you about Regulation 17. You don't know about Regulation 17? Then you aren't Franco-Ontarian. Even if you have spoken French from childhood onwards, if you do not know about Regulation 17 or sense its implications, you are not Franco-Ontarian. Regulation 17 was about schools. It is the central event around which the modern sense of a Franco-Ontarian community developed. More than for any other part of our society in Ontario, the school has been at the centre of consciousness of French-speaking Ontarians since before the turn of the century. The history of how all this came about is too long to recount in detail. Instead we shall attempt to see how the historical vision of the past shapes the education of Franco-Ontarians today, how progress has come about, and what problems remain for the future.

The legacy of Egerton Ryerson for Franco-Ontarians is a mixed one. Despite his own early record in expressing support for French as a language of instruction, he is known to the Province as a whole for his role in creating the basic infrastructure of a modern educational system, in particular the institutional framework of central direction that was to widen accessibility to public education, strengthen standards, and ultimately lead to the creation of the broad tax-supported system of education that we enjoy today. Like his contemporaries in other jurisdictions, he developed the role of the state, converting a private good into a public service. The final direction taken by the new public service was imbued with a 19th-century progressivism that became increasingly more intolerant of cultural diversity and, in particular, of Roman Catholicism; the intolerance was, of course, reciprocated. The progress of the secular state in asserting control over education must be understood as a struggle in which a certain view of the world lost out.

In that struggle, the Franco-Ontarians were only partly protected in their rights by legislation that dated back before Confederation, in particular the Separate Schools Act of 1863, a statute of the united province of Canada. The rights in existence then were confirmed by the British North America Act of 1867. What this proved to mean in practice was that the religious basis of schooling was protected – in the sense that control was vested in Roman Catholic householders who elected trustees to "manage" their schools. Ryerson is remembered, at least in part, for his role as a participant in the process by which, through a series of administrative measures and convoluted legal battles, provincial authorities asserted control over most of the essential elements of modern education, including the power to dictate what language be used for instructional purposes. The first consequence of this process was to cause the majority of Franco-Ontarians to switch from public schools into separate schools in the last years of the century. Referring to the rights of Roman Catholics, a later judicial ruling found that "(their) right to manage (the separate schools) does not involve the right of determining the language to be used in the schools" (*Trustees of the Roman*

Catholic Separate Schools of the City of Ottawa v. Mackell et al. (1917), A.C. 62).

A series of regulatory steps taken by the provincial authorities with respect to separate schools in Ontario culminated finally in 1912 with Regulation 17. From that date onward, it was forbidden to use French as a language of instruction beyond Grade 2, even though French-speaking residents had always had the right to have their children educated in the French language in elementary schools. The effect of this regulation was to mobilize Franco-Ontarian opinion into an unremitting battle. The ACFEO (Association Canadienne-Française d'Education d'Ontario), which was founded in 1912, led the fight for French-language rights in schooling; it became the principal organization speaking for the community in all fields down to the present day. (The word "Education" was dropped from the name in 1968.) A so-called "gentleman's agreement" in 1927 put an end to nearly 15 years of bitterly resented enforcement of Regulation 17 and paved the way for French to be used as the *de facto* language of instruction for most of the elementary schools attended by Franco-Ontarian children. French remained in a merely tolerated status without official sanction for another four decades. Because it was held that the rights of separate school supporters extended only to control of education through Grade 10, at the time of Confederation there was never any question of using French as a language of instruction in public secondary schools. Throughout this period, access to French-language education beyond Grade 10 was provided by a network of church-supported Roman Catholic secondary schools; only a small elite went to them, the nucleus of the community leaders up until only a decade ago. (For an authoritative historical overview, see *Royal Commission on Bilingualism and Biculturalism*, 1968.)

Regulation 17 remains down to this day the symbol of intolerance and oppression for Franco-Ontarians. Few outsiders can truly appreciate the emotional weight that this symbol had for several generations of French-speakers in Ontario. Its memory is alive even in the young people who grew into adulthood in the 1970s: some acquaintances have recounted to me personally how their grandparents felt it important to lecture them repeatedly about the Regulation and its evil effects. Its one positive effect was indirect: by providing a clearly defined target for mobilization of opinion, it forged a sense of community that geography would probably have kept the Franco-Ontarians from otherwise achieving.

Other essays in this volume chronicle the general progress of Ontario education up to the present, including the massive expansion of access to secondary education during the period after the Second World War and to post-secondary education during the 1960s. This is the backdrop against which one can judge the consequences of the policies directed towards first eliminating and then limiting the use of French as a language of instruction. Because of this massive, province-wide growth, most general reviews of educational developments pay little attention to the Franco-Ontarian minority. This group accounted for slightly less than 10 percent of the school-age population in 1941, a proportion that declined to about 5 percent in 1981. In terms of the Province as a whole, such small numbers are easy to neglect in describing general trends.

The importance of the Franco-Ontarian school problem can be grasped adequately only in its relationship to Canada as a whole and to the other provinces. According to the 1981 census, 475,605 persons having French as a mother tongue lived in the province of Ontario. This may well be only 5.5 percent of the provincial population, but it accounts for 50.5 percent of the French Canadian population of Canada living outside Quebec. Whatever happens to them and their culture will affect decisively the future shape of Canada and will determine what role French-speaking Canadians can expect to play outside the Province of Quebec. At the same time, the simple educational problem of dealing with their needs takes on its true dimensions in terms of the following comparison: in 1981-82, there were 94,210 Francophones enrolled in public elementary and secondary education in Ontario; this is the equivalent of approximately 50 percent or more of the school-age population in each of four provinces (Alberta, Nova Scotia, New Brunswick, and Saskatchewan) and is larger (of course) than that of a fifth, Prince Edward Island. In half of our provinces, in other words, a group the size of the Franco-Ontarians would make up half the school enrolment and, presumably, receive a major share of public attention to their educational needs.

The heritage of Regulation 17 was revealed in bold, public terms during the 1960s by two very different pieces of educational research. The first was the so-called Carnegie Study, which charted the educational destinies of a sample of Ontario students over a period of years, starting in 1959. It revealed a massive difference in the way Franco-Ontarians succeeded in school as compared to their non-French fellows. The study was a major input to the report of the Royal Commission on Bilingualism and Biculturalism (published 1968).

A second study, a doctoral thesis by R.A.M. Carlton at the University of Toronto, received front-page treatment in its day. This study of educational achievement in a small, unnamed community in northern Ontario documented how Franco-Ontarian students were shunted into dead-end educational streams and pushed out of secondary school by social forces while their English-speaking comrades went through "successfully." The thesis gave human meaning to the Carnegie Study figures on secondary schooling in a way that helped stir opinion favorably towards the reforms then in gestation. A provincially appointed committee on French-language schools in Ontario, the Beriault Committee, had not completed its report before Premier Robarts announced a total revision of provincial policy, the recognition of French as a language of instruction, and the decision to allow its use for instructional purposes throughout the secondary school curriculum. This capped a series of changes during the mid-1960s that had seen French recognized as a language of instruction for teaching history and geography in addition to the traditional instruction in *français* as a mother tongue.

The enthusiasm provoked by these changes has caused public attention to forget the consequences of the period that went before. As diagnosed by the Royal Commission on Bilingualism and Biculturalism, the problems occurred because students who pursued their education in French during the elementary years were faced with an almost impossible obstacle when suddenly forced to switch mainly into English. The Carlton study showed how streaming and other influences magnified the difficulty of this initial transition into so-called "bilingual" schools, where a few courses (français, history, geography, and Latin) were sometimes offered in French. The 1976 census gives an indication of the size of the problem thus engendered: 31.7 percent of adult Franco-Ontarians in 1976 had only a Grade 8 education or less, and a goodly number of these were younger persons who did not attempt the transition to English-language secondary schools when such schooling became commonplace for the rest of the population. Nearly twice as many Francophones as non-Francophones were in this group (31.7 percent versus 16.7 percent). These persons were more or less left out of the official statistics and other studies comparing secondary school performance between the two groups. In a very large number of localities in the north and east of the Province today, 40 to 50 percent of the adult Franco-Ontarian population have a Grade 8 education or less. As for those who did try to go on to secondary school, the results were catastrophic (even ignoring these pre-secondary dropouts). Let us consider two groups of 100 students each enrolled in Grade 9 at public high schools in 1963-64, one group Franco-Ontarian and the other non-Francophone: two years later, 72 of the non-Francophones entered Grade 11; only 30 of the Francophones entered that Grade–in other words, 70 percent were already dropouts. By Grade 13, in 1967-68, 33 of the original non-Francophones were enrolled, as compared to only six Francophones. Thus, in public secondary schools, the Franco-Ontarians only had *one-fifth* the chance of English-speaking students of entering the year of schooling that prepared for university. (The Carnegie Study, which included private school students of both groups, estimated the chance at slightly better than one-fourth by comparison with children from English-speaking families.) The implications are staggering: the 16-year-olds who dropped out in 1968 from Grade 10 are today 32 years of age and have some 30 years of work life ahead of them before retirement. Having an inferior education is a heavy burden to carry and

---

J'ai fait ma douzième année dans un collège privé pour filles. Je savais que l'année suivante j'aurais à subir les examens standardisés du "Département de l'éducation." Je croyais que la plupart des religieuses n'étaient pas assez compétentes sur le plan académique pour nous préparer à y réussir suffisamment pour entrer à l'université. C'est pourquoi je me suis inscrite à l'école secondaire dite bilingue.

"Bilingue," ça voulait dire qu'on avait un cours en français: le français! Tous nos autres cours étaient avec les étudiants anglophones.

Cependant, il y avait une façon de nous identifier. L'administration regroupait les étudiants francophones dans les classes-foyers où l'on se retrouvait au début et à la fin de la journée. Comme par hasard, ces "home-rooms" (identifiées par les lettres de l'alphabet) portaient toutes un "F." Ainsi, toute l'école savait que les classes 9F, 10F, 11F, 12F et 13F contiendraient une bonne proportion de "French kids." En général, les anglophones n'étaient pas trop contents d'être placés dans ces classes-foyers.

Les quelques professeurs francophones nous organisaient en "clubs culturels" pour qu'on se retrouve en-dehors des classes pour des sports, des danses, des sorties, mais les étudiants étaient très conscients d'être marginaux et essayaient beaucoup plus de se fondre dans le groupe majoritaire que d'en ressortir.

Plus tard, quand les cours d'histoire, de géographie et de latin ont été offerts en français, je crois que le sens du groupe et la fierté de parler français se sont probablement améliorés.

DENISE PAQUETTE
13F — 1965

---

its economic price is high. *One Franco-Ontarian adult in three has an education of Grade 8 or less; nearly two out of three have a Grade 10 education or less*. This is the price they paid for unilingual English-only secondary schools. The younger ones in their thirties today will still be paying in the year 2014 the price of the heritage of Regulation 17. I call them the "lost generations."

The 1967 announcement by the Ontario government that recognized French as a language of instruction for both elementary and secondary schools was the beginning of a long series of reforms that continue down to the present day. Not a single year has passed without some significant initiative to improve Franco-Ontarian education. Space, however, does not permit a detailed analysis of the entire range of policy changes in the intervening years. Consequently, our analysis will deal with the main directions of the reforms and with the persistent, still unresolved problems that have reduced their effectiveness: the so-called "mixed" school problem and the issue of minority control of schooling.

The effects of the change in Ontario policies might well be termed an "educational renaissance." The initial policy announcements involved two essential changes: the legitimation of existing practice in elementary schools and the creation of a new French-language educational system at the secondary level. Until 1979, Ontario policy recognized two types of high school offering instruction in French: "mixed" schools attended by both Francophone and non-Francophone students, each free to choose credits in either French or English, and "homogeneous" schools attended only by French-speaking students. Legislation, amended and revised several times since then in order to strengthen Francophone rights, required school boards to provide education in French whenever certain numbers of French-speaking students were present and their parents requested it. School boards were left considerable freedom in deciding whether to house the students in a separate school building, in a wing or other part of a school building, or in individual classrooms intermixed with classes in otherwise English-language schools. For elementary education, the practical consequence was to launch the process of setting up classes and schools in areas of very low relative density of Francophone population (particularly in the south of the Province), a task made necessary by the gradual drift of population towards these areas. In other words, the effects were important but did not touch the community as a whole. But at the secondary level, a total transformation ensued. Homogeneous French high schools were created *en masse*, and existing English schools began to offer classes, courses, and programs (later credits) in French. By 1976, there were 24 homogeneous French high schools and 36 mixed high schools in the Province. In 1969, the first year after the reform was official in law, nearly 22,000 French-speaking high school students were enrolled in programs partially or entirely taught in French, and the percentage of them going into the upper grades (except Grade 13) was rapidly approaching that of the remainder of the population. This dramatic shift in transition ratios between grades demonstrated, beyond a shadow of a doubt, the cause and effect relationship between language of instruction and educational participation (see Footnote).

These results were not achieved without considerable soul-searching on the part of provincial politicians. Much has

---

Footnote: Some observers have objected that the low transition rates in the pre-1968 period were simply part of a Francophone culture and were similar to the ratios in Quebec. This viewpoint attempts to shift the blame to the Franco-Ontarians for their problems and perpetuates the idea that their dropping out of the system was voluntary. The enormous differences between the public educational structures of Quebec (where a central ministry of education was only created in the 1960s) and those of Ontario at the period concerned rules out such comparisons: the French-speaking citizens of Ontario were kept out of the mainstream of educational events that affected all other groups (Native American Indians excepted), including those who shared their religion. The change of policy in Ontario had an effect similar to the rupture of a dam: a wave of students flowed through the secondary system, demonstrable proof of an unmet educational need–unmet because of a policy, not because of the absence of demand.

been written about the difficulty of carrying out reforms without provoking a "backlash" from public opinion of the English majority. (This appears to be a universal problem of educating minorities.) The similarities of the problems and of the policy solutions adopted in Ontario and in other jurisdictions deserve to be mentioned. The expansion of educational opportunities for the French minority at the high school level was also pursued actively in the same period by two other Canadian provinces, Manitoba and New Brunswick. The Manitoba situation remains in a state of flux, but to consider New Brunswick – perhaps in part because of the greater concentrations of Francophones in some districts and also because the Province's francophone population constitutes a relatively large proportion of the total electorate, New Brunswick has pursued a far-reaching set of policies that go well beyond those of Ontario, including the adoption of French as a second official language and the creation of unilingual school districts, a policy solution put into place only progressively during this period.

The national "change of heart" that coincided with the 1967 Confederation centennial celebrations was, in fact, part of a much larger pattern. The dilemma of Ontario political policy in the late 1960s resulted from two contradictory, but widespread, tendencies that affected most of the industrialized countries. At the same time as decisions were being made to help Franco-Ontarians, other policies were being developed to decentralize control of education, increasing the power of locally elected school trustees. Essentially this meant that the implementation of the reforms at the local level was handed over to school boards which, with only a few exceptions, were dominated by local, English-speaking majorities. Francophones were not in a position to play effective roles in decision-making except in a few localities (mainly in the "border" counties along the frontier with Quebec). As revealed in a recent comparative study of finance, organization, and governance of education for linguistic and cultural minorities, conducted under the aegis of the Organization for Economic Co-operation and Development, most jurisdictions in this situation have been forced to admit that minorities require some form of central protection and intervention if their interests are to be safeguarded against the pull of local majorities. As a general rule, the higher the degree of central intervention, the more likely the minorities are to benefit from the policies decided in their favor.

The climate of opinion in the country at large continued to develop during the 1970s in directions that favored the reinforcement of minority rights. The election of the Péquiste Government in Quebec threw down a gauntlet to the political leadership of the remainder of Canadian provinces and to the Federal Government. Operating from behind the scenes since the early 1970s, the Federal Government had "oiled" the creaky machinery of development of minority-language education by a system of formula grants to provinces. The grants to all provinces for the period 1970-71 to 1980-81 totalled slightly more than one billion dollars, of which Ontario received some $220 million; an additional $245 million was allocated to provinces for the costs of second-language teaching of the second official language, English in Quebec, French in the other provinces. In a famous declaration made at a meeting of First Ministers in St-Andrews-by-the-Sea (N.B.) in 1977, the ten provinces undertook to provide access to education in the minority language, wherever numbers were sufficient. The way was opened thereby to bring a similar guarantee into the constitutional amendments that were being actively discussed. The final text of Article 23 of the Canadian Charter of Rights and Freedoms retained a similar restriction, so that the right to education "applies wherever in the province the number of children of citizens who have such a right is sufficient to warrant the provision to them out of public funds of minority language instruction."

Thus it was against a backdrop of broad international trends favoring minorities and of Canadian developments moving in the same direction that Ontario policy on minority-language education emerged during the period after the reforms. Several times after the passage of the original legislation in 1968, major public disputes erupted in connection with what became the major issue of French-language secondary education: how to get majority English-speaking public school boards to agree to set up secondary school programs in French outside the framework of so-called "mixed" secondary schools. The failure of provincial policies to deal adequately with this problem, ostensibly the topic of many public debates in the period, has raised a much larger policy matter that is currently the "hottest" issue of all: the degree to which the French-speaking minority should be allowed to control their own schools.

The interplay between the mixed school problem and that of minority control of education was already clear in the recommendations of the Symons Commission. As a one-man Commission on French-language Secondary Schools, Dr. T.H. Symons helped solve one of the first major disputes over creation of a homogeneous French secondary school (in Sturgeon Falls) and provided the framework for major legislative reforms. The new legislation had three main effects: (a) tightening up the mandatory requirements for providing instruction in French; (b) creating so-called "French Language Advisory Committees" (FLAC), bodies elected by the local Franco-Ontarian population which had to be consulted by school boards in relation to decisions affecting the schooling of their children (the creation of a FLAC was made mandatory only for boards operating secondary schools, thereby avoiding the delicate issue of changing the existing powers of trustees of Roman Catholic separate schools); and (c) establishing a mechanism for mediation and, in some cases, resolution of conflicts, known as the Languages of Instruction Commission of Ontario. The upshot of these changes, quickly enacted in legislation, was to provide the Franco-Ontarians with a means of clarifying issues, raising them to the public consciousness by appealing to a provincial "tribunal," and holding the attention of public authorities. In short, they had the means of political mobilization that would enable even relatively small communities of Francophones to make themselves heard.

The mixed secondary schools problem has usually been treated by English-speaking school trustees as being an issue of costs. In a given locality, there are only a few Franco-Ontarians (comparatively speaking); they are receiving some instruction in French in a mixed secondary school and the expansion of such courses or housing the students in a separate building (existing or totally new, depending upon circumstances) would be "too costly." Since the beginning of the reforms, public opinion among English-speaking Ontarians has persistently confused education for Franco-Ontarians with the idea of "bilingual" education; it is assumed that the purpose of the reforms is to permit both English and French children to learn each other's language by going to the same schools – an ideal almost never realized in practice. In the heat of debate, opinions sometimes are expressed that it is "un-Canadian" to want schooling in separate facilities, but such views tend to be set aside as the opinion of a small proportion of the trustees who oppose changes favoring the Franco-Ontarians. Indeed, debate is usually couched in terms of "helping" improve their education, and most boards decide, when pressured, to take limited steps to improve course offerings in mixed schools. The Franco-Ontarians' view of the issues was first presented on their behalf by the Symons Commission, which noted that "much more often than not, the mixed or so-called 'bilingual' school, is a one-way street to assimilation for the French-speaking students."

Even if the main impetus for change throughout the period has been the insistent demands of the Franco-Ontarians themselves, additional help has often been provided by research under Ministry of Education sponsorship – either internal staff studies or externally contracted research. The study most directly connected with the central problem of mixed schools – namely, costs and services – resulted in a scorching indictment of the programs of these schools. Most of those studied offered only minimal programming in French, even when the French-speaking students constituted a sizable minority, or even a majority, of the students attending; the program offerings served essentially to shift the French students taking most of their Grade 9 courses in their native language to studying mainly in English just one or two years later. Enrolments and other indicators suggested distinct parallels with the socially based streaming of French students found over a decade earlier by the Carlton study – except that in the 1960s the secondary system was acknowledged to be intended to function almost exclusively in English. The same study also demonstrated that, even though Franco-Ontarian students had important unmet educational needs and the school boards received grants intended to alleviate the special problems of their education, in almost all of the school boards examined, more money was being spent on education of English-language students than on the French. Other parallel studies documented the differential cost requirements of school boards delivering bilingual education. Such studies paved the way for a major revision of the provincial grant system, which now required school boards to demonstrate differential expenditures in favor of Francophones in order to qualify for extra subsidies. In turn, the research was part of a larger review of provincial policy that led to a whole range of measures intended "to improve services and resources necessary to ensure equal educational opportunities to students in French-language schools" (Ministry of Education, Ontario, *Elementary and Secondary French-Language Education in Ontario*, Review and Evaluation Bulletin: Vol. 1, No. 4, 1983).

In 1979, the eruption of yet another major dispute related to mixed secondary schools, this time in Penetanguishene, led to a new elaboration of policy – the creation of so-called "French-language entities." A sort of halfway house, the policy involved splitting up a mixed secondary school into separate "entities" under their own principal, one English and one French; they continued to share the same buildings and physical facilities but were nominally expected to function autonomously. Although the entity proved insufficient for Penetanguishene, where a homogeneous French language secondary school was eventually established, provincial policy, down to the present, continues to encourage the establishment of French-language entities where separate schools appear too costly; but since decisions remain with school boards, complaints and disputes continue to be rife. It is not uncommon for school boards to reject recommendations from the Languages of Instruction Commission of Ontario as well as direct requests from the Ministry of Education. In one dispute (Essex County) during the mid-1970s, a special law had to be passed by the provincial Legislature to force a school board to create a homogeneous French secondary school. Meanwhile, various indicators continue to show that the Franco-Ontarians in the remaining mixed secondary schools (in 1982-83, 30 schools with an enrolment of 6,197 Francophones – about 24 percent of the provincial enrolment of Francophones) suffer from serious problems of inadequate, sometimes almost non-existent, programs in French.

More than any other factor, the failure to find a lasting, satisfactory solution to the mixed schools problem provided the Franco-Ontarian community with the visible political rallying point necessary to raise an even larger problem: their right to control the educational system serving their children. An analysis prepared from documents of the Languages of Instruction Commission of Ontario showed 15 cases in 14 school boards where attempts by parents to obtain services apparently guaranteed them by provincial policy and legislation were rebuffed, hindered, or delayed by school boards dominated by English-speaking trustees. The records covered only referrals to the Commission and did not, of course, treat the numerous instances where initial rebuffs were followed eventually by compromises that avoided a formal appeal; nor did they include most of the disputes that occurred before the Commission was established. The main conclusion to be derived from this record is that, in a large number of instances, spread over wide geographical areas of the Province, the French-language minority could not count on the elected local trustees to deal sympathetically with their problems; instead of receiving positive treatment at the trustees' hands, they have been rejected under conditions that, in some cases, were absolutely appalling. On more than one occasion, school boards have simply voted to do away with education for the minority – e.g., by cutting off bus services required to send them to a nearby district offering French-language services. In fact, just as this book was going to press, the provincial authorities were attempting to persuade a northern Ontario school board to rescind a decision whereby it refused to provide education to some 60 pupils from a neighboring town, effective the following September. Whereas this might be interpreted as a bargaining ploy to force negotiations on issues the local trustees consider important, it is hard to think of a set of circumstances – other than education of Franco-Ontarians – where an Ontario school board would deliberately decide to cut off education of a significant number of pupils and refuse further responsibility. Nor is it possible to judge the long-term psychological impact of situations where hostile local majorities refuse to recognize minority rights and create situations where children and young people are made to believe that studying in their mother tongue is considered controversial, "anti-English," or even "un-Canadian" by elected local officials – and, therefore, by a majority of their neighbors.

The battle over Francophone control of French-language education is being waged currently on several fronts. Following the filing of a suit by the Association Canadienne-Française de l'Ontario contending that the constitutional guarantees of minority language education include the right to minority control of the educational establishments, the Attorney-General for Ontario made a referral to the Court of Appeal in the Supreme Court of Ontario to resolve this and other legal questions related to the provisions of the Canadian Charter of Rights and Freedoms. Judging by the otherwise positive attitude taken by the provincial authorities in recent years, it would appear that the referral by the Province is intended to validate its own constitutional prerogatives and thereby retain its freedom to reach whatever agreement it feels best with the representatives of the Franco-Ontarian community. Negotiations on the matter of governance have been conducted in several forms over a period of years, culminating with the publication in 1982 of a report by a committee including representatives of both the French-language population and the provincial authorities. The report proposed measures to ensure guaranteed Francophone representation on public school bords (not Separate School boards) where they constitute a significant local minority (10 percent or more) and to give the Francophone trustees control over the most important aspects of education offered to the minority (*Report of the Joint Committee on the Governance of French-language Elementary and Secondary Schools*, 1982). With numerous modifications in detail, the governmental White Paper published in the spring of 1983 followed the general orientation of the joint committee and, among its proposals, made suggestions for legislation to ensure such guaranteed representation. Not surprisingly, the 20 or so school boards affected by a proposal to diminish their powers and modify their structure unanimously rejected the White Paper during the succeeding months. However, faced with a firm provincial determination to push forward, the parties have been forced back to the bargaining table, and it is expected that proposals to ensure guaranteed representation will be published and enacted in 1984. An important factor in the equation is that an agreement in principle has been reached by the Ontario Separate School Trustees Association and the

Francophone trustees (Association Française des Conseils Scolaires de l'Ontario) that would permit the Provincial Government to extend its proposals also to the separate schools.

Given the number of factors intervening, there is no certainty as to the form that the final solution will take. If the Supreme Court of Ontario were to uphold the viewpoint of the Francophones in a firm and definitive way, the situation would be set for the creation of so-called "homogeneous school boards" – i.e., school boards of Francophones elected solely by Francophones. This would give Franco-Ontarians approximately the same status as the French-speaking citizens of New Brunswick and English-speaking citizens born in Quebec. Anything less than this solution, whether obtained judicially or through negotiation, appears likely to be a compromise that will not fully satisfy all the Franco-Ontarians. It remains to be seen whether this will provide an enduring settlement or be treated as the next round in a continuing series of struggles to achieve "parity" with the minorities in New Brunswick and Quebec.

In a period of a little more than 15 years then, Franco-Ontarians have moved from the status of an oppressed minority at least to the level of a tolerated nuisance. Several factors suggest that they may rise beyond this and may, in time, reach the level of an accepted minority with a legal status providing nearly equal access to education at the elementary and secondary levels. The elements of a solution are already clearly visible and require only perhaps a few more months of hard negotiation to bring them into legislative and practical reality:

The provincial White Paper of 1983 included a proposal to do away entirely with the clause limiting rights to situations "where numbers warrant"; this will eliminate most of the discretion of local authorities to deal with minority requests for educational services. Legislation was introduced in the last session of the Provincial Legislature and allowed to die on the order paper. The Government is committed to reintroducing it and passing it in 1984.

A second proposal of the White Paper has also been carried through the stage of initial introduction as legislation: the strengthening of the powers of the Language of Instruction Commission of Ontario. For the first time, the Minister of Education will receive the right to order a school board to comply with recommendations of the Commission.

The proposals for guaranteed representation appear almost certain to eventuate in significant changes permitting much stronger and more direct control by Franco-Ontarians over their education.

Even if the present provincial policies fall short of providing homogeneous school boards, they appear to lay the groundwork for eliminating the major political obstacle to developing full equality of access for Franco-Ontarians to secondary education: namely, the foot-dragging and various other impediments resulting from refusals by local English-speaking majorities to accept provincial laws and policies.

The proposals will not solve all the problems of Franco-Ontarian education. Rather they may set up a situation where the true long-term issues can be addressed. Among these issues are the following:

Guaranteeing individual rights to an education (rather than "where numbers warrant") will not ensure that the rights are effectively implemented. The bulk of persons affected by this new guarantee are those who live in areas where Francophones are an almost invisible minority (less than two percent, often only a fraction of one percent) – i.e., in areas administered by school boards with few or no employees who even speak French. Some mechanisms will have to be found to provide easy access and what one might call "user-friendly" ways to help interested parents and children to avail themselves of new opportunities.

Franco-Ontarian school populations have been shrinking at a much more rapid rate than those of the rest of the Province, and so their schools are destined, even in areas of high density of population, to be much smaller than average. Multi-grading is likely to be the norm in many parts of the Province. In almost every locality, means will have to be sought to organize equitable educational opportunities despite very small numbers of pupils.

Assimilation is an ever-present problem. More and more children start school with a very inadequate knowledge of French, often with English as their dominant language. Franco-Ontarians are basically bilingual, and their educational needs require very special measures if their group is to survive into future generations.

The low general average education of Franco-Ontarian adults means that their children are laboring under a severe disadvantage. Special measures are required to encourage them to participate in the upper levels of education, particularly Grade 13 (or the equivalent under reorganized credit systems now being introduced) in order that larger numbers will be qualified to go on to university.

Unfortunately, the educational system from K to 13 is not a sufficient basis for solving the educational problems of a minority such as the Franco-Ontarians who suffer under socio-economic and cultural disadvantages. No matter what is done in the schools, the problems will not be solved, because their roots are elsewhere, outside "The House that Ryerson Built." Here are what appear to be the priority issues to be dealt with by public authorities in the coming years:

Franco-Ontarian educational rights end at Grade 13. After that, they have limited access to severely limited programs in community colleges and universities. Their participation rates in university are very much lower than those of the rest of the population. They are lowest in those fields of study where instructional programs are not offered in French by any university in the province – particularly engineering, sciences, mathematics, computer science, advanced technology, and medicine; in short, in all the areas that provide high status and promise for leadership in the world of tomorrow. The current structure of universities and community colleges has proved inadequate to fulfill their needs, in part because of the autonomy of individual institutions, almost always controlled by non-Francophone boards of governors and English-dominant administrations. The recent proposals of a provincial committee of enquiry on university education in northeastern Ontario bear a striking similarity to the steps that have been taken by the Province in the last decade to change elementary and secondary education, right down to the proposal for guaranteed Francophone representation on the Board of Governors of a new University of North Eastern Ontario.

Cité des Jeunes, a French secondary school in Kapuskasing — founded 1970

Education in French must be buttressed by community services in French. The current provincial policy direction has been to expand the use of French in key areas such as in the provincial judicial system. Much more thorough-going measures are necessary, probably with financial encouragements and legal obligations, for municipalities to provide services. Unless French is widely used in public administration, its role will appear progressively more limited. At the same time, as services appear, they will provide a long-term job market that will be a powerful incentive for young Franco-Ontarians to maintain their language and seek higher qualifying education.

Who can say whether these measures will be enough to provide a right for French-speaking Canadians to look upon Ontario as a land that "belongs" to them? Yet conserving a viable, living Franco-Ontarian culture is a prerequisite to conserving a Canadian identity that transcends ethnic and linguistic rivalries, that reaches beyond the instincts of building ever-higher barriers between our provinces, and that calls upon our young people to look forward to a future where they can all feel equals. For this reason, one final issue cannot be avoided: Will Canada long survive if Ontario maintains its refusal to consider official bilingualism, even as an option for the future? Could a commitment to having two official languages be announced for final implementation after a transition period of, say, 16 years – in time for the year 2000? The symbolic act of proposing such a measure would finally legitimate the existence of Franco-Ontarians as equal citizens, legitimate the rights of 50 percent of Canadian citizens who are considered "French Canadians" rather than Francophones from Quebec. Interestingly, it would bring history around full circle, using the liberal, progressive instrument of the state, forged by people like Egerton Ryerson in the 19th century, and turning it into the means to conserve a culture that it once used to combat. It would be a great way of demonstrating that the Ontario bicentennial is intended to mark a new beginning.

Something really to celebrate, for everybody.

STACY CHURCHILL is an associate professor at OISE and at the School of Graduate Studies, University of Toronto, specializing in problems of linguistic minorities and computer-assisted instruction. Prior to entering academic life, he worked as a journalist and, later, in the computing industry, living and studying in Chile, France, Finland, and the United Kingdom. A graduate of the Institute of Political Studies, University of Paris, he obtained a doctorate from the London School of Economics and Political Science, joining the staff of OISE in 1967. He was the first director of a major computer-assisted instruction project, subsequently the largest in Canada. From 1976 to 1981 he was coordinator of Research and Development at OISE, where he founded the Centre for Franco-Ontarian Studies. In 1983, he was appointed as a member of the Languages of Instruction Commission of Ontario.

The arrogant justification
Of men putting down womankind
Is based on the age-old assumption
Of a vastly superior mind.

Yet comparing a man and a woman,
One awkward conclusion remains:
That although their anatomies differ,
They are born with identical brains.

THE SCHOOLING OF GIRLS

DORMER ELLIS

Egerton Ryerson intended education to be for girls as well as for boys. In his 1850 report as Chief Superintendent of Schools, he expressed concern that there were still "nearly one hundred thousand children of school age in Upper Canada not attending any school," and stated that "This awful fact furnishes a hundred thousand arguments to urge each friend of Canada, each friend of virtue, of knowledge and of civilization, to exert himself to his utmost until the number of children attending our schools shall equal the number of children of school age." Figures in this report indicate that of the one hundred and fifty thousand children who were enrolled in school, 44 percent were girls.

By 1871, the vigorous campaign of Ryerson had been so successful that there were free elementary schools throughout Ontario, and parents were required by law to have their sons and daughters attend for at least four months a year between the ages of seven and twelve. Later in the 19th century, legislation was passed to strengthen attendance requirements throughout the school year and to raise the age of compulsory attendance to 14 years. After the First World War, the Adolescent School Attendance Act raised the age of compulsory attendance to 16. In 1950, the Royal Commission on Education in Ontario pointed out that improvements in transportation had removed any valid reason for not requiring the attendance of younger children and recommended that the period of compulsory attendance be from 6 to 16 years. It is interesting to note that throughout this long period, there was never any distinction made between boys and girls in school attendance requirements. Today, Ontario elementary and secondary schools are free to boys and girls alike, and all children must attend until the age of 16.

There is ample evidence that schoolgirls fare better than schoolboys, at least as far as their rate of progress through the grades is concerned. For decades, the annual reports of the Minister of Education for Ontario included tables showing the age distributions of boys and girls in each grade. A statistical study of these sex-age-grade distributions during the quarter century 1936-61 found two characteristics that had not changed over the years. One was the equal numbers of boys and girls in all grades from 1 to 12, and the other was the faster pace of girls. Although there was virtually no age difference at the Grade 1 level, in every other grade the average age of girls was less than that of boys, and this age difference became more pronounced as the children moved upward through the grades. In Grade 6, girls averaged three months younger than boys, by Grade 9 the difference had

89

increased to nearly four months, and by Grade 12 to five months. Suggested explanations of this lasting phenomenon were based on the assumption that there must be some subtle factor built into the school system which enabled girls to succeed at the required tasks more quickly than boys and thus be promoted to higher grades at a faster rate. Among the factors suggested were stories in primary readers being about home life (presumably of more interest to girls than to boys), the large number of women compared to men on the teaching staffs of elementary schools, and the tendency of teachers to give rewards for obedience and tidiness, traits assumed to be more common in girls than in boys.

The first large-scale educational research project undertaken in Ontario was a province-wide study of all students who were in Grade 13 during the 1955-56 school year. The research was funded by the Atkinson Foundation and carried out by researchers in the Department of Educational Research, Ontario College of Education, working under the supervision of W. G. Fleming. Nine thousand students completed questionnaires, groups of teachers rated them on personality traits, their marks on Grade 13 examinations were made available as were their scores on academic aptitude and achievement tests, and information about degree of success in the earlier grades of secondary school was obtained from each student's file.

Although the sexes were equally represented in the lower grades, there were three boys to every two girls in Grade 13. The boys averaged about half a year older than the girls. The girls were given higher ratings on desirable personality traits than were the boys. The academic attainment of the girls was greater than that of the boys. In spite of the indications that the Grade 13 girls had a better chance of success in university than their male counterparts, a much smaller percentage of them went on to university studies. Commenting on this, Fleming expressed the prevailing view about such differences when he wrote: "It is generally felt that society benefits more by educating a boy

---

I have frequently been asked whether I considered it desirable that girls should study Latin in the Grammar Schools. It is, in my opinion, most undesirable; and I am at a loss to comprehend how any intelligent person acquainted with the state of things in our Grammar Schools can come to a different conclusion. . . . Since I became Inspector, I have not met with half a dozen girls in the Grammar Schools of Canada by whom the study of Latin has been pursued far enough for their taste to be in the least degree influenced by what has been read. Aesthetically, the benefits of Grammar Schools to girls are *nil*. . . . It may perhaps be said that although they have for the most part made but little progress in Latin up to the present time, a fair proportion of them may be expected to pursue the study to a point where its advantages can be reaped. I do not believe that three out of a hundred will. As a class, they have dipped the soles of their feet in the water, with no intention or likelihood of wading deeper into it. They are not studying Latin with any definite object. They have taken it up under pressure at the solicitation of the teachers or trustees to enable the schools to maintain the requisite average attendance of ten classical pupils or to increase that part of the income of the schools which is derived from public sources. In a short time they will leave school to enter on the practical work of life without having either desired or obtained more than the merest smattering of Latin, and their places will be taken by another band of girls who will go through the same routine.

REV. GEORGE PAXTON YOUNG,
(FROM A "REPORT ON THE GRAMMAR SCHOOLS," 1865)

than a girl at this level." Such a sexist statement if made in 1984 would surely be challenged, but at the time of the publication of the Atkinson reports, it was accepted as self-evident. How did it come about that education in the final grade of the school system had a different value for girls than for boys?

Ontario has a long history of co-educational secondary schools. Even before 1850, a few young girls of social standing received their elementary education in so-called grammar schools because their families did not want them to associate with the lower class children attending the common elementary schools. However, the senior pupils at the secondary level in these grammar schools were almost always boys. Around the time of Confederation, there was still considerable opposition to co-education in the secondary schools, but Egerton Ryerson struck a compromise with grammar school trustees by establishing a secondary school grant formula which equated two girls to one boy and which led to legislation making public high schools co-educational. Nevertheless, some places held out. In Kingston, for example, "the promiscuous attendance of the sexes at the same school" was considered a great evil, and ten years passed before the collegiate finally admitted female students, having first constructed a separate room for them.

It was not unusual to have separate rooms and even separate entrances for girls well into the 20th century. When my father attended a mixed secondary school in Toronto in the 1910-14 period, not only were classes sex-segregated but also it was strictly forbidden to speak to a student of the opposite sex in the corridors or on the school grounds. A boy who walked to or from school with any girl other than his sister risked expulsion.

The strict rules of conduct gradually relaxed as co-educational secondary schools became common in Ontario. Nevertheless, except where small schools and low enrolment in the optional subjects of the higher grades made mixed classes an economic necessity, single-sex classes

"... *every young woman should know how to make her own hats."*

were, for many years, still considered preferable, and it was certainly not the case that all courses were equally open to both sexes – for example, the industrial and vocational courses that were established by secondary schools in the larger communities during the period between the two World Wars were intended exclusively for one sex or the other as they reflected society's expectations concerning the future roles of the schools' graduates.

In the early 1940s when I was enrolled in the academic stream of a technical school in Toronto, one industrial or vocational subject was included in the curriculum of each of the first four years of the five-year program. The boys chose their optional subjects from among several courses in machine shop practice, electricity, carpentry, and draughting, while the girls took cooking, home nursing, dressmaking, and millinery in successive school years. Although I had the highest academic average of any student in my year and had already decided to study engineering after graduating from secondary school, my request to take a course in machine draughting rather than millinery produced a shocked "Certainly not!" from the form teacher and precipitated an interview with the principal, who explained in a fatherly way why every young woman should know how to make her own hats. There were no career counsellors or guidance departments in the secondary schools of that era but, near the end of the fifth year of studies, two speakers came to the school to discuss university programs. One was a man from an engineering faculty; the other was a woman from a faculty of household science. When I tried to attend the lecture for prospective engineering students, I was ridiculed by the presiding teacher and sent off unceremoniously to join the girls in the home economics room.

Although there have been guidance facilities in Ontario secondary schools for over a quarter of a century, girls who want to enter fields of study that are non-traditional for their sex do not always receive encouragement. In the autumn of 1976, a questionnaire survey was undertaken in which the research subjects were all the women students enrolled in the first year of any engineering program at 10 Ontario universities. These 163 women were asked who had encouraged them in their choice of post-secondary studies, who had attempted to dissuade them, and the reasons given for so doing. Only 2 percent mentioned a high school guidance teacher as having provided encouragement to prepare for the profession of engineering, and 25 percent identified guidance teachers as individuals who had not approved of this career choice. Although the young women had demonstrated their ability and interest in mathematics and science by earning high grades in these subjects at secondary school, guidance teachers who attempted to dissuade them from engineering suggested such traditional alternatives as nursing or home economics. The questionnaire survey was repeated in 1981, by which time the number of young women enrolled in the first year of engineering programs at Ontario universities had more than doubled. Almost half of these students reported that a secondary school guidance teacher had approved of engineering as a career choice, and only 15 percent said that guidance personnel had deliberately tried to dissuade them. This is a dramatic change in just five years, and reflects rapidly changing attitudes both in the schools and in society. It is only comparatively recently that efforts have been made to broaden schoolgirls' career horizons to include non-traditional occupations and to plan for long-term employment.

It may be that the Royal Commission on the Status of Women in Canada provided the initial impetus. As the Commission moved across the country receiving briefs and holding public meetings, facts began to supplant traditional myths about working women. Previously, evidence that was contrary to the myths was treated as "the exception that proved the rule." The Royal Commission drew the public's attention to such facts as the following: women comprise about one-third of the labour force; over half of working women are married; the number of women who never return to paid employment once they have left to raise a family is rapidly declining; and women generally work in a few occupations labelled "female" and earn less money than do men who work in a much broader spectrum of occupations. The Commission observed that occupational segregation by sex had existed for so long that society took it for granted. Among the recommendations in the report of the Royal

Commission on the Status of Women in Canada were that girls be made more aware of the long-term consequences of their subject choices at high school and that they be encouraged to plan realistically for their working future. This was a challenge to the schools.

During 1975, International Women's Year, special programs and activities in Ontario schools drew the attention of students and teachers to the few women who were in non-traditional occupations in the hope of getting more girls to look beyond their usual narrow range of employment possibilities. There were posters and pamphlets with the heading "You're a what?," each one depicting a young woman in an unusual occupation – driving a truck, operating a crane, surveying, draughting, and plumbing.

Following the recommendations of the Royal Commission on the Status of Women in Canada and the spotlight on women during International Women's Year (together, no doubt, with other changes that have taken place in society as a whole), determined efforts have been made to reduce the stereotyping of women and girls in school books. In the past decade, texts in all subject areas have been rewritten to avoid sexist language, and children's readers now include women in roles other than housewife, teacher, or nurse. Although blatant sexism has been removed, the more subtle forms remain. Recent research by Priscilla Galloway involved an examination of seventeen hundred literary works on English courses in Ontario secondary schools (see her book, *What's Wrong with High School English?*). The sample of schools was geographically representative and included rural and urban, large and small schools. Dr. Galloway found that eight times more of the literature was written by men than by women and that some English courses had no literature written by a woman. She also found that there were seven times as many male protagonists as there were female, and she commented that there was little reason to suppose that a biased curriculum was being taught in an unbiased manner.

Social custom and traditional beliefs are slow to change.

In spite of commendable efforts by the Ministry of Education to eradicate sexist language and the stereotyping of women in textbooks, schools are essentially conservative in the message they pass on to students. Numerous research studies have documented the traditionality of a girl's career choices and her unrealistic expectations concerning her adult life. The probably erroneous but unquestioned assumption that she will be in the work force for only a short time before meeting the man who will provide for her for the rest of her life still leads many teenage girls to drop challenging courses in mathematics and physics in favour of acquiring an immediately saleable skill like typewriting.

Surveys of girls in the early grades of secondary school have shown that their occupational expectations are either traditionally feminine (and hence are likely to be low status and low paying) or fantastically glamorous but requiring little academic preparation. The number of girls who hope to be a private secretary to a young, handsome, single lawyer makes this career goal statistically improbable of achievement. The strong influence of the media becomes obvious when girls suddenly aspire to an occupation that has previously been unmentioned. A television series about an attractive young woman engaged in enjoyable activities in exotic locales, surrounded by admiring, eligible men, but apparently needing no specific educational background, led some high school girls to describe their career plans as being the cruise director on a "Love Boat." One should not underestimate the magnitude of the task faced by school career counsellors who try to raise girls' aspirations while keeping them realistic.

Because role models with whom they can easily identify may be scarce, girls in certain social classes or belonging to particular ethnic groups may require additional assistance before they can envision themselves in non-traditional, well-paying positions. In 1972, with research funding from the Ministry of Education, a province-wide survey of students in the first year of Ontario's French-language

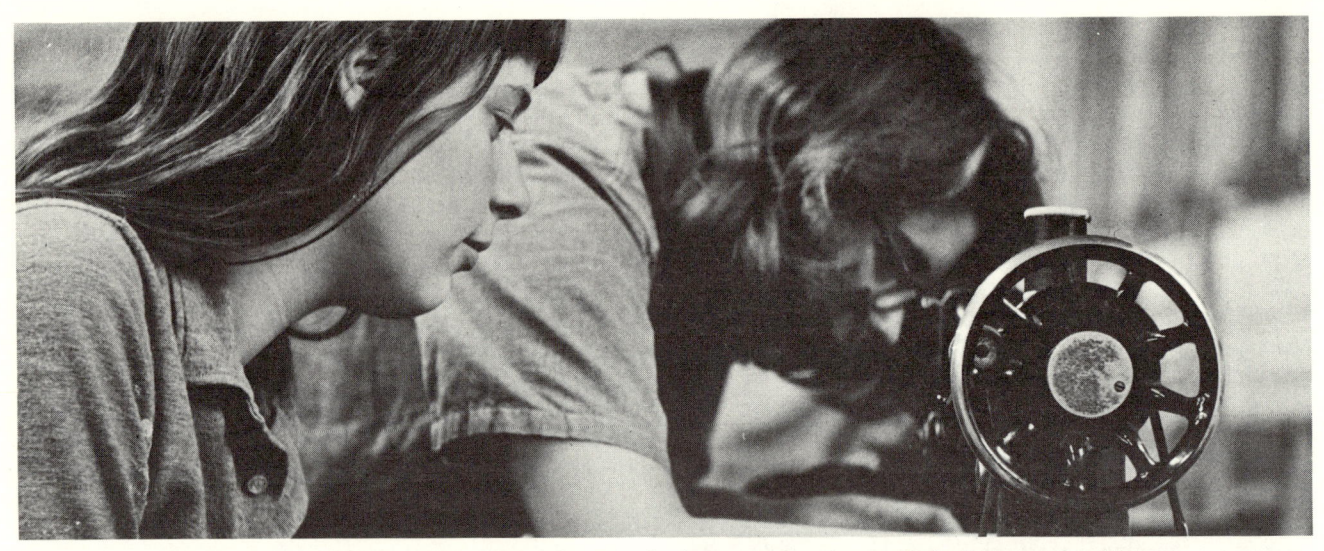

Traditionally, girls had little choice but to take home economics as their vocational subject

secondary schools was carried out. The questionnaire that was administered to a representative sample of two thousand students included items about educational plans and occupational expectations. Although there was little sex difference in the length of time students intended to remain in school, girls were considerably lower than boys in the occupational status they expected to attain. Even girls who indicated that they planned to graduate from Grade 13 went on to say that after completing their schooling, they would likely work as a waitress, store clerk, or hairdresser. When the survey was repeated four years later, by which time French-language secondary schools had become more established in the Province, the career aspirations of Grade 9 boys were found to be higher than those in the earlier study but Grade 9 girls still did not expect to be employed in any but very traditionally feminine occupations. None of the thousand girls surveyed aspired to an occupation which required a knowledge of senior mathematics or science – not one mentioned pharmacist, accountant, dentist, engineer, physician, or biochemist. Nurse, elementary school teacher, and secretary were the most common choices, but some just recorded "homemaker," thereby indicating that they did not expect ever to be in remunerative employment.

Doctoral theses in the Department of Applied Psychology at the Ontario Institute for Studies in Education have documented the fact that many girls in secondary school still believe the traditional myths about women's lives. Lynda Sayer studied the career awareness of Grade 9 girls in a large school in Metropolitan Toronto which draws students from a wide range of socio-economic levels. The data collected did not suggest that serious inroads had been made in the traditional attitudes and beliefs of adolescent girls. Girls' perceptions of their parents' preferences appeared to play a large role in educational plans. Almost all the girls expected to marry, but many thought that they would work outside the home, perhaps on a part-time basis, after all their children were in school. Very few intended to prepare for a high status, well-paying profession. Most expected to work in a predominantly feminine occupation. Experimental research on the relative effectiveness of various short-term career awareness programs (one period a day for five days) led to the conclusion that none was very effective in altering the attitudes and beliefs of 14- and 15-year-old girls to the extent that they would look beyond a narrow range of low status occupations. The researcher felt that programs of longer duration, preferably integrated with the regular school curriculum, would have to be provided if girls were to be given the opportunity to develop their full career potential.

Eleven hundred girls in the final grades of secondary school in southern Ontario were the research subjects of a doctoral study by Avis Glaze. They were selected in such a way that the influence of such factors as rural or urban residence, ethnicity, socio-economic status, and religious affiliation could be investigated. For one aspect of the research, the girls took a multiple-choice test about women in the work force, the correct answers being those consistent with statistics published by the Women's Bureau of the Ontario Ministry of Labour. It was apparent that although they were approaching the completion of their secondary school education, these girls were very poorly informed about the realities of the working world and still believed myths about women's lives. Their answers to questions about the average number of years women spend in remunerative employment, women's average earnings as compared to those of men, and the relationship between education and employment revealed appalling misconceptions. The majority of these senior high school students believed erroneously that 40 percent of women who are university graduates never marry and that housewives are less likely to become divorced than are married women who work outside the home. It was concluded that even though the statistics on the participation of women in the work force are so revealing and the centrality of work in the lives of individuals so well established, girls who were soon to graduate from Ontario secondary schools continued to be myopic in their career planning. This is hardly surprising when one considers how little they knew about the employment status of women. The majority of the subjects of this research said that at no time during all the years they had spent in Ontario elementary and secondary schools had they been provided with a forum for the discussion in a detailed and systematic way of women's experiences in the work force. They were unaware of the effects of sex-role stereotyping and of the economic disadvantages women face if they need to support themselves and their dependents.

Why is it that these basic facts are not taught to students in Ontario schools? It would be unfair to be too critical of the school system in this regard, because it is an integral part of society. Although schools may lead in social change, they cannot be drastically different from the communities they serve. Could it be that educators are themselves caught up in a system which unintentionally but systematically discriminates against women? Even a casual observer cannot help but notice that women teachers greatly outnumber men in the lower elementary grades, but their ranks become progressively thinner as one moves upward through the senior elementary and secondary grades. Women and men are certainly not equally represented among school principals, department heads, and senior supervisory personnel. Does the status of women in the educational system reflect the status of women in society at large?

During the early years of the 19th century, teachers in the common elementary schools of Ontario were all men. The advent of women teachers began about mid-century, and by the time of Confederation there were about equal numbers of men and women teaching school. Soon after, women began to outnumber men, and by the turn of the century, there were four times as many women teaching as men. The

High school girls are now encouraged to take machine shop courses such as welding

proportion has declined during the present century as teaching salaries have improved. Ontario teachers now earn salaries that depend only on their academic qualifications and years of service, there being a single salary scale applicable to both sexes. However, the average salary paid to men is greater than that paid to women because men are much more likely to be in supervisory or administrative positions which have higher salary scales than those of classroom teachers.

The historical development of teachers' federations in Ontario has led to fragmentation. The Federation of Women Teachers' Associations of Ontario (FWTAO) was organized in 1918, the Ontario Secondary School Teachers' Federation (OSSTF) in 1919, and the Ontario Public School Men Teachers' Federation (OPSMTF) in 1920. *L'Association des enseignants franco-ontariens* was established in 1939 by teachers in French-language elementary schools, and the Ontario English Catholic Teachers' Association was organized in 1944 for teachers in the English-language Roman Catholic separate schools. In 1944, the Ontario Teachers' Federation (embracing these five affiliates) was formed, and legislation was passed to ensure automatic membership and deduction of fees from teachers' salaries. Every person teaching in a publicly supported elementary or secondary school in Ontario is required to belong to the appropriate affiliate.

It will be noted that three of the five affiliates have both male and female statutory members, while the two that serve the public elementary schools do not. Efforts have been made in recent years by the OPSMTF to amalgamate with the FWTAO, but although they have changed their name to the Ontario Public School Teachers' Federation and although a few women teachers have joined as voluntary members in addition to their obligatory membership in the FWTAO, so far they have been unsuccessful. What is the status of women in the teachers' associations and in the school system itself? Findings from several studies carried out by affiliates or by researchers working in co-operation with them throw some light on this question.

During the 1981-82 school year, the Ontario English Catholic Teachers' Association used a random sampling technique to survey members' opinions on matters of concern to the Association. The demographic information collected showed that although women teachers greatly outnumbered their male colleagues, principals were five times more likely to be male than female and those women who were principals tended to be in charge of smaller schools. Also, the stereotype of the "old maid" schoolteacher was not supported by the statistical picture that emerged from this research. There were twice as many married as single women, and the majority of the single women were still in their twenties. There were significant sex differences in the responses to some questionnaire items. Irrespective of age and years of experience in the teaching profession, men were far more likely than women to have taken part in collective bargaining training sessions. Responses to items about conferences for incumbent and aspiring supervisory personnel revealed a preponderance of men not only among members who had already participated but also among those indicating future interest. There was no evidence that the sex ratio among principals would change very much in the near future.

The strong tendency for women to remain at the classroom level is not a peculiarity of any one teachers' association; and insofar as there are sex differences in aspirations, this cannot be attributed entirely to lack of opportunity for promotion. Beginning in 1968, three successive cohorts of student-teachers attending Ontario's two French-language teachers' colleges in Sudbury and Ottawa were the subjects of research undertaken in co-operation with *L'Association des enseignants franco-ontariens*. Four out of five student-teachers were women,

---

My Grade 6 teacher was probably the ultimate in schoolmarm stereotype. Unmarried (in those days, spinster), with horn-rimmed spectacles and flashing dark eyes, she created an impression of absolute severity which left students quivering.

But every Thursday afternoon, she would break out from that crusty shell and, through a vehicle she called simply "author's club", allow us to soar. Those of us who were so inclined could read aloud stories, poems, or prose that we had written in our spare time. The rest would simply relax and listen.

It could be something as simple as a ten-line verse or as complex as an ongoing saga with a thickening plot of bizarre weekly twists. The only condition was that the story had to be completed by year-end.

I thrilled to science fiction tales from one fellow student who could fly from tall buildings and swim twenty thousand leagues under the sea in the same week. For my part, I wrote a book entitled *Great Stamina*, involving the classic story of a crippled horse and how its master fought to ensure its survival.

For all of us, author's club wasn't school. It was a chance to dream, to dare, to imagine. For that, I am ever grateful to Miss Gravelle.

SHEILA COPPS, MPP,
HAMILTON CENTRE

---

and as a group, they were superior to their male classmates in academic achievement at secondary school, grades in teachers' college, and scores on a test of general intelligence. When asked what grade level they would prefer to teach, the student-teachers gave replies that were strongly related to their sex. Only rarely did a woman indicate a level beyond Grade 5, and the primary grades were the choice of the majority. The men, with few exceptions, envisioned themselves as teaching in Grades 6, 7, or 8, and commonly added a comment that they would like eventually to specialize in a subject area or move into a supervisory position.

The aspirations of male francophone student-teachers are congruent with the results of a membership study carried out in 1969 by the Ontario Public School Men Teachers' Federation. A salient finding of this questionnaire survey of seven thousand men was their preoccupation with accumulating credits towards the bachelor or arts degree, which would make them eligible to take the first step up the ladder of school administration. In giving their reasons for choosing the teaching profession, the majority made no mention of the classroom instruction of children; instead they looked to the opportunity to continue their studies on a part-time basis with a view to promotion to higher-paying positions in the school system.

In complete contrast to the OPSMTF study are the findings (published in 1970) from several studies conducted by the Federation of Women Teachers' Associations of Ontario. The female elementary school teacher was described as "a perpetual incumbent of the lowest rank in the hierarchy." The term "a perennial classroom teacher" seemed to be appropriate for over 90 percent of FWTAO members. Most women teachers were not interested in positions of leadership and so did not prepare for them; they expected to remain classroom teachers throughout their working lives. Demographic information included the fact that two-thirds of the women teachers were married and that half of the married women were mothers. In a typical year, about 4 percent of FWTAO members left the classroom to take up household duties, and about 4 percent returned from a period of full-time homemaking. Over half of those returning to the classroom had been absent for less than four years.

An FWTAO study of women teachers-in-training found that almost all expected to marry and become mothers. They planned to teach until the arrival of their first-born and to return to teaching when there was no longer a pre-school child in the home. Three-quarters of the women student-teachers indicated that teaching had been their first choice of occupation and that they had decided to become teachers when they were still elementary school pupils. Information about the background of women teachers and teachers-in-training compiled by the FWTAO showed the typical teacher to be white, Anglo-Saxon, and Protestant. Almost 90 percent were Canadian born, most of the others having emigrated from England, Scotland, or the United States. Two-thirds grew up in communities of fewer than 25,000 people. Typically, the woman teacher came from a lower middle class family, and her mother had a little more education than her father.

In general, the woman who is a classroom teacher in an elementary school is in a predominantly feminine occupation which has traditionally been socially approved as very appropriate for a person of her sex. She expects to remain a classroom teacher throughout her working life. Such a description of the typical woman teacher should not, of course, obscure the fact that a small but important minority of FWTAO members do aspire to principalships and other supervisory positions, succeed in earning promotion, and carry out their responsibilities very well. Other experienced and ambitious women teachers prefer to be in a consultative rather than an administrative role; they become specialists in primary methods, oral French, or some other aspect of the elementary curriculum. An alternative route to positions of leadership and influence is through election to office in a teachers' federation. In contrast to all other affiliates, the president and executive officers of the FWTAO are always women.

The fact remains, however, that the typical woman teacher in an elementary school does not aspire to positions of leadership; and if she is herself without career ambition, is it reasonable to expect that she will somehow inspire her female pupils to strive for non-traditional careers where they would be in direct competition with men?

Men and women who teach at the secondary level belong to the Ontario Secondary School Teachers' Federation. *Do Not Erase*, the story of the first fifty years of the OSSTF, provides evidence of the participation of women in the organization right from the start: as the announcement of the inaugural meeting in 1919 stated, "The interests of both men and women teachers will be carefully considered." However, lists of attendees at meetings and other information in the book show that women have been vastly outnumbered by men in Federation activities. Of the first fifty presidents of the OSSTF, only six were women.

In terms of numbers, women are well represented in today's secondary schools. Nevertheless, insofar as men and women are not equally likely to be teaching in all subject areas or to be heads of departments, vice-principals, or principals, there are significant differences in their roles. Teachers of physics, chemistry, and calculus are very likely to be men, whereas teachers of English and other languages are often women. Even in subject areas where women teachers are not uncommon, the department head is likely to be a man; for example, 80 percent of English departments are headed by male teachers. Women principals of secondary schools are rare indeed. What subtle message is being conveyed to girls who spend five of their adolescent years in Ontario's public secondary schools?

In 1980, the Ministry of Education collected course enrolment data by sex. Although all courses are intended to be equally accessible to boys and girls and although guidance counsellors are available to advise students about which courses are best suited to their abilities and career goals, sex differences in subject selection were vast. Female participation rates significantly exceeded those of males in consumer studies, languages, world religions, art, family studies, music, and dramatic arts. Male participation rates substantially exceeded those of females in physics, general science, physical geography, calculus, environmental science, geology, urban geography, algebra, relations and functions, chemistry, computer science, and all the technological courses. The findings were brought to the attention of secondary school teachers in the February 1984 issue of *Forum*, their Federation's magazine, the accompanying comment being that "female students, through course selection, are limiting their chances of entry into technical and professional fields."

The facts are not new. What is new is the recognition by school authorities and the general public that the sex differences in subject choices do matter. This is a direct result of increased awareness of the length of time that women actually spend in remunerative employment. In 1950, the Ontario Royal Commission on Education (on which men outnumbered women by more than four to one) made the statement: "The vast majority of girls will make homemaking a career, although they may for a limited period engage in some other occupation." This "limited period" in the work force is now calculated to be about thirty years for women who marry and have children and even longer for those who remain childless. The economic consequences, both to individual women and to society at large, of subject choices made in high school are now beginning to be recognized.

In 1981, the Science Council of Canada held an invitational workshop in Ottawa to seek the causes of the low participation rate of Canadian women in the scientific and technological professions. The papers presented by educators and scientists (all women) have been edited into a book entitled *Who Turns the Wheel?* which includes practical suggestions for increasing the enrolment of girls in science subjects. (Copies of *Who Turns the Wheel?* may be obtained free of charge from the Publications Office, Science Council of Canada, 100 Metcalfe Street, Ottawa, Ontario, K1P 5M1.) The scarcity of same-sex role models was a problem recognized by the participants in the Science Council's workshop. Few secondary school girls are personally acquainted with women who have achieved success in

> Childhood memories take me back to the Kawarthas' famous floating bridges. I was from a little rural school, and we senior pupils were travelling in a big cattle-truck to visit the Quaker Oats factory, St. Peter's Cathedral, and the Riverside Zoo in Peterborough.
>
> Our successful day was ending, and we were on our way home. When we reached the Chemong floating bridge, it went down with the weight of 30 pupils in the back of the truck. One foot of water came up on the wheels. But our driver was cool and undaunted.
>
> Chivalry was everywhere in the 1930s. The solution was simple. The boys were told to climb down and walk across the bridge ahead of the truck, and the remaining pupils. . . . Well, we girls rode like ladies safely across the bridge.
>
> CLARA TELFORD,
> PRESIDENT OF OASWT FOR 1983-84,
> LOCAL PETERBOROUGH CHAPTER

occupations dependent on a knowledge of mathematics and science. The National Film Board of Canada has recently released a beautiful film called "I Want to be an Engineer." There are no actors or actresses in this film; each person plays himself or herself. The film is intended for showing to secondary school students of both sexes, to their parents, and to guidance counsellors. It features five young engineers – two married couples and a single woman. One of the couples has four children. Because the film exhibits the personal, family, and professional lives of enthusiastic, attractive, successful women, it is much in demand for career guidance sessions in secondary schools as a way of presenting role models to girls hesitant about considering careers based on mathematics and science. The Women's Bureau of the Ontario Ministry of Labour has produced a poster which is also popular with guidance counsellors. It shows a bright young girl repairing her bicycle and declaring, "I want to be an engineer, just like my mom." This poster cleverly conveys the dual message that a girl can aspire to a non-traditional occupation and that a woman in a predominantly masculine profession can also be a mother. (To request a copy of this poster, write to Women's Bureau, Ontario Ministry of Labour, 400 University Avenue, Toronto, Ontario, M7A 1T7, or the Northern Office, 435 James Street, Thunder Bay, Ontario, P7E 6E3.)

Of course, live role models are even more effective than those presented vicariously. To encourage women to follow a career in science or engineering, Women in Science and Engineering (W.I.S.E.) was established in Toronto in 1977 and now has chapters in Ottawa, Sarnia, and Waterloo and members-at-large in other communities. Most of the members are young women who are successfully combining interesting and financially rewarding careers in engineering or the related sciences with the joys of family life. They are role models *par excellence*. Typical of the educational activities in which W.I.S.E. members participate was a Saturday conference organized by the Toronto Board of Education in November 1983 for girls in the senior elementary and secondary grades. Mathematics teachers, counsellors, and parents were also invited. The purpose was to persuade the girls to keep mathematics in their timetables by exposing them to women working in occupations highly dependent on secondary school mathematics. As well as plenary sessions, the program provided opportunities for small groups of girls to chat with individual women about the work that they did, the academic background required, and the remuneration received. Questions from the girls in these sessions were as likely to pertain to dual career families or child care arrangements as to information about the specific mathematics background needed for a particular type of work. The collegiate where the conference was held was decorated with posters of women in non-traditional, mathematics-based occupations – everything from accountant to astronaut. (Further information about W.I.S.E. can be obtained by writing to P.O. Box 6067, Station 'A', Toronto, Ontario, M5W 1P5.)

In January 1984, the Ontario cabinet minister responsible for women's issues announced an innovative program: the recruitment of women who are successfully combining non-traditional careers with marriage and motherhood to go into schools to talk to teenagers of both sexes. The goals include encouraging girls to set their occupational sights beyond the steno pool and the department-store counter by taking appropriate subjects in secondary school, showing them that it is not necessary to forego marriage and motherhood in order to have an interesting and rewarding career, and preparing boys for an adult world in which men and women will work together even in jobs traditionally thought to be the preserve of men. The program, called "Open Doors", will start in Thunder Bay, Sault Ste Marie, North Bay, London, Peterborough, and Kingston, but will likely be extended to schools in other regions of Ontario.

The school system is intended to provide equal educational opportunities for boys and girls. Schooling is free throughout the elementary and secondary grades. Students of both sexes can select from a wide variety of optional subjects in the senior grades. Great efforts have been made to render textbooks free of sex-role stereotyping. The final step is for schools to combat lingering myths about women's lives so that girls as well as boys can take full advantage of the educational opportunities provided by the Province.

DORMER ELLIS is both a registered professional engineer and a qualified educational researcher. She was educated in the Ontario school system and at the University of Toronto. She is an associate professor in the Department of Measurement, Evaluation, and Computer Science and in the Department of Adult Education at OISE, and she is the national president of Women in Science and Engineering.

A new computer in our school,
Though threatened with the strap,
Would only program upside down
And stirred up quite a flap.
The principal at length declared,
"It's got a handicap."

They packed it off to Special Ed.
For care by experts who
First turned to physics, then to God,
And then Bill 82.
But still it programmed upside down
Whatever they might do.

Yet what resource such experts show,
Their know-how on the line!
"The fault," they said at Special Ed,
"Lies with your class design.
"Suspend the children upside down,
The NOCI's doing fine."

SPECIAL EDUCATION

ROBERT MacINTYRE

The development of special education programs might be imagined as the saga of "these couple of kids." Consider the following scene in which a teacher is talking to a school administrator:

"I have these couple of kids who just don't seem to be learning in my class. I really can't reach them."

"Why not? Do you have any idea about what may be the cause of their problem?"

"Well, most of my instruction involves lectures and student recitation. These deaf children just don't have the abilities needed to learn in my class. Can't we do something special for them?"

And so we do, but soon we hear about:

"These couple of kids really need some kind of special help. They can't be taught to read. They can't write. They can't even see what I put on the blackboard."

"What sort of problem do they have?"

"It's a visual problem. They can't see. They really can't be expected to learn from the readers and workbooks which the other children in my class use."

"I suppose we could set up a special program for blind children also."

So we do, and all is well until:

"These couple of kids are just making it impossible to teach. They don't follow instructions. They disturb the class – and me. They act up and act out. They're just a pair of delinquents and shouldn't be in with the other children."

"I guess you would like us to have a special school for these delinquents, set up somewhere else so that you can concentrate on the other students."

"Of course. It would be better for everybody."

Then, with the blind, deaf, and delinquent children safely in schools and classes of their own, another problem becomes apparent:

"We really have to do something with these couple of kids. They just can't keep up with the class. It's not fair on the rest to have to wait for these children; and it's not fair on them to expect that they can do the same sort of work as the others."

"Would special education for the retarded, maybe with an emphasis on vocational training or crafts, be a good idea, do you think?"

"The very thing."

"Could you teach one of these classes?"

"No. I think these children need a special teacher and special teaching. I haven't had that kind of training."

More recently, the problem has shifted to a new group:

"I have these couple of kids who aren't benefitting in my classroom. We have to do something about it. The parents are upset, and what I'm doing just isn't working."

"What's the problem now? These children aren't retarded or disturbed or blind or deaf are they?"

"No. And they're not from poor families or from ethnic minority groups either; we have programs for those children. No, the ones I'm talking about seem to have trouble learning the basics, no matter what I do. Maybe they have a learning disability."

"And you would like us to set up a . . ."

". . . special program for learning disabilities. The parents would like it, and I could concentrate in my classroom on the children who benefit."

Perhaps, some time in the future, we will hear:

"You know, there are still these couple of kids who don't seem to be learning in my class. Could we set up a special education program for boys?"

✻ ✻ ✻

Perhaps all this is a bit fanciful, and certainly it is oversimplified. The development of special education in Ontario has been a process of extending education services to larger and larger segments of the population and of identifying more and more children in need of special help. The culminating development in recent times has been the "Education Amendment Act, 1980" (Bill 82) which makes a school board responsible for providing an education for all children in its district. Previously, boards did not need to accept special students if they could not provide an appropriate program. Special education services, when available, were often provided in separate programs, sometimes quite distant from the referring school.

In Ontario, children with serious sensory defects were the first to be offered a special program. Both the Ontario School for the Deaf in Belleville and the Ontario School for the Blind in Brantford were established in 1873. Consistent with the feeling at the time that the handicapped needed a protected and healthy environment, the School for the Deaf was located on a farm, which provided the residents with dairy products and vegetables. Over time, the school developed a series of vocational programs emphasizing practical skills, beginning with those needed around the farm and house and advancing to such trades as wood working and shoe repairing. Printing trades were also taught, partially under the assumption that deaf individuals would be particularly suited to working in the noisy environs of print

"Could we set up a special education program for boys?"

Students stripping cane at the Brantford Institute for the Blind, c. 1900

shops. At first, the School for the Blind concentrated on Braille reading and writing. Eventually it too developed vocational programs in such skills as sewing and music. Piano tuning was thought to be a particularly appropriate skill for the blind.

Facilities for retarded children were being demanded by the Inspector of Asylums, Prisons, and Public Charities in the early 1870s, and in 1876 the Orillia Asylum was reopened as a custodial institution for those who, in the medical terminology of the times, were called idiots. Previous to this time, those severely retarded individuals who did find themselves in custodial care were either in jails or in poorhouses. Before 1873, even the asylums for the insane were unable to serve people suffering from "congenital idiocy" even if they were certified to be insane also. Presumably they lived in private homes, unable to qualify for existing services; and ironically, a hundred years later, the movement to normalize the environment for the retarded has begun placing individuals in settings more nearly like homes than institutions.

The Orillia Asylum was headed from 1877 to 1910 by Dr. A. H. Beaton, who had strong feelings about the need for training rather than simple custodial care. He continually campaigned for funds and facilities, and by 1888, the Orillia facility had become a training institution for feeble-minded children, with a head teacher and assistant, Miss M.B. Christie and Miss Jennings, and with 75 pupils in the institution's school. By 1897, the educational staff had increased to seven, but a government swing towards financial restraint gradually cut back the staff to four (in 1898) and finally to two (in 1902), and the school was closed. It was reopened in 1904 with Miss M.V. Nash as principal and an enrollment of 92 children. This effort ended in 1907. But again the school was reopened and continued until

Beaton's retirement. In spite of his persistence and the efforts of the women who were doing ground-breaking work, education for the retarded got off to a rocky start in Ontario.

Similar residential programs were next developed for delinquent children. The training institution for girls was opened at Mercer in 1880, and a similar facility for boys was opened seven years later at Victoria. The opening of a facility for girls before one for boys marks one of the few times that girls have led boys in the need for special education services.

It is possible that the really delinquent boys of the time found their way to jails or that the society had less tolerance for acting out behavior in girls than in boys. The Bowmanville School for Boys was founded in 1925 and took over services from the Victoria Industrial School when it was closed in 1934. The program for girls shifted to Galt in 1933 and later to Cobourg.

Although many of the residential facilities opened in the late nineteenth century have continued into this century and

AO S1422

ASYLUM FOR IDIOTS, ORILLIA.

even to the present, the major special education focus since the early 1900s has been the establishment of day-class programs, with the emphasis in the programs changing as new developments in both education and health care have evolved. Early programs reflected the strong medical involvement in exceptionality, and retardation and physical health problems were given attention first.

In 1910, an open-air school was started on Toronto Island for children with tuberculosis. The program was operated by the Hospital for Sick Children. In the same year, the Toronto Board set up two classes for mentally retarded students. The Department of Education legitimized this program the following year under "An Act Respecting Special Classes" which allowed special classes for children who were abnormally slow in learning or who, for physical or mental reasons, required special training. The Toronto Board used this authorization two years later to set up "Forest Schools" for malnourished children in High Park and Victoria Park. Under pressure from developing advocacy groups and Dr. Helen MacMurchy, the Legislature in 1914 followed up the 1911 Act by the first relatively detailed special education act. The Auxiliary Classes Act, as it was known, established entry requirements (including the necessity for a full examination), provided for residential schools, and defined the general structure and size of the special classes.

Dr. Helen MacMurchy, a major figure in the early establishment of school programs for the retarded in Ontario, was a medical doctor with a specialty in medical welfare for children. Beginning with her participation in a British Royal Commission on mental deficiency in 1905, Dr. MacMurchy engaged in a series of reports, petitions, and employments through which she pursued her objective of expanded educational programming for the retarded. In 1906 she was appointed Inspector of the Feeble-Minded, and later she was appointed by the Toronto Board as a School Medical Inspector to identify retarded pupils. This position brought her in conflict with Chief Inspector J. L. Hughes and with the Board's Chief Medical Officer, setting the stage for strained relations between the medical and educational professions which has continued to mark special education. Following the 1914 Auxiliary Classes Act, for which she was largely responsible, Dr. MacMurchy became the first Provincial Inspector of Auxiliary Classes. Her first reports in this position continued her criticisms of what was being done, or not being done, in most boards, and her dedication and insistence that special classes were her responsibility continued to create conflicts with educational professionals in the system. In spite of these conflicts, she was able to provide for special classes the general framework which lasted through the end of the Second World War and to establish the legitimacy of such classes. As a result of her encouragement, progressive boards in the larger cities were successful in establishing some programs. In 1915 and again in 1919, she provided summer training for auxiliary teachers, using a pattern of lectures, guest experts, and practicum experiences. By 1920, when she left her Ontario post to work with the Canadian Government in public health and child care, she had managed to set up the basic structure of special education and to influence public opinion towards its implementation, despite her limited success with particular school boards and with establishing the number of classes which she felt to be necessary.

Programatically, MacMurchy saw the problems of retardation as essentially medical and social ones. In common with many other professionals of the time, she was concerned with eugenic control of retardation through incarceration or control of retarded women of child-bearing age. Her educational guidance to teachers was minimal and emphasized medical understanding.

In 1921 a retired educator, Dr. S.B. Sinclair, became Inspector of Auxiliary Classes, bringing with him a solid background in educational administration and an interest in the developing techniques of psychometric assessment of the intellectually handicapped. The following year, Miss Helen Delaporte, who had worked both as a teacher and as a physical therapist with handicapped war veterans, was appointed Assistant Inspector. Together, these two were responsible for changing the identification of mental handicaps from a medical to a psychological and educational model. Initially, Sinclair and then Delaporte did most of the testing, but guidelines were soon developed to show teachers how to identify candidates for auxiliary classes. Still later, auxiliary teachers were taught to administer the new Binet tests which formed part of the identification process, although Sinclair or Delaporte made the final placement decision.

At this time, the educational program for the children in the auxiliary classes was better defined than in MacMurchy's era. There was a heavy emphasis on sensory-motor training and on developing social skills and health habits. Academic work was limited, sometimes by means of elaborate formulae, based on measured IQ, to what was considered proportional to the student's ability. Nowhere was there any suggestion that these children could catch up or that the goals of regular education might be appropriate for them too.

The scope of Sinclair's and Delaporte's work was greatly extended by the Adolescent Schools Attendance Act of 1919, which made compulsory education a reality for the first time and which raised the school-leaving age to sixteen. The students either returned or introduced into the system by this Act were often the delinquent, disturbed, deprived, or retarded for whom the regular program was neither appropriate nor effective. Indeed, Dr. Sinclair saw the value of auxiliary classes as much in the removal of these disruptive children from the regular mainstream as in the educational programming it provided them.

Under Sinclair and Delaporte, services for the mentally handicapped were expanded in number and, through vocational schools, were extended to the secondary level. The 1924 amendment to the Vocational Education Act of 1921 allowed interaction between special education and the vocational program. In 1924, the first school for retarded adolescent boys and girls was set up in Toronto at the Jarvis Street School, and similar schools were established in Hamilton and Ottawa.

Granted that progress had been made, Sinclair, in his last report before his retirement in 1928, raised three issues which are still of concern to special education: cost, stigmatization, and coverage. First, he noted that the classes required regular classrooms and teachers, yet were limited to sixteen students; this made them nearly twice as expensive as regular programs. Second, he protested against the stigmatization of the pupils, pointing out that all had IQs above 50

A Grade 9 science teacher in a vocational school was having difficulty moving students back to their desks. They were reading at only about a Grade 3 level and were thus experiencing problems in all their subjects. They all wanted her to check their last day's work, and they all wanted to be first.

She asked them to sit down and told them she would call them up one-at-a-time. A few complied immediately. As she was trying to get the others to sit down, those already seated started coming back, worried that they were missing out on some of her attention. Finally, she got them all seated except for one student Joe whom she asked to remain in order to mark his work.

She spoke to them all about patience, about waiting their turn, about being patient, patient, patient. All the while Joe gazed seriously at her. When she had finished, he looked at her and gravely spoke, "I know, miss, patience is a virgin."

JOHN BOICH, EXECUTIVE DIRECTOR,
THE ONTARIO ASSOCIATION OF EDUCATION
ADMINISTRATIVE OFFICIALS

and that half had IQs above 70; evidently the problems of defining exceptionality by IQ level and of the negative connotations of low mental functioning were apparent almost from the first although 50 years were to elapse before concerted professional and public objections were raised. Third, he noted the lack of programs in rural Ontario and the lack of practical alternatives for providing services outside the major cities.

Other exceptionalities, although fewer in number than the retarded, also benefitted from increased services in this era. Sight-saving classes, using large print books, were begun in 1921. Convalescent children in hospitals and sanatoria received education in special classes beginning in 1923. Speech-correction and lip-reading classes were begun on a limited basis by itinerant therapists, and visiting teachers were provided for home-bound children and those in children's shelters. Classes for the physically handicapped also experienced a slow growth. The summer course for auxiliary teachers was established with a new format in 1921 and was taught regularly from then on.

In spite of a tendency towards overcrowding and a need to lower costs, the program at Orillia also improved. The school program began again in 1922 under Miss M.K. Harvie, and by 1926 there was a staff of 12, serving the needs of the more able children placed there.

In 1929, Dr. H. Amoss took over as Inspector of Auxiliary Classes, with Helen Delaporte continuing as Assistant. The next ten years, covering the period of the Depression, were marked by reorganization of the system and improvement in the directions provided to teachers. Amoss and Delaporte published *Training Handicapped Children* in 1933, and this text became a standard classroom aid. Auxiliary training classes for retarded children at the elementary level were renamed "opportunity classes" and increased to 174 classes, while over 2,000 retarded students in rural areas were served by individual opportunity units. The secondary program grew to 136 classes in what were now called special industrial schools. A start was also made towards remedial special education, with an experimental academic vocational class in 1937 for children in the slow-learner category.

The Second World War and the post-war era saw continued slow growth in programs, hindered until about 1950 by a shortage of teachers. The Inspector was then Dr. C.E. Strothers, who encouraged some new types of service. He supported parent groups in their efforts to get financial aid for schools for the trainable mentally retarded, resulting in provincial assistance in 1953 and a growth of such school units to 37 two years later. He also supported the establishment of special classes at the secondary level for children who had not been able to pass the Grade 8 examinations but who were over age for elementary school. But in spite of his efforts to increase the variety of specialists in the Auxiliary Branch of the Department of Education, he was caught in a trend during this period towards greater local control of special education and diminished provincial participation.

With increased urbanization and industrialization following the war, the need for and the number of special classes burgeoned; from 1954 to 1963, opportunity classes increased from 343 to 902. Some of this growth was due to centralization of rural school boards and some to general growth of educational services. People also became aware at this time of the special education needs of children with cerebral palsy and with rarer conditions such as cystic fibrosis and muscular dystrophy. In the larger population centres, programs were begun for learning disabilities attributable to neurological impairment, aphasia, and dyslexia – categories which were to give rise to much debate in subsequent years.

Under Ministers of Education J.P. Robarts and, later, W.G. Davis, services were expanded through diversification of the secondary education program to better serve slow learning youngsters and through the formation of Township School Areas having access to local taxation monies. The

"... *programs were begun for learning disabilities....*"

problems of lack of service for rural areas and of secondary-level alternatives persisted, but at least they were being acknowledged and worked on.

Hospital schools were also expanded. Orillia, now housing about 2500 patients, was joined by Smiths Falls in 1951 and Cedar Springs in 1961. In spite of this increased capacity, the hospitals continued to be overcrowded and only accepted the more severely retarded. Educational programs at these hospital schools were supervised and supported by liaison between the Departments of Health and Education, and for the first time hospital teachers could gain experience credits towards their teaching certificates.

Special Education classrooms are places where the curriculum is often the last thing that students learn.

While teaching students with emotional problems, I learned never to confront these kids with their misdeeds in front of the rest of the class. Since they did not want to be seen as backing down and since I didn't feel like it either, these confrontations would sour the classroom atmosphere. Therefore, I had to become adept at defusing conflicts by asking students to leave the room for a talk. These talks would usually begin as follows: "You seem to be having a problem today. Can I help?"

I spent one ugly November morning hollering at everyone in the class. The merest infringement of the rules would bring on my terrible torrent of acrimony, until all eight students had ceased to listen, ceased to work. One of the students, Alex, a kid who hadn't learned a spelling word since the beginning of September, asked if he could speak to me in private. Just what I needed! Another wanting to leave school early for a dental appointment!

"No, really, I have to talk to you. Outside."

"Yeah, what is it?" I barked, when we got into the hall.

"You seem to be having a problem today. Can I help?"

So you see what I mean. That kid would never learn anything I wanted him to learn, yet he was nonetheless an expert at Special Education.

KENNETH KLONSKY,
SPECIAL ED. RESOURCE TEACHER,
SCARBOROUGH BOARD

The late 1960s and 1970s continued the pattern of expansion of services for the handicapped, along with the expansion of education in general. New demands were made as parent groups became more insistent on the provision of appropriate services. The Ontario Association for Children with Learning Disabilities joined its voice with that of the older Ontario Association for Retarded Children in campaigning their respective causes. Increasingly, vocal groups pushed for more and better programming for gifted children, and special programs for these children were started.

Although the summer courses continued under the direction of the Ministry of Education, teachers were also receiving special education training through the faculties of education and graduate instruction at the Ontario Institute for Studies in Education. The continued crowding of the hospital schools and the movement towards normalization of services for the retarded resulted in a shift of population out of the larger institutions and into smaller group homes and foster-care facilities in local communities. In 1974, the Ministry of Education set up the Special Education Branch to deal with

Listening lessons to treat dyslexia at the Child Study Centre, University of Ottawa

all the complex aspects of programming for exceptional children.

Also in this period, the Ministry of Community and Social Services became responsible for the provision of some educational services to children with learning disabilities in situations where the school boards were unable to do so. This unusual development followed a court case in which an ex-student was found to have a reading level below that needed for vocational training, although his parents testified that they had not been told about the problem. The judge ruled that the boy was entitled to basic special education to bring him to the required level. Parents of learning-disabled children, especially in rural or sparsely populated areas in the Province, were quick to take advantage of this new source of funding.

In 1980, the current Minister of Education, Dr. Bette Stephenson, introduced Bill 82, responding to pressures to clarify the special education responsibility issue. This legislation, when fully operative in 1985, makes the local school boards responsible for providing (or arranging for the provision of) appropriate educational programs for all school age children in their districts. Funding from the Ministry of Community and Social Services will then come to an end and, for the first time, handicapped children and their parents will have a recognized right to service from the Ministry of Education and local boards. The Bill 82 Amendments to the Education Act provide for the most comprehensive definition of services and programs for the handicapped to date in Ontario. Since the program is not fully in place and all of the necessary administrative memoranda have not been written, it is not possible to predict exactly how special education in Ontario will develop under this new legislation. But based on the history and experience of special education in Ontario, some general observations about likely developments are possible.

There will be continued pressure for more services for exceptional individuals and complaints that the existing facilities are overcrowded and/or understaffed.

There will be continued cooperation, interaction, and (sometimes) conflict between medical-clinical and educational approaches to the handicapped.

There will continue to be discussion and disagreement about identifying exceptional individuals – the tools to be used and the persons to authorize them.

There will continue to be concern about the costs of the special education programs, especially as compared with those of other programs.

Service in sparsely populated areas will continue to be expensive, scarce, and hard to deliver.

There will continue to be strong-willed individuals campaigning for one or other service, program, exceptionality, or profession.

And, of course, there will always be "those last couple

of kids" who just don't seem to fit the programs we have for them.

We've come a long, long way in providing education for this group of "outsiders" in the last hundred years. The problems which persist and the new ones which arise simply indicate both the complex and resistant nature of the problem of individual exceptionality for an educational system dedicated to mass education, and our continued progress in becoming more and more inclusive in our definition of who has a right to education and to what kind. I hope the next two hundred years will see as much excitement, growth, concern, and democratic conflict as has characterized the last hundred. It would, or course, be dull if we had all the answers and all the programs.

ROBERT MacINTYRE began in special education as a student teacher of the retarded in New York City and later became a research psychologist in Tennessee and California. He was on the graduate faculty of the University of Southern California, starting their special education department, and was a founding director of Special Education Instructional Materials Center Network and assistant director at the ERIC Clearinghouse in Washington, D.C. A new Canadian, he has been an associate professor in OISE's Department of Special Education since 1974.

I need hardly explain
About Dick, about Jane,
'Cause most of you met them in reading.
But that, as you know,
Was a long time ago
And the years have a way of receding.

They matured very quick
Did our Jane, did our Dick,
And though I've no wish to affront 'em,
Without any warning
They married one morning
'Cause nobody else seemed to want 'em.

Then in passion sublime
They invested their time,
Two kids their investment returning;
Which delighted the twain
All except for our Jane
Who was high on continuous learning.

So illiterate Jane
Started Grade 1 again
And read of herself with enjoyment;
While our Dick stayed in bed,
And to bring home the bread,
Their kids took on casual employment.

There lies buried, I think,
Underneath all this ink
A moral for teachers and sages:
That our Dick and our Jane
Had done well to remain
Entombed in their reading books' pages.

P.S. I forgot
To make mention of Spot.
His running and jumping abated,
Now his only desire
Is to sleep by the fire
Caninely content and castrated.

THE EMERGENCE OF A SYSTEM OF CONTINUING EDUCATION: 1945–1984

ALAN THOMAS

Nothing alters a school or a university or, indeed, an entire system of education quite so radically as a change in the character and composition of the student body. Occasionally, as in the onslaught of war veterans on Canadian universities in 1945, the results of such changes are highly visible and dramatic. During the succeeding four to six years, the press revelled in accounts of huge classes, uncomfortable instructors, and "experienced" students, impatient with what they believed to be the unneccessary ritual of academic life. During that period, the principal refuge of the academic establishment was their belief that the invasion would soon be over, after which life would return to normal. It never did. The student "veterans" had barely made their way through the system when the huge numbers of the late fifties and sixties, characterized by their own types of prickly rebelliousness, began to appear.

More often, however, the changes are slow and barely visible. Indications that they are taking place are usually concealed in other disturbances, such as accusations about lowered standards or "apathetic" students. The true nature of such changes are seldom revealed until they have achieved large proportions.

These changes can be of several kinds. Frequently, more than one kind occurs simultaneously. There may be a shift in the balance of places traditionally held by men and women. There may be a slow alteration in the social or cultural background of students entering the system. (In an immigrant society like Canada's, this sort of change tends to have been an historical constant, although, until recently, it has been most evident in the elementary schools.) Finally, and most profoundly, there may be a change in the age of the student body. In this circumstance, it is usual to find increasing numbers of older students seeking educational credentials. What is of special significance is that, at least at the outset, these older students participate in educational environments designed primarily for the young.

School systems were created to control change in society. In particular, they were intended to be the principal instrument for coping with the changes experienced by successive generations, ensuring a "common" experience for all the children no matter how diverse the lives of their parents. For the most part, this diversity is most obvious at the lowest levels of the system. At the upper or post-secondary levels, either as a result of the successful socializing of the young carried out by primary and secondary schools or by the application of varying standards of admission, a much greater homogeneity of attitude and ambition is expected and achieved. However, when several major changes in the nature of the student body occur simultaneously, the traditional strategies of assimilation by an educational system are strained beyond their limits. What then happens is that there is a loss of sense of purpose or direction.

Since the end of the Second World War, all three types of change outlined previously have been taking place in the educational system of Ontario. As the most popular destination for immigrants to Canada, the Province has been obliged not only to cope with the shifts in background of immigrant children but also to meet the rising aspirations of immigrant parents both for their children and for themselves. The success of the educational system in establishing its credentials as the chief basis for employment has meant that those aspirations can be achieved only in educational terms. Simultaneously, there is abundant evidence of the increased participation of women in all levels of education, with every prospect that they will soon outnumber men as students at every level. In turn, the increased number of women is linked intimately with the last of these three changes: the steady upward movement of the median age of the student body – at all levels of the educational system and among both full- and part-time students.

An additional problem is represented by the way in which students choose to participate in the system. The change in composition of the student body, particularly the change in age, reflects an increase in the number of individuals who wish to pursue their studies on a part-time basis and who therefore combine the role of student with all of the other roles and responsibilities of an adult citizen; so what has been emerging in Ontario – slowly, inevitably, often painfully, and clearly inequitably – is a system of continuing education. It has been doing so for more than forty years.

In this context, the term "continuing education" is used in a sense that is itself now gradually emerging. The term originally meant the provision of, and participation in, education beyond the limits of the formal system – as in "continuing education in the professions." Originally these activities were associated largely with universities. More recently, the term has been applied to the education of individuals who return to educational pursuits abandoned before completion. This additional meaning (which can be associated with any level of education or any teaching agency) has led to a considerable broadening in the use of the term. The legacy of the campaign for compulsory education conducted at the end of the last century was a widespread

"... these older students participate in educational environments designed primarily for the young"

> Continuing education is no mirage in the desert; it is no dream of a religious prophet. Hard-headed, unsentimental engineers, doctors, lawyers, manufacturers now understand that they must continue to study and learn, just to keep up with the demands of their calling, as well as accept the obligations of public responsibility. The late President of the Canadian Association for Adult Education, Father M. M. Coady of Antigonish, used to say, "The man who has ceased to learn ought not to be allowed to wander around loose in these dangerous days." Make no mistake, the day for continuing education has come, even if all of us who are presently working in adult education fail to realize it, fail to make common cause with our new allies and colleagues, fail to claim the position that is ours. People want what we have; if we don't supply it in ways that are satisfying to them, they will go elsewhere or produce for themselves.
>
> ROBY KIDD,
> (FROM "THE GOALS FOR ADULT EDUCATION," 1959)

belief that adult education at levels below the university was generally unnecessary. Thus, until recently, provision for adults by school boards was regarded as remedial and occasional rather than developmental. However, the introduction of what can be termed new "basics" (for example, computer literacy), and their inclusion at the elementary level, has resulted in greater prominence of school boards in continuing education. What this means is that individuals can and do continue their education at different levels (including elementary schools) and in programs that are related to their previous educational experience. Therefore, the child who moves from Grade 5 to Grade 6, the young person who moves from secondary school to college or university, or the adult who returns to any level of education after years of absence from the educational system can all be said to be *continuing* their education. The measure of success of such a system is that a person can cope with the changes in himself or herself resulting from a learning experience and, at the same time, maintain continuity in his or her life.

The enhanced meaning of the term "continuing education" itself reflects a real shift in educational behavior in Ontario, as in the rest of Canada. The enhanced meaning is, in full:

> A system(s) of education which includes formal and non-formal education, that is defined with respect to its various parts and agencies (elementary schools, secondary schools, colleges and universities, for example) in terms of specific educational objectives to be fostered, rather than in terms of the age or circumstances of the learners. The system is available to persons of any age, part-time, full-time, voluntary or compulsory, and is financed by a mixture of private and public resources. It is distinguished from other educational activities in the society by the possession of the exclusive right to provide public recognition or certification for those completing its program, though not all of its programs lead to such certification. (*New Reflections on a Learning Society*, Department of Adult Education, OISE, 1981)

The evolution of this system in Ontario has not been easy or comfortable. However, if we are to survive for another 200 years, the evolution is inevitable. The character of contemporary society is such that it demands more learning from more people over longer and longer periods of their lives. Only a system of "continuing education" can cope with these demands. For these reasons, it is important for us to understand fully how these developments occur and how the stresses associated with them might be reduced or modified.

Information on the ages of students has not until

recently been collected either by institutions or by Statistics Canada. For that reason, trend data are not available. In 1981, Statistics Canada reported that 40 percent of all university students in Canada were 25 years or over. In 1983, Statistics Canada reported that 12.7 percent of full-time college students were over the age of 24. These figures, plus a report from the same source that between 1970 and 1979 the number of part-time graduate and undergraduate women students increased by 250 percent, confirms there was an increase in the number of older part-time students, most of whom were women. It also reinforces the contention that a system of continuing education is very much better suited to women's lives, and it is that pressure from older women applicants for admission that has played a significant part in forcing the emergence of a continuing education system in Ontario, as in the rest of Canada.

Changes in the character and composition of a student body impinge on educational agencies in two ways. The first relates to internal matters of curriculum, course structure, and teaching styles. During the initial phase of such changes, when traditional objectives tend to be stoutly defended, the internal practices must be adjusted to the differing backgrounds, expectations, and aspirations of the new student body. Even if the prevailing educational view does not concur with Dewey's belief that you must start where the student is, the student has no alternative. These adjustments usually result in public concern for falling standards and in demands for more student counselling. Both responses are clear indications that teachers are either providing unsatisfactory instruction or failing to adjust to changing needs. The subsequent phase of this process is a gradual change in the objectives of the educational agency so that they are more in accord with the aspirations and objectives of the student body.

In the early 1950s (in Ontario and, indeed, in the whole of Canada), a new generation of young people from lower socio-economic backgrounds was moving into the higher grades of the secondary schools. Up until then, the secondary school had functioned as a preparation for the universities, systematically eliminating at successive grade levels students who were unable to meet university-imposed standards for admission. High school graduation was synonymous with university entrance. However, this new generation needed high school graduation for a variety of other purposes. School credentials were becoming increasingly important in gaining employment; and secondary schools began to respond to these pressures, with the result that the objective of university admission was becoming "adulterated" – or so it was argued. The alarm was sounded by Hilda Neatby, an historian at the University of Saskatchewan, in her book *So Little for the Mind* (1954). It was heard with clarity in Ontario. As the title suggests, the concern was expressed in terms not of legitimate competitive demands upon the secondary school but of the declining intellectual preparation of university applicants.

The subsequent preoccupation of the late fifties and sixties with increased numbers of students at all levels of the educational system, coupled with concerns for greater freedom of entrance to university, tended to obscure the issues raised by Neatby, although recently they have been re-asserted with renewed vigor. The peculiar character and function of the Canadian secondary school means that it, more than any other unit in the educational system, reflects and expresses this type of change in the student body.

The demands of a booming economy in the 1950s, '60s, and early '70s for more skilled workers — or at least for individuals who could learn a diversity of skills in the workplace — placed new pressures on the secondary schools to provide exits at different levels of achievement. The same demands were grounds for the establishment of the colleges of applied arts and technology (CAATs).

The second and more significant result of changes in the character and composition of student bodies is that of major alteration in the relationships between the teaching agencies, the educational system, and the communities they serve. These relationships are more complex and more diverse than their outward political forms – such as elections of trustees or appointments to boards of education. They are the vehicles whereby it is determined what shall be taught, and how and by whom; who shall pay for what; who shall determine the success or failure of the students and of the system; and, finally, who shall the students be. It is not always clearly understood that the last decision determines all the others. Each student comes from some particular community in the society, and each manifests some aspect of the relationship between the teaching agency and that community. For example, the traditional, and usually unarticulated, basis of the relationship between a school board and the community it serves is that those who support the board's activities (voters, taxpayers, and professional staff) do so always in the interest of others – that is, of their children and other people's children. However, as the school board makes itself available to adults, who are themselves voters and taxpayers, the relationship with the community must alter. In the context of such relationships, two major developments have taken place in Ontario that warrant mention.

First, the establishment of the CAATs has created relationships between the educational system and new groups who had previously not experienced post-secondary

Students discuss an assignment with their teacher at the Kirkland Lake campus of the Northern College of Applied Arts and Technology

education. Second, there has been a rapid growth in numbers of part-time and full-time students who, for the most part, are older than the conventional students. This growth occurred first at the college and university level, but recently it has also been occurring at elementary and secondary schools. What this means is a whole new relationship between student life and adult life – more and more students are combining the characteristics of student life with the demands of full adult responsibilities. Slowly but relentlessly, these new combinations are coming to dominate the culture of teaching agencies. Although these students are still a minority, their influence, based on the possession of skills that the system indirectly presumes to teach, is already omnipresent. In short, they are bringing about a radical alteration in the relationship between the teaching agencies and the community. It is one perspective, as a citizen, to view the educational system – a secondary school, a college, or a university – as a resource for one's child or the children of others. It is quite another to view it as a resource for oneself.

Coupled with actual changes in the composition of existing student bodies, there have also appeared new groups of potential students. These are individuals who might wish to become students if different providing agencies or programs were created. For example, it was for "potential students" that the CAATs were created – for the thousands of successful secondary school graduates who could not or did not wish to go to a university but, at the same time, needed further formal instruction to obtain employment in an increasingly technological economy. The establishment of these colleges created new student bodies of a nature much more diverse than the Province had witnessed before.

Similarly, the same demand for technical skills was steadily creating student or "trainee" roles entirely outside of the educational system. As early as the 1930s, the then glamor industry – the oil companies – had found it necessary to engage in its own research to develop its specialized technologies. The inevitable result of engagement in any kind of research is that individuals must be trained to implement the results. When the research has been private, so must be the training. Barely visible, this kind of private education and training moved beyond the oil industry and, for a variety of reasons, has become a dimension of all large organizations, public and private. In contemporary Ontario, it would be impossible to find an organization of any size which is not engaged in some form of training and/or education. In 1980, a study of a large "high tech" company revealed that it maintained 19 instructional centres in the Province, providing a variety of programs for more than 20,000 "students" per year at an expenditure of between 50 and 100 million dollars. Few countries in the world (and Canada is no exception) collect adequate data about these activities, but most acknowledge the continuous growth and increasing scope of such private programs. The "continuing" student, therefore, can easily move from formal school to almost-as-formal instruction with an employer and back again. Often the student will participate in employer-sponsored education and some form of part-time formal education at the same time. Consequently, with education and training no longer the exclusive domain of the formal system, the implicit conviction that what is not taught by that system is not worth learning is gradually being discarded. Programs of "cooperative education" (originally peculiar to the post-secondary system but now spreading to the secondary level) together with novel efforts at developing "equivalent" credentials are beginning to create bridges between the two – formal and "employment" systems. But except for students who move back and forth between them, they remain on the surface essentially parallel and isolated from one another. The genuine exchanges are underground, but they are there.

Beneath the political and administrative problems that emerge as these relationships change are more subtle and pervasive issues, issues relating to what can be called the "culture" of education. All teaching bodies pursue their

An enthusiastic class of adult and teenage students at Bathurst Heights Secondary School

activities on the basis of three sets of assumptions. First, there are assumptions about what the students will have learned before they are admitted; second, there are assumptions about how they will learn, what the agency is prepared to teach, and, perhaps more important, what they are learning concurrently beyond what the agency is teaching; and, third, there are assumptions about what they will learn after they have completed the program provided by that particular agency.

To consider the first assumption, teaching agencies outside the compulsory system (mainly post-secondary) can impose their expectations by setting admission standards. If the prospective student cannot demonstrate some specific skills and/or knowledge, he or she is simply refused admission. There is constant debate over what these standards should be, and how and by whom they should be measured. The CAATs were introduced in Ontario to allow for the further development of skills and knowledge that the universities were not competent or inclined to provide. The elementary and secondary systems have no such luxury of control; they must take any child of the proper age who is resident in the community. Thus a constant adjustment is forced on these systems, since they must respond to cultural or socio-economic changes in the learning background of each generation of children, and, at the secondary level, deal with admission standards of a post-secondary system which shows much less disposition to adjust.

In addition, a number of circumstances have combined to create an increasing demand for admission from older students who are re-entering the educational system at all levels after some years of absence. The higher educational qualifications required by employers, a decline in total numbers of the conventional student age groups, the increasing number of married women whose children have reached school age, and more people with more spare time (sometimes as a result of unemployment) – all of these circumstances have resulted in substantial numbers of older individuals re-entering the educational system on a part-time or full-time basis.

Under present circumstances, the entrance qualification obtained 20 years ago is equal to the qualification obtained last year. Common sense, however, tells us that the qualifications of two individuals separated by 20 years are not at all the same in terms of their previous learning, and although the differences may be of a kind that escape academic measurement, they can deeply affect attitudes and behavior. When we consider, too, the steady increase in the number of older students and the enormous variety of experience they represent, then the dimensions of the problem – or opportunity – become clearer.

While the first assumption presents itself as a problem of admission and is therefore primarily the concern of educational administrators, the second is the very "stuff" of the lives of all teachers. For whereas the official tradition of the educational system is to attend only to what is learned as a result of what is taught and to dismiss as inconsequential what is learned elsewhere, every teacher knows that such intellectual "imperialism" is impossible.

In the elementary schools, much time is taken in relating classroom content to what the child has learned and is learning elsewhere. Also at this level, there are Home and School Associations where information is exchanged about the needs of the two communities. The school tries to win the support of the parents for its procedures and objectives. As students move up the system, the power of the family diminishes and that of the outside community grows. The schools respond at both secondary and post-secondary levels by developing a "culture" which surrounds the student and dominates most of his or her time. This culture, which is dominated by the influence of peers, helps to protect and support the educational goals of the schools. Thus schools, colleges, and universities alike try to create "communities of students" in which the stimulus to learning is directed to common goals. These two sets of dynamics – one towards "studentship" and the other towards a supportive "membership" – must be kept in a careful and delicate balance. It was the loss of that balance through the temporary supremacy of community "membership" that characterized the universities in the 1960s. However, the disruptions were less evident and less explosive in Canada than in other countries, partly because of the smaller size of the student communities.

Numbers are critical in the "culture" of education. In Ontario universities, the principal experience controlling concurrent learning (that is, in maintaining the most effective cultural balance) has been gained primarily from working with full-time students — in effect with young students who have had little experience outside of the educational system and whose lives have been bound up in activities associated with one teaching agency or another. With the increase in number of part-time students and older full-time students, the balance is again being disturbed. With the older students, they are rarely engulfed by the institutional culture. They have too many other responsibilities; and even if they do participate, they bring with them years of experience outside the educational system. With part-time students, they seldom get the opportunity to experience much of the culture; but they do bring with them, on every class occasion, on-going experience about the impact of what they are being taught on their diverse worlds.

Examples of two students might be helpful. The first student is a woman who left school some years ago to marry and raise a family. Her children are young, but she is studying accounting part-time in preparation for a return to public life. She brings with her to class experience of adult life, experience of small children and other domestic responsibilities, and perhaps some lack of assurance about coping with the demands of formal education once again. The second student is a man who also left school some years ago to take a job. He is now studying accounting in order to obtain a degree which will help his career. He brings experience of adult life, perhaps a similar lack of assurance about coping with the demands of being a student, and, in addition, daily experience in the specific application to his job of what he learns. Each of these students was admitted to the program on the basis of equivalent preparation, each will likely achieve a similar degree, but the learning outcomes and the impact of each on the regular class meetings will be very different. Furthermore, although they will carry an apparently identical imprimatur of knowledge and competence, their impact on the society will be profoundly different. Such students are increasingly typical of the Ontario educational system.

The third assumption deals with what the student will learn after he or she has completed the program of the particular teaching agency. Traditionally, the major preoccupation has been with information passed back to the teaching agency either by more advanced teaching agencies or by employers about the capabilities of those graduates they have received. This information was used, if at all, to alter the experience of present or future students; none of it helped the graduates themselves. However, as the opportunities for re-entering the educational system have increased, the likelihood of graduates returning to their original teaching agencies has done likewise. This is particularly true of the post-secondary level where, for example, continuing education for "professionals" has become a major responsibility. But, as has been pointed out, it is also true of the elementary/secondary levels, where many who left before completing (or even entering) secondary school and who cannot improve their lives without upgrading their educational status are returning. The return of its graduates tells something about the initial success or failure of that level of education – something of which both professional educators and graduates are now becoming aware.

In summary then, it is these changes in the composition and character of the student body that are bringing about a profound alteration of the educational system of Ontario – bringing about a system of continuing education. Administratively and structurally, the process has been slow, but it has maintained momentum. It has come about in two ways. One has been the creation of new teaching agencies: the colleges of applied arts and technology in the public domain and training units in large non-educational organizations. The other has been the burgeoning numbers of older citizens seeking entry into the traditional teaching agencies – elementary and secondary schools, universities, and the new colleges.

But it is the pressure on the culture that remains to be met and accepted. As a result of this pressure, the formal system of education, particularly in the upper levels, seems adrift, without a clear sense of mission or purpose. Various agencies do not seem to know who their student bodies ought to be or what they should be taught. They are not particularly responsive to the compositions that actually exist. They seem unwilling to acknowledge the extent to which learning and instruction have spread beyond the boundaries of the formal systems, and they continue either to ignore that spread or to deprecate its significance in efforts to regain their pre-eminence.

It is even less clear who should pay for students in the formal system. More assistance is being claimed by less conventional groups. Looming over all this confusion is a federal initiative represented by the Task Force on Skill Development. To meet the demands suggested in the Task Force's report (*Learning and Living in Canada*), the capacity of the present formal system is obviously inadequate. Consequently, if the report were to be implemented, all of the present pressures would increase for a fully developed system of continuing education.

Reluctance to acknowledge these pressures victimizes the students, actual and potential. For those who participate in any one of the present systems, continuity exists only

> The great mass of the (Canadian) people are at present completely ignorant even of the rudiments of the most common learning. Very few can either read or write; and parents who are ignorant themselves, possess so slight a relish for literature and are so little acquainted with its advantages, that they feel scarcely any anxiety to have the minds of their children cultivated. . . . They will not believe that "knowledge is power," and being convinced that it is not in the nature of "book-learned skill" to improve the earnestness of their sons in hewing wood or the readiness of their daughters in spinning flax, they consider it a misapplication of money to spend any sum in obtaining instruction for their offspring.
>
> E. A. TALBOT,
> (FROM A SERIES OF LETTERS PUBLISHED IN 1824)

marginally. Conflicting admission standards, differences in transfer regulations, and variations in assessment of formal and informal experience – all impede satisfactory utilization of the systems even by the most willing and industrious students. Even more serious are inequities in the opportunity to participate, particularly among older students. An individual who has succeeded in the early years of schooling is almost guaranteed success at later stages; more and more alternative educational opportunities will be open to him or her. For those who fail initially, remedial opportunities are few and not very effective. Witness the functional illiteracy rate in Canada: the figures are scandalous and few steps are being taken to remedy them.

From one point of view, the existing situation is a tribute to the elementary and secondary system. Those who succeed there demonstrate that they will very likely succeed in the post-secondary system and in the careers for which that success has prepared them. Above all, they demonstrate a capacity for continued learning under those conditions common to formal schooling. Since, as a society, we are increasingly dependent upon the competence and willingness to learn of such individuals, it cannot be a question of reducing their opportunities for further learning. But such opportunities must not be at the expense of the large numbers of others who do not succeed in the early stages but who demonstrate the willingness and ability to profit from such opportunities later in their lives. It is likely that the formal system cannot succeed with everyone when they are children and young people. Therefore, it is an indictment of the society as a whole if nothing is done for the substantial numbers who are presently denied second or even third chances to re-enter the competition for success. We cannot afford to have an inner and outer society, a society made up of those who can move forward and those who are left behind. We cannot afford it for reasons of simple justice. But we also cannot afford it because of the serious loss of imagination, intelligence, and commitment. Our first task, then, is to be aware of the inequities and to attempt to remedy them. The opening up of the elementary and secondary schools and the provision of financial assistance to such people is a beginning. But it is only a beginning. Other steps must be taken associated with the larger problem of accepting and accelerating the development of a genuine system of continuing education.

First, many types of financial and administrative arrangements for participants must be developed and encouraged. Most of our experience in the provision of education has been garnered from systems based on the compulsory attendance of dependent children or young people. Only the relatively small university system has acquired different experience, and even then, until a few years ago, it was considered that the universities acted "in loco parentis." In addition to more varied sources of financial support, a continuing education system means a greater variety in patterns of attendance and in provision of programs. To be simpler for the students, the system will have to become more complex for the administrators and providers. For example, it would be a constructive advance to abandon entirely administrative distinctions between part-time and full-time students. Such a development has already begun at secondary and college levels.

"Many types of financial and administrative arrangements for participants must be developed...."

Second, we must develop much improved systems of information gathering, monitoring, and evaluation. The information-gathering bodies of Ontario must acquire systematic and continuous data about the extent of participation in education in the Province. Since the flexibility inherent in a system of continuing education means that participation by providing agencies and by students will vary from time to time and from place to place, the need for regular and extensive information is paramount. A semi-independent organization like the Ontario Economic Council is needed to provide such service and to report annually. Information about educational participation is at least as important as much of the economic information that is reported so assiduously. It is of importance not only to public but to private bodies as well, particularly those that are engaged in education and training and in the employment of skilled labor.

Third, the same organization could engage in evaluation in the sense that it could report an overabundance of some opportunities and shortages of others. Information about the ease of transfer between one educational program or agency and another would, if reported regularly, go a long way towards reducing inequity and promoting continuity in the lives of students. It would also encourage teaching agencies to examine constantly their admission standards and procedures (since these would be open to public scrutiny) and to forge relationships with non-educational agencies engaged in training.

Finally, efforts must be made to broaden the availability and distribution of educational information immediately useful to potential learners. A good deal has been accomplished in the collection and sorting of educational information by various computer-based systems operating at the "wholesale" level. But little progress has been made at the "retail" level, where the individual students (potential and actual) are to be found. The naiveté among educators about the scope and speed with which information travels,

Photo by Blackhall, Scarborough

not just in Ontario but in Canada as a whole, is confounding. To an alarming degree, they seem to think that their only task is to communicate with existing students. How such individuals find their way to becoming students is their own concern. Recent competition, particularly among post-secondary agencies, has helped, but the information provided is mostly institutional exhortation. "Learning Centres," particularly for women, have sprung up; but there are not many in Ontario, and little systematic progress has been made.

Learning will always outdistance education, particularly in societies committed to high rates of change and development, and it is both proper and desirable that this should be so. This is not an argument for greater control and direction over learning by the educational system. Nevertheless, the relationship between learning and education, both at an individual and an organizational level, must be the object of constant examination, reflection, and adjustment. It appears to be seriously out of balance at the present time.

What the change in composition and character of student bodies means is that the sources of new learning on which future teaching must be based are far more various and complex than they have been in the past. One of the principal sources of this new learning are the students themselves. For that reason, students must play much larger roles in the development and determination of the educational system in which they participate, and they must play their roles openly, responsibly, and consciously – rather than covertly and sometimes unconsciously, as at present. The 1960s and early 1970s provided some examples of superficial attempts by students to enlarge their roles within their providing agencies. Partly they succeeded, but the types of changes involved are far more sweeping and expansive than the achievement of a few places on the governing bodies of providing agencies. They reach to the concept of who and what a student is or is expected to be, and this concept must be shared equally by students and agencies. The sharing of a mutual enterprise which not only allows but also insists on the exercise of differing roles and authority within it (but which, in the long run, is responsive because students are also citizens, voters, and taxpayers) must suffuse the classrooms and administrative offices of the particular agency.

In a society in which change is encouraged, indeed worshipped, the composition of groups of individuals who choose to be students will likewise be subject to continuous change. However, a system of continuing education as described is best equipped to respond continuously to those changes. Ontario has gone a considerable way towards developing such a system, but the Province has still to acknowledge that fact and to realize the consequences. In particular, the leaders of the existing agencies – schools, colleges, and universities – have to rethink their roles in such a system and to arrive at new statements of their purpose and function. Education is a moral enterprise. It has always been so in Ontario, and it must continue to be so. How much greater the challenge is when it is not just the children who are involved but the whole population. What that means is that the relationship between the state, which must involve substantial numbers of its citizens in learner and student roles, and the citizens, who must voluntarily embrace these roles, is subject to such moral considerations as truth, honesty, and justice. Learning cannot be coerced. It must be won and deserved.

ALAN THOMAS attended Upper Canada College, the University of Toronto, and, at the graduate level, Teachers' College, Columbia University. Throughout his working life he has been involved in adult education in Canada — with the University of British Columbia, the Canadian Association for Adult Education, the Canadian Government, and, in recent years, at OISE. His attention has been focussed on the larger programs of adult education, including education within industry, the corrections system, and the labor movement, and of late his concern has shifted to "learning" (as distinct from "education"). In 1974, he was elected to the presidency of the Canadian Association for Adult Education; and in 1982, he was made a Member of the Order of Canada.

127

A place to stand
And a place to grow.
You may go far.
How far you go
Depends much less
('Twas always so)
On who you are
Than who you know.

UNFINISHED DREAMS: EDUCATION AND THE OPPRESSED

PAUL OLSON

There is a special symbol used at traditional Chinese weddings that translates to "double happiness." 1984 is Ontario's 200th anniversary; and in Ontario, we have been twice blessed to have witnessed the marriage of a stable and comparatively peaceful polity to a very wealthy society.

Our provincial resources are epic: a land mass four times that of Great Britain; some of the richest mineral deposits in the world; a shore line to the south along the largest supply of fresh water in the world and a shore line to the north surrounded by the ice wonders of Hudson Bay. We have timber, farmland, water, minerals, power, and a host of other natural riches, making us among the wealthiest areas in the world. Our cultural wealth is also impressive. We shelter Canada's capital and the nation's largest metropolis; we are the financial heart of the country and its industrial core. The "nation's newspaper" is here; and so are the broadcast centres of radio, television, and film. We make cars, planes, tractors, computers, and communication and guidance systems. We have a rural heart too and fashion, with traditional craftsmanship, such artifacts as fine furniture.

On the whole, we are the most dominant province, causing one historian, upon reviewing Canadian history, to protest: "When historians speak of Ontario history, it is always 'Canadian history.' When they speak of anywhere else, it is always 'regional history'."

But beyond material wealth lies our population. It is a platitude, but it is also true: Ontario is its people. Our ethnic diversity runs the gamut of humanity. Toronto, our capital city, is the most diverse network of first generation ethnic communities anywhere. And central to harnessing the vast cultural, social, and economic power of our people and of our Province is our educational system.

It is in vogue, and perhaps rightly so, to rail against the failings of our schools; but if one takes a historical perspective, it is difficult not to be impressed by the prevalence and universality of our schools and by their sociological impact. Schools as an institution are an immense success. This is a fact often overlooked even by schooling's more ardent supporters. Consider, too, the sheer magnitude of the enterprise. In the past quarter century, "education" has consistently been the single largest line item in our provincial budget. The highly skilled manpower deployed in Ontario education's service is a veritable army. In the elementary and secondary stream, there are nearly 100,000 teachers and principals, together with a significant support group (janitors, lunch staff, secretaries, board and ministry personnel).

And these workers are joined by others both above and below the K-13 level – for example, by infant day-care workers and by university professors. Education is a major industry.

Most impressive of all is the universality of the enterprise. What other institutions (other than mortuaries and hospitals) process such a universal cross section! Almost as impressive is the quality of the learning given – for example, despite the colossal numbers that schools assimilate (and civilize) they "fail" far less often than they are portrayed as doing. Literacy among our younger generations is all but universal, and most of our population is minimally numerate. In short, the teaching of basic skills in Ontario is comparable to the best anywhere in the world; and contrary to popular misconception, there is no evidence that the standard of basic skills has deteriorated during the last decade.

Then, at the top of the educational hierarchy, the theme of our accomplishments is equally worthy. Fifteen percent of the appropriate age group attends university, and nearly a quarter receives some form of post-secondary instruction. Within these gross figures, all our Ontario universities compare favorably to North American norms, and our colleges of applied arts and technology enjoy a worldwide reputation. Given then that Ontario's educational system has accomplished much, the chief purpose of education – one that is taken so often for granted as to be forgotten or trivialized – needs, perhaps, to be stated: that is to achieve the goal which Carlyle so eloquently epitomized as "letting each be all they may." And in our bicentennial year of reflective celebration, it is important and appropriate that this purpose not be overlooked. Much has been done, but there are dreams unfinished – both personal and collective – and it is vital that we examine what they are and how they have come to be if we are to come closer to fulfilling the promise of all our people and ourselves.

* * *

Discussing the oppressed is a curious business, for to speak of them is to speak of our failures: it invites the uncomfortable, and reactions to the topic reflect this fact. Those who consider the topic at all tend either to express *moral* rage or (the other side of anger's coin) to adopt a posture of piety and self-righteousness, dismiss calls for redress as "bleeding heart," and blame victims as if they, mystically or psychologically, wished failure down upon themselves – or worse still, they deny the truth of human dreams and reject reform and change as even needed since "people are where they are because they belong there." One component surely missing in both these mainly moral or ideological accounts is, I believe, a systematic, historical understanding of who the oppressed are and how they became oppressed.

So, who *are* the oppressed in Ontario? There are several ways to approach this seemingly straightforward question. The first, and most common, is to generate a litany of oppressed groups. Who one includes in such a list tends to be arbitrary, but among the groups coming readily to mind are women, ethnics (especially visible minorities), the poor, children, those in various forms of "special" education, linguistic minorities, those with class or cognitive styles varying from school norms, and those who desire vocational education; those who hold dissident views, have an unconventional sexual orientation, or who otherwise transgress social norms; and those with inadequate literacy skills, those innumerate, and those about to be dismissed as "computer illiterates."

But rather than review the arguments why individuals can be said to be oppressed in this brief list I have suggested, I would first like to propose a theory of how oppression occurs; I would then like to cite some case histories from research to exemplify how oppressive processes work in lived practice; and I would finally like to discuss options for what might be done to ameliorate these processes and to allow us to achieve our collective goals for the education of our children.

* * *

As I have previously suggested, when we speak of the "oppressed," we tend to treat them categorically: by this, I mean we frame the dilemma of women or of minorities or the poor as a state or a singular condition. The gist of such "analysis" usually centres on features we like or don't like about these groups. What is evoked is a tacit embodiment of our own *individual* reactions to these features. For instance, if we believe that poor people are conditionally the way they are because they are lazy or stupid, we are unlikely to be sympathetic to social welfare programs for their benefit. Conversely, if we believe that the poor are struggling but unfortunate souls, another reaction is evoked. What both these individual reactions share in common is an attributive causal and moral response to status conditions. Such moral polarization seeks to establish blame – blame on the schools or on society or on the oppressed themselves. Correction of what is perceived as the offending cause follows closely upon the heels of such posturing.

This pattern, I suggest, describes how we psychologically relate to oppression. Thus, discussion of the oppressed is quickly transformed from description or analysis into moral judgment. Now moralizing about education has been a central preoccupation throughout Ontario's history. Egerton Ryerson, as a notable example, wanted to establish a universal public school system partly to put the fear of God into what he perceived as the drunken, unruly Irish and German Catholic immigrants. Hence the Ontario school system, which has served so many so well, was born – kicking and screaming and railing, as evidenced by written tracts which now read as racist and religiously bigoted about what should be done for "other people's children." From this nativity, Ryerson's Ontario system bore two siblings: one, the legitimate scion destined to educate for betterment; and the other, an illegitimate child born to carry on social control and devoted to marginalizing the oppressed.

One of the most formidable obstacles to the universal diffusion of education and knowledge is class isolation and class exclusiveness — where the highest grades of society are wholly severed from the lower in responsibility, obligations and sympathy; where sect wraps itself up in the cloak of its own pride, and sees nothing of knowledge or virtue, or patriotism, beyond its own enclosures; and where the men of liberal education regard the education of the masses as an encroachment upon their own domains, or beneath their care, or notice. The feeble and most needy, as also the most numerous classes, are thus rendered still feebler by neglect, while the educated and more wealthy are rendered still stronger by monopoly. Our Municipal and School System, on the contrary, is of the largest comprehension — it embraces in its provisions all classes and all sects, and places the property of all, without exception, under contribution for the education of all, without respect to persons. Thus every man, whether rich or poor, is made equal before the law, and is laid under obligation, according to his means, of education the whole community (*sic*).

EGERTON RYERSON (1851)

That schooling is more than a straightforward mix of neutral curriculum and antiseptic pedagogy should not be surprising. For the *contents* of the curriculum (be they secular or religious; mental or manual; whether they deal with our own culture or someone else's) coupled with the *forms* of pedagogy (be they authoritarian or permissive; directive or participatory) are root, trunk, and branch moral issues whose implementation forms the core image of what we perceive as sacred and profane, valuable and worthless. These issues telegraph through their curricular codes, both overt and covert, how we should be socialized. It is unfathomable, therefore, that they could be anything but moral issues at their deepest levels.

Nonetheless, I should like to argue that these "moral" components implicit in our curricula are themselves dual and contradictory forms, whose effects vary depending on our usage of the term "morality." For instance, in treating schooling as essentially a moral situation – one where people are slotted as a categorical response to issues – at least two interpretations of the term "morality" are manifest.

The first is the very real and important activist interpretation of morality that shakes us from lethargic indifference and directs us to looking at and altering what is wrong. To seek causation and to effect remediation has a positive intent and is based upon an important truth – that social status is neither fully given nor solely individually achieved but instead is largely constructed from social actions and by social relations. The drive to be moral, in this respect, is positive because it affirms our mutual responsibility and ability to have volitional control over our collective social circumstances.

The second interpretation of morality – the drive to be *imposingly moral* – seeks to localize the attribution of status to individuals and to strait-jacket both causes of oppression and solutions. When this appears in schools, the "moral act of educating" becomes, I submit, a central apparatus of maintaining ideological practices supportive of oppression. Sorting out which moral enterprise we are pursuing in our educational practice determines whether we are helping people or frustrating their achievements and dreams.

Our tendency to treat oppression as a moral dilemma that is both categorical and individual leads to inherent logical, methodological, and practical inconsistencies.

In terms of logic, if we do view people in categorical ways – as women, as ethnics, as handicapped, and so on – we are in fact not noting their collective conditions by responding to them as individuals. Through training,

> Whether all social systems produce some basic human anxieties or the rapid change and economic insecurity of capitalism in particular generates them, current victimology research indicates widespread public unease. This seems to focus especially upon strangers, immigrants, outsiders, and in particular, I would suggest, the young, perhaps the quintessential strangers in our midst. Inordinately concentrated in the ever-threatening working class, the young are seen as unappreciative of our past, unsocialized, menacingly strong and healthy, and seductively sexy. With crime and delinquency as the third-ranking issue of concern to Canadians after inflation and unemployment, moral reproduction becomes fertile material for the reconstruction of domination.
>
> W. GORDON WEST
> (FROM "EDUCATION, MORAL REPRODUCTION, AND THE STATE," *INTERCHANGE* VOL. 12 2/3, 1981)

educators look to help individuals, but such an approach is severely limited in handling general status problems since the root of such problems lies in structural social relationships rather than in random individual circumstances. Understanding what these structural relationships are and how they operate is therefore a necessary step in any meaningful discussion of oppression.

The second inconsistency of the individual/categorical status approach to dealing with oppression is methodological and (more important) is itself a moral constraint. Oppression by commission is the methodological error of reductionism – or treating diverse, and sometimes contradictory, phenomena as if they were the same. This tendency to substitute belief or logical theory for lived experience is a critical failing not only in much of the traditional educational treatment of oppression but also in overly structural approaches which want to substitute for the serendipitous surprises of life the neatness of articulated moral or theoretical positions. People (happily) are always doing things they are not supposed to, and knowing this universal truth is part and parcel of understanding much of the richness of life. If educators and theorists have shared a single common greatest fault in addressing the oppressed, it lies in their failure to grasp the complexity of *lived experience* and to face critical examination of what, how, when, and where abstractions come to be full blown in day-to-day life.

This tendency towards reductionism – to treat people not in the richness of their own lives but as icons or images projected from various theories, beliefs or prejudices – is a moral tragedy because it denies aspects of common experience and because it trivializes others and ourselves. It leads to our being unwilling or unable to evaluate either how the common underlying elements in our lives interconnect or how it is that impulses and responses in others are the human ones we share. This approach tries to strait-jacket experience into an image, which then allows dismissal of others and our shared responsibilities; for morality, ultimately, is a shared or social position, and as the golden rule reminds us, how we treat others is how we should expect others to treat us.

To be moral in the first positive interpretation necessitates that we comprehend both structurally how oppression comes into being and, in day-to-day life, how oppression is experienced. What gives rise to oppression is a source of considerable debate, but (to reduce my own argument to its essence) I would claim that oppression's roots lie in our basest impulses – in greed to exploit the labor of others; in our own insecurities about ourselves (and therefore about others different from ourselves); in our sexual anxieties; and in our hidden (sometimes not so hidden) fears that others' misfortunes may become our own. On the surface, I am offering a psychological explanation for oppression, but I would also suggest that the structural foundations bear the scars of conflict arising out of material and social self-interest. These interests, however, are seldom evident (particularly in education) as a direct intentional manifestation of power. Instead, the structure of repressive power – the systematic ability to keep others from fulfilling their potential – rests in more indirect sets of institutional and ideological practices which act quietly but effectively to mediate between what are oppressive interests and practices structuring what people become.

What this means in terms of educational settings is that no one (or hardly anyone) ever maliciously intends to oppress others, especially children. Being clear on this point and how structural power finds its own agency in institutional processing (doing what Dorothy Smith has called "institutional ethnography") is vital to understanding how oppression can enter our schools. Teachers and administrators are frequently uncomfortable in their dealings with oppressed groups and approach them warily, guiltily, or with millennial zeal. In Ontario, I believe, most educators do sincerely try to help children reach their potential. Hearing charges that they "oppress children" or are the silent agents of ideological forces defies their conscious intentions. Nonetheless, as I shall illustrate later, the institutional, bureaucratic, and classroom practices of teaching – what those in the "new sociology" of education have dubbed *the hidden curriculum* – do act to inculcate ideology, to sort out children, and to provide an agency for oppression.

Part of what it should mean to be authentically moral – the litmus test – is not merely that our intentions as teachers not be maniacal but that we consciously strive to hear that which is not audibly spoken, that we examine our own practices – and those of society – to find the roots of oppression, until we can assure ourselves and others that each child has reached his or her own potential. To do less is a disservice to education; to do less is to deny the collective and social potential in ourselves; to do less is not good enough.

How the hidden curriculum works in schools to engender oppression is now well known. One primary device whereby schooling telegraphs specific ideological messages is through what Basil Bernstein has called codes – or systems by which different groups understand one another. In linguistic terms this means, for instance, that working class children tend to use more pronouns than middle class children whose speech tends to be noun specific. This variation has the effect that particularistic codes (working class) tend to draw upon specific contexts for their meaning while universalistic ones (middle class) reference general forms. The content of each speech is identical and neither is richer nor more intelligent than the other. What becomes important in this distinction, however, is not the issue of using one or the other as a pedagogical device (teaching working class children to speak in universalistic codes) but that speech forms learned in the home are used to devalue and segregate children, thereby driving a tragic wedge between home and school. Thus, what these nominal linguistic differences do is to perform as legitimating surrogates for very real power differences – and, for educators, sadly act to abrogate what ought to be a duty to instruct each child to his or her full potential.

As an ideology of failure, this labelling process is given further tragic substance by the fact that these institutional divisions become parts of the biography of children's careers, which are then used to stratify the curriculum so that what and how children are taught varies within what are nominally uniform public schools.

There are some important recent ethnographic studies of education from Australia (by R. W. Connell) and from the United States (by Jean Anyon) which forcefully illustrate that schools *do* make a difference as to how people perform – both in school and in their later careers. What is transparently clear in both studies is that the amount and level of technical information given to working, middle, and upper class children vary dramatically (as does parental control over schooling): for working class children, psychological issues – motivation, attitude, etc – dominate pedagogy whereas for middle and upper class children, the transfer of technical skills is top on the pedagogical agenda. Control devices analogous to the curricular ones discussed above also come

"Wayward children, those who resist authority, are likely to be dismissed as 'learning' problems."

in the forms of pedagogy. Working class schools are characteristically authoritarian (and adversarial between teachers and pupils). Values held by working class children are systematically undervalued in schooling (with predictable resistance from the children), and the children are subjected to systematic forms of non-teaching by rote, reinforced by sledge-hammer discipline. Middle class children, by contrast, are given far more self directed and permissive forms of pedagogy; they are encouraged to examine problems not as "right or wrong" but as they bear on their own lives. The result of such imposed cultural forms and learning styles is that the gap between working and middle class children widens with the years spent in school.

Examples of such processes abound in Ontario's educational history. For instance, Francophones in the last century controlled their educational system in many central and northern Ontario communities. Bilingualism prevailed in both separate francophone schools and the affairs of the community. Certainly a Franco-Ontarian system does exist in many parts of the Province to this day, but during the later part of the last century and the early part of this century, conscious efforts were made to devalue both the French language and its associated culture. Towns which once bore French names were altered to English names; and in schools, the media, and community affairs, French was systematically downplayed.

Equally insidious, use of the French language was equated with "the Quebec issue," calling for the adoption of Quebec (or even French) curriculum materials and texts – texts that said nothing about Ontario geography or history found in conventional English texts. The tacit message in this curricular practice was that Franco-Ontarians were aliens in their own land. Lost in these curricular "accommodations" was the essential role which, demographically and historically, Francophones have played in shaping Ontario. The net legacy of this alienation, the practice by inference of making our neighbors "strangers" in their own land, has been

". . . Francophone ethnics converting to English as their first language in the home."

devastating. Herbert Gurthier's 1982 Statistics Census, for instance, indicates that between 1960 and 1970, the rate of "Anglicization" (of Francophone ethnics converting to English as their first language in the home) was 26 percent in Ontario. Stated another way, one in four families of French ancestry who had started that decade speaking French as their first language concluded it speaking principally English.

To be sure, important progress has been made in Ontario recently to revitalize Franco-Ontarian education and to assure French language rights. Nevertheless, the process of alienating our children's heritage from their education continues in too many instances. Two very interesting studies, for instance, done at the Ontario Institute for Studies in Education, analysed teacher report cards sent to immigrant parents from Jamaica and Portugal. Both indicate that we are far from achieving the multicultural goals to which both our Canadian and Ontario Governments are officially committed.

In the study of those of Jamaican ancestry (among whom the Creole dialect is commonplace), teachers systematically reported the problems that they experienced with dialects as "learning" or "intelligence" problems of the children. These children were recommended – in numbers statistically out of proportion to their numbers in school – to remedial or "slow learner" classes. Analysis of report cards showed highly patronizing teacher comments such as "Your children would be better if they had grown up with English." English, of course, is the language of Jamaica; and while dialect is a serious issue in teaching immigrant children, suggesting to parents that their own native tongue is a foreign language is hardly an efficient route to achieving harmony between school and home.

The results from the study of Portuguese immigrant children produced much the same kind of evidence. Portuguese mothers (most of them Roman Catholic and conservative) were told that their daughters would be better if the family paid more attention to "their daughters' morals." Children themselves reported that their teachers had little comprehension of their home life and that when they tried to tell this to their parents – Portuguese parents, who, like Jamaicans, come from a very strict authoritarian system – they told their children to "do what your teachers say." Simultaneously, teachers complained that the parents "don't care about their kids," while parents complained that "teachers are supposed to teach our children; it's their job, and they don't." The children's response was a curious Portuguese-Canadian hybrid – namely, to be cynical toward both parents and teachers as "not knowing what's happening" and to reference their peer subgroup for values and legitimacy about the world. Predictably, school dropouts are disproportionately high among this cohort.

In these two examples, there lies a theoretical principle about how structure intrudes in education as an agent of repression: instead of resorting to direct repression or the exercise of concerted power, schooling in various of its curricular practices comes to bureaucratize or treat categorically what are human problems. By treating what are differences in culture, value, social belief, and power as if they were neutral technical questions, schooling practice – the bureaucratic processes that allow us to *help other people's children* — acts to generate or exacerbate social division and oppression.

* * *

My claims to this point are admittedly abstract and undocumented. Proving such claims is plainly beyond the scope of this paper, but I would like to give four selected examples from Ontario and other Canadian research literature to exemplify how schools' bureaucratic processes actualize oppression by carrying out seemingly neutral or technical schooling procedures.

Equal instruction for all children – Most teachers believe that they teach all their students equally, and as I have suggested, this is certainly their intention. In Ontario in particular, we have made great material strides towards equality, notably in our tax basis where major differences in funding between school boards do not exist – in contrast to the United States where school boards differ radically in the materials (and quality of teachers) that they make available to children. Consequently, many have claimed that Ontario provides equal (or nearly equal) education for all. At one level it does.

But recently, Professor Ann Manicom of Dalhousie University, following up on theoretical work done by Dorothy Smith in Toronto, has looked closely at what happens in actual teaching practice in Ontario (and Nova Scotia). What Manicom finds is that how well a child performs in school depends in large measure not simply on the teacher or the child's competence but on the work of parenting (usually mothering) done at home. For example, when a primary teacher teaches painting to elementary school children, the extent to which mothers have had the materials, time, money, and ability to teach children such lessons as the "red paint goes in one can while green goes in the other – otherwise you will get a muddy brown" affects how well the teacher herself can teach. For those who have learned these lessons at home, the teacher can get past the rudiments and on to teaching finer points of art. For those who haven't, these essentials must be dealt with. Manicom reports similar findings with geoboards and other text materials.

It is, of course, hardly news that not all children bring the same skills to school. What is interesting are the teachers' responses. Teachers, using ostensibly "equivalent" techniques, see the children who are "easier" to teach (i.e. who know where the brushes go) as "brighter" or with a better aptitude for art. It may be argued that these variations in homes and in society cannot be fully compensated for in schooling. While this is true, it also is another matter to say that one child is "bright" while another is not when, in fact, what is at issue is an ascription arising out of differences in experience. A far more equitable test of "brightness" (if "brightness" truly matters) is how well each child copes with a situation given his or her own biographical information level. What is most insidious about this practice of confusing intelligence with social variance is that tracking decisions about "where people fit" are made on just these kinds of evaluations, and subsequent curriculum content and forms of pedagogy are adjusted accordingly. In short, this confusion of past practice and experience with intelligence is among the most persistently oppressive mechanisms in schooling and is a principal example of how the apparently neutral cultural norms act to produce and reinforce forms of structural inequality.

Middle class homes with single parents – How structural forms and institutional values help create invidious distinctions is not limited to differences of social class. Consider the case of many middle class women who are "single parent" mothers.

The oppressed status of women – historically, in traditional law, and in job mobility – is now well documented and widely acknowledged. The most common way of glossing over women's structural oppression (or that of our other oppressed groups) is to blast forth shot-gun volleys of "throw-away statistics." In Canada, for instance, a woman is raped every seventeen minutes; women earn between fifty and sixty cents in the dollar for the same work as men. These statistical profiles embody what are profoundly consequential lived realities in the lives of various women, and surely issues like violence against women and equal pay are among the most important and visible in the feminist movement for equality. Yet, whereas most educators desire to eliminate such gross inequities, there are subtle practices which reinforce patriarchal stratification and inequality within the schooling process. The treatment of single parent families is just one such case.

Alison Griffith, carrying out research on single parent families in Toronto and Vancouver, found that the label "single parent" acted as a key word or code which helped to classify children (and mothers) along patriarchal lines. How this career slotting device works is interesting.

"Single parent" is, on the surface, a nominal category without rank, stigma, or status, but in practice, "single parents" are disproportionately women. Teachers and administrators say they use the single parent label only as a nominal category to state facts about family type. Not all those from one parent homes, however, become reported on official records as "single parents." "Widows," for instance, are infrequently noted as "single parents." Even more telling, those who already possess a more encompassing label – for instance, "welfare mother" or "native mother" – are seldom classified on records as single parents. This pattern becomes further disoriented because when the child is doing academically well in school, the single parent label is invariably absent from the child's institutional biography. Those who are classified as "single parent," therefore, are a distillate of children who come largely from middle class families, have one parent (a mother), and are deemed to be unsatisfactory in school. The results of these techniques for determining on official records who is a "single parent" and who is not sometimes border on the bizarre. For example, in one documented case a single mother has two sons: on the school records of her first son, who is academically gifted, she is never listed as a single parent; on the records of her second son, who is academically and behaviorally more troublesome, her single parent status is consistently listed as a contributing explanation for his behavior.

Griffith provides an interpretation of these findings. She argues that "single parent" is a second order sorting device used in bureaucratic processing agencies (e.g., schools, police and welfare agencies) to code how a child should be processed. "Single parent" is therefore not a neutral or nominal category at all but is an *attributive* device to causally explain the child's "failure" by locating it in the mother's marital status. The school thereby frees itself from responsibility for the child's failure while simultaneously reinforcing the conventional model of a patriarchal family as the only authentic one.

This mode of processing is itself "secondary" to other more powerful sorting devices such as class and ethnic status in establishing how children arrive where they are and how they are to be dealt with. For it is only in their rejection of an idealized family form that these single parent women differ from any other middle class mother. By selectively reporting only "failures", the processing practices appear to establish what is in fact a spurious correlation between single parenting and delinquency. What the repetition of this practice does as a hidden agenda is to reinforce patriarchy by telegraphing the message that women alone are incompetent to raise children and "fit" mothers are in nuclear families with fathers.

No one conspires in schools to transfer patriarchy (or oppression); but some of our most routinized procedures bear witness to how deeply forms of prejudice and oppression run in our schooling forms. Breaking through conventional wisdom to establish valid facts about how schools work and how people fit in them ought to be part of our educational agenda. We must not only read and report the symbols that we use to categorize one another – we must understand their structural origins and their lived consequences.

Symbols of popular culture: the media in schools, or how we assess who we are – Recently there have been some most interesting analyses of how images of self, group, and the world are presented in popular culture, the media, and schools. Ed Sullivan at OISE has carefully examined Toronto's three major English language dailies – the *Globe and Mail*, the *Star*, and the *Sun* – to see how minority or oppressed groups are prevalently portrayed. He has then evaluated the popular presentations of these newspapers against research findings about minority and oppressed groups.

What Sullivan has found is that varying images of why and how people relate in terms of social power are portrayed in each newspaper. The form of reporting also varies, depending upon which audience the newspaper targets. In the *Globe* and *Star*, for instance, a similar model of causation for oppression is portrayed. In this model, groups are presented not as structurally subordinate but as somehow (for whatever reason) deficient or lacking in material, social, or cultural capital. There is no innate or structural reason why people should vary except for the vagaries of their histories. However, what needs to be done to remedy perceived differences is clear: to "equalize" varying groups, one must transfer capital – usually psychological or symbolic – to the oppressed group. What underlies the remedial action in this model is a correctionalist view for the oppressed – or what Sullivan calls a "mug and jug approach." We take some skill or feature missing in the oppressed group and give them this until they are equivalent to the other group.

This correctionalist approach is interesting because it conforms most closely to the views about dealing with oppressed groups held by most educators. If minorities were unable to get jobs, for instance, we would (following this logic) transfer skills to them until they were equal to those with jobs. Minorities in this presentation, therefore, "must learn to think like small business," or minorities "must sacrifice to get their children professions," or we need to provide incentives to business to help minorities. Plainly, education is a primary transfer device in this correctionalist model.

The *Sun*, by contrast, targets a very different, less intellectual audience. Why the oppressed are where they are, according to the *Sun's* world view, is a virtual inversion of what the evidence suggests in the literature. In the power matrix, the dominant groups are portrayed as victims.

Minorities are taking over Canada. Women are pushy and burn bras. The poor are on "pogey" and are the source of economic decline. Criminals and the handicapped get everything.

While he notes that the pictures presented vary sharply in each of these newspapers (the *Globe* tends to address a more analytical audience than the *Star*, for instance), Sullivan contends that the underlying process of portraying images is, in its most important respects, the same in all of them. First, each focusses its reporting on how groups should be treated in society. Second, the structural power relationships which generate differences in the first place are never discussed; for example, that racism is a structural feature of many Anglo-Canadians and that this (and not just lack of skills) may be the reason for minorities' oppression is not a central focus or theme. And third, the victim is always portrayed as the source or agent of oppression. At best (our "moral" side), we "help" the oppressed. But our own practices and social relations as dominant groups remain silent.

Understanding how oppression is portrayed in this way is important for two reasons. First, it is in the repetition of the images of popular culture that we begin to construct popular wisdom about who people are and why they are where they are. Second, following from this, we construct policies to remedy perceived problems. But if we have mislocated the true social relations and causations, if we believe, for instance, that the way to multicultural harmony is simply to upgrade minority skills and to ignore structural racism, we are likely to produce unsatisfactory programs, doomed to failure because they have taken no account of the underlying causes of oppression.

This pattern, I suggest, is a common one in education. We start some remedial program to right wrongs (we tip the jug towards the mug), but we ignore the larger social whole from which the inequality arises. We set out, for instance, to "teach girls math," but in so doing, we do little to control for home or media or job market. In the end, some girls may be marginally better, but because of piecemeal reform programs, most remain where they were. Exhausted (and doubtless no longer funded), our piecemeal project is now cited as an instance of reform that has "been tried" but has "not worked." In examining oppression, it is important that we always bear two things in mind: first, that we examine relations for their fullest structural causes; second, that we do not underestimate how powerfully and deeply prejudice and inequality can run. It is a mistake based on arrogance to assume that because a piecemeal approach has not succeeded that the struggle should not continue.

The definition of self: secondary deviance and how others' views of us shape what we are – One of the most interesting efforts to redress long standing injustices toward the oppressed in Ontario is taking place in special education – in particular, the passage of Bill 82, which facilitates a parent's right to have a child's special education needs met. The reforms associated with Bill 82 are especially important because they are not piecemeal and because they are backed by a concerted systematically funded attempt to aid those with special needs. But much can be learned by looking at the institutional practices which processed special education children in schools until very recently.

The first and most symptomatic process is embodied in the category "special education" itself. On the surface, this title looks straightforward enough, but if one examines it carefully, it is rather vacuous. Special education may mean that one can't deal easily with the child because the child has no arms or legs; or it may mean that regular classroom teachers can't deal with the child because they are afraid of being knifed; or it may mean that the child is so bright that it is intimidating to teach the child. There is no uniform meaning to the label "special education" except that, for whatever reason, the child doesn't fit into our orthodox perception of how a standard classroom should look. We offer special education as help, but at the most fundamental level of organization, what we are saying is "you don't fit."

This apparently callous analysis of special education brings out a major issue among those advocating rights for handicapped, retarded, delinquent, and other special education groups (including the gifted). This is the issue of secondary deviance. What the analysis of secondary deviance applied to special education children says, in essence, is that a great deal of why special education children are different is because we *label and treat them differently*.

What we are increasingly led to think is that the school system — with Opportunity Class as its dead-end division — just isn't set up to be meaningful for our kids. It doesn't relate to the things they know about and care about. It doesn't touch the world as it's experienced by people who don't have much money, who are forced to take society's hard and boring jobs, who are constantly threatened by unemployment, who are harassed by welfare officials or the police. It doesn't understand what it means to be a person with integrity under these circumstances, or where you find life and friendship. So the kids slide away, and turn their minds and their hearts off. And many of those who turn off the most end up in Opportunity Class.

TREFANN MOTHERS' BRIEF TO THE
TORONTO BOARD (1970)
(FROM *CITY KIDS BOOK,* OISE PRESS, 1979)

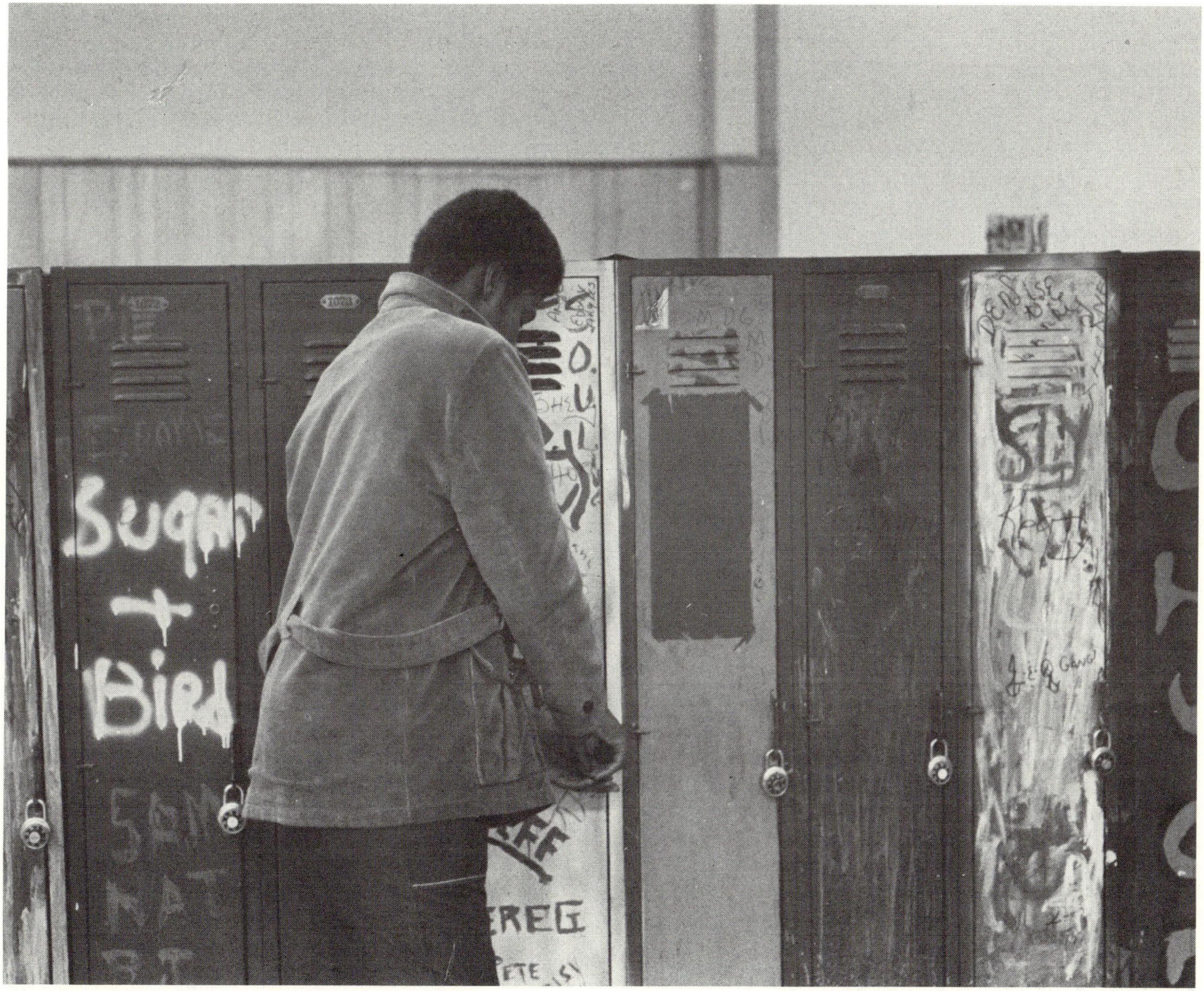
Sugar
+
Bird
SLY

Paraplegics, for example, were traditionally sent to special schools and isolated. Other children were never exposed to those in wheelchairs (except in charity campaigns which trumpeted the "tragedy" of their being) and predictably developed stereotypical prejudice.

According to the theory of secondary deviance, this notion of difference (and ultimately of incompetence) becomes self-fulfilling prophecy because we deny opportunity to all those tagged blind or deaf or "special." This label carries with it not only the assigned notation of what are very real problems but also unwarranted abrogations of the individual's right to integration and self-attainment within the larger society. Bill 82 bears the fraternal twin marks of hope and fear for the future. It allows all, particularly those oppressed by their "special" status, finally to receive the materials and instruction they need to become as self-sufficient (and as educated) as possible. But the legislation also presents a danger of fostering new labelling programs. When we "identify" problems (as is called for under interpretations of sections of Bill 82), it is all too easy to label social problems as "learning disabilities." Minorities, wayward children, those who resist authority, and those who come from working class homes are liable to be dismissed as "special" or "learning" problems. The care and dignity with which we implement legislation like Bill 82 are every bit as important to ameliorating and eliminating the stigma and failure of those with non-traditional needs as is the very important passage of the legislation itself.

* * *

I have tried to show that everyday routinized processes, both in schools and in society as a whole, help to shape the standards, curriculum content, and values we hold – and that they lie at the root of oppression. Yet the examples I have considered are far from exhaustive of the oppressive role of education in our Province. We have, for instance, a long history of undervaluing manual versus mental work, such that our vocational systems (which reach largely working class children) have never fully realized their potential. The substance (and availability) of what is offered to whom is also an issue full of subtle machinations. Recent work by Jane Gaskell on how technical skills are taught to girls and how girls' business curricula systematically lead to very general but unrecognized skills in the workplace is an instance in point. So too are issues of self-esteem: how subjectivity and structure penetrate each other. Work by Roger Simon at OISE has been helpful in illustrating how certification for job attainment blocks many students from going on (and becoming certified) in areas in which they are already competent. And the list goes on.

There is much in our schooling practice which must be altered if we are to allow all our children to achieve their potential. But while this is imperative, it is not of itself sufficient to end structural oppression. I would like in this respect to return to some concepts at the beginning of this essay.

In practice, society often looks to schools to end inequality. Certainly schooling is vital to bringing about reform and to achieving self-actualization. And as I have been trying to argue, how we process children in schools – how we meet their real needs and evaluate their real abilities – is vital to this success, requiring that we constantly monitor our own practices, both material and psychological, as educators. Nonetheless, education is an area where issues of structural inequality and oppression have been addressed more thoroughly than in almost any other governmental or private institution. This is important to remember because it suggests that schools alone cannot fully compensate for society. But then there are different ways to interpret this statement. To some, it means that schools should not be blamed for programmatic failure. To me, it means that, as society looks to us for solutions, those of us in education must struggle with society to give us the means to achieve our ends, and while redoubling our efforts, we must recognize that what is valued in the larger society, how we are funded, where our children go, and what images they see and hear immeasurably affect our perceptions and our ability to do our jobs.

School and society are integrally bound, and it is vital that we comprehend how social processes shape what we do as educators and whom we receive as students. Most of the examples in this essay have been drawn from internal school practice, but what we teach and to whom is not solely a classroom or individual matter; it has to do with struggles and power relations in the wider society. If we are to face oppression head on, looking at school forms in isolation is necessary but not enough. For until all of our children come to us with respect for their own language, culture, and states of body and mind; until we abate the larger oppressive forms in society itself – we will be unable to say unashamedly that all our children have reached their potential.

PAUL OLSON is an assistant professor in OISE's Department of Sociology. He has written extensively about inequality, research methodologies, social theory, and school implementation processes. He is currently researching the sociological aspects of bilingual learning, in particular French immersion about which he is writing two books, and the sociological impact of the use of computers in schools and homes, concerning which he is conducting a comprehensive ethnographic study.

I do not like the U. of T.
Its size does not appeal to me,
Which sentiment is also true
Of Western. As for Waterloo
I think I'd rather cross the way
And sulk at Wilfrid Laurier.
Then R.M.C. and Guelph — forget
Except for brigadier or vet;
And only one who courts disaster
Would ever contemplate McMaster.
Queen's has its Golden Gaels I ken
But stands too close to Kingston Pen;
And Lakehead out at Thunder Bay
Is miles too many miles away.
Ryerson has merits, some agree,
But lacks respectability;
And as for Windsor and Laurentian —
In charity I give them mention;
To pass on Brock without a word
For fear of seeming too absurd.
There's arguments I've heard for York
But lacking substance, full of talk,
While everything I know of Trent
Is tinged with discord and dissent.
Carleton remains, and so does Ottawa —
From them, I thank my stars, I gottawa
To bask in ignorance all day
Sans work, sans learning, sans B.A.

ONTARIO AND ITS UNIVERSITIES

ROBIN HARRIS

Very early in their history, the people of Ontario through their elected representatives in the Legislature made the decision that higher education should be available to them and that public funds should be allocated for its support. Throughout the 19th century, pursuit of this policy took the form of efforts to establish a single provincial institution that would adequately serve the needs of its citizens, understood at this time to involve the provision of a liberal education to its young men (and, from the 1880s, its young women) and of preparation for the recognized professions: initially law, medicine, and the Church but, by 1900, including agriculture, dentistry, engineering, music, and pharmacy as well.

In the 20th century, with the addition of research and community service as essential university functions and with the further proliferation of professions for which a university education was deemed appropriate, the search has been for a network of provincially supported institutions which in concert would provide for the burgeoning needs: hence an expansion from one provincial university in 1900 (with about 2,000 full-time students and a handful of part-time ones) to 16 in 1984 (with about 170,000 full-time students and almost as many part-time).

The 20th century has also seen the replacement of the term *higher education* by the term *post-secondary education*, embracing programs that lead to diplomas or certificates rather than to university degrees. Thus, in Ontario in 1984, there is a parallel network of post-secondary institutions – 22 colleges of applied arts and technology, 4 colleges of agricultural technology, an institute of medical technology, and several others – with a combined enrolment of 150,000 full-time and over 400,000 part-time students. All of this is reflected in the increase of public funds expended on higher or post-secondary education: from $100,000 in 1900 to $2 billion in 1984.

Throughout the 200 years, the tradition in Ontario has been that it is the responsibility of the Legislature (in practical terms, the government in office) to determine the amount of public funds to be allocated for higher education, and it is the responsibility of the universities to decide how these funds are to be spent. That a university must be autonomous as to who should be admitted, who should teach, and what should be taught has been generally accepted; exceptions (notably, at the turn of the century, when there were instances of the then Minister of Education interfering with staff appointments at the University of Toronto) have been rare. In the last 10 years, however, as the costs of

> **I**t makes me laugh to think back ten years and remember the imagery conjured up in my head by the word "university." It was such a *big* word. *Big*, formidable looking buildings on huge campuses where you could get lost in the corridors, never to surface again. Inside: people with *big* brains. Professors: *big,* ferocious men wearing gowns. (I knew they didn't really wear them anymore it was just the idea.) Needless to say, I wanted nothing to do with such a place.
>
> Things changed, however. I got fed up with playing housewife out in the boonies and so, trembling in my boots, I entered into one of the smallest of the big institutions around: Trent University. A wonderful place but nevertheless you can imagine how disappointed I was to discover the truth about the situation. Take professors for instance: not only did they not know everything, they didn't even know many things that I knew. In fact, they were despicably normal — thick-headed, opinionated, half of them too friendly, others misogynists.
>
> After two years, I decided I'd had enough, and I escaped to the real world again. Five years later, I'm back to finish off and collect my letters, this time at U of T, the biggest of the big. The only intimidating thing about that place is the bureaucracy. I guess, all in all, university is much better than I had imagined it to be. I'll be glad to see the end of it, but I must confess, I have had some fun.
>
> MIRANDA OLIVER,
UNIVERSITY STUDENT

supporting universities have risen dramatically, the question of accountability has been of increasing concern to the Legislature and has given it second thoughts on the matter of university autonomy. Can the universities be permitted to admit any student they deem qualified if provincial funds are insufficient? To take a concrete case, should 10 universities be permitted to operate faculties of education when the same number of students could be accommodated at five, particularly when the demand for qualified teachers in the Province's schools is substantially lower than the number of applicants. Then again, should any Ontario student who wishes to enrol in a teacher training course and has the academic qualifications be denied the opportunity?

This issue — essentially accountability versus accessibility — is one of many which the Government has asked a three-person Commission on the Future of the Universities of Ontario, appointed in December 1983, to consider in the process of "developing a plan of action to better enable the universities ... to adjust to changing social and economic conditions." The Commission is required to report by 15 November 1984. Thus it can be safely assumed that the "University Question" will be debated in the Legislature in 1985, as it has been regularly since 1797.

* * *

The establishment of a "college of a higher class" in the colony was advocated by its first Lieutenant-Governor, John Graves Simcoe, even before he embarked for Canada to take up his duties, and he continued to press for it – though without success – throughout his five-year tenure of the office. But a year after his departure, in 1797, the Legislature of Upper Canada petitioned the British King, George III, to assign a portion of public land as an endowment for educational purposes – specifically for the establishment of district grammar (secondary) schools and of "a College or University, where the youth of the country may be enabled to perfect themselves in the different branches of liberal knowledge." The request was approved, and of the 500,000 acres set aside, about half was designated the University Endowment following the granting, in 1827, of a charter for the establishment "at or near Our Town of York, in our said

Province of Upper Canada ... (of) one College, with the style and privileges of an University ... for the education and instruction of youth and students in arts and faculties, to continue forever, to be called King's College." In the best romantic tradition, "for ever" turned out to be just over twenty years.

"... to continue forever, to be called King's College."

The university charter contained no restrictions with respect to the race, color, or creed of students in the arts, medicine, or law, but candidates for degrees in divinity were required to be members of the Established Church of England and Wales, as were the chancellor, president, and all staff members, these together constituting the governing body of the institution and therefore in control of the endowment. This arrangement proved unacceptable to the three other major religious groups in the Province, each of which had as many or nearly as many adherents as the Church of England. The opening of King's College was consequently delayed until 1843, by which time three other universities were in operation: the Methodists' Victoria College at Cobourg, the Presbyterians' Queen's at Kingston, and the Roman Catholics' Regiopolis also at Kingston. For the balance of the decade, the Legislature carried on an almost continuous debate (four separate bills were introduced) as to whether the endowment should be used to maintain a single provincial university or divided between the four. The conclusion was that it should not be divided but that it should be assigned to an institution without denominational connection. As of January 1, 1850, King's College was abolished, and a non-denominational University of Toronto was established in its stead and with its charter.

The hope was that the other colleges would associate themselves with the Provincial University as affiliates, and while they continued to be entirely responsible for work in theology (an area from which the University was specifically barred), they would prepare their students in all other subjects for the University's examinations and degrees. As further encouragement, in 1853 another University of Toronto Act was passed whereby the University's functions were restricted to those of examining and degree-granting and its teaching responsibilities were assigned to "a provincial college" (University College) to which its teaching staff were transferred. All students in the Province would thus have access to the Provincial University's degrees, either through the non-denominational University College or through one operated by a religious denomination. By 1853, these religious colleges also included the University of Trinity College at Toronto, which the Anglicans had promptly established as a replacement for the abolished King's; and by the time of Confederation, there were Roman Catholic colleges at Ottawa (the University of Ottawa), Toronto (St. Michael's College), and Windsor (Assumption), a second Methodist college at Belleville (Albert), and Baptist and Anglican colleges at Woodstock and London which ultimately evolved into McMaster University at Toronto (chartered 1887) and the Western University of London (chartered 1878). By 1867, three professional schools had also been established: the Ontario Veterinary College at Toronto (by a Scotsman named Andrew Smith) and two medical schools organized by local doctors in Toronto and Kingston and affiliated respectively with the University of Toronto and Queen's.

Support for some, though not all, of these "outlying colleges" was provided by the Legislature in the form of annual grants. This practice was introduced in 1842 with respect to Victoria, which had opened the previous year, and during the 1840s was extended to Queen's and Regiopolis. Subsequently, Trinity, Ottawa, Assumption, and St. Michael's were added, as well as the medical schools at Toronto and Kingston and, curiously enough, Victoria College's affiliated medical school, which was located outside the Province in Montreal. The grants ranged from $750 (to the medical schools) to $5,000 (Queen's and Victoria) and, in 1867, totalled $22,550. There were no annual grants to the University of Toronto or to its teaching arm, University College, on the grounds that the University Endowment was sufficient for their needs.

At the time of Confederation, access to higher education was, in geographic terms, readily available to the Province's male youth; there were seven chartered universities and as many other post-secondary institutions, and with the exception of Hamilton, all the major centres of population had at least one institution offering education beyond high school. There was, however, little demand. Total enrolment in all these institutions combined was below 1,000, with only the University of Toronto, Trinity, and Victoria having as many as 100. The diploma courses in agriculture and engineering which University College had introduced in the 1850s had attracted less than a dozen students in more than a decade. Despite the legislative grants, all the denominational colleges were in financial difficulty, the endowment of the Provincial University had been largely expended in the construction of its main building, and the professional schools were no more than holding their own. This financial position worsened in 1867 when the Legislature decided that grants should be made only to institutions which were not under denominational control – a policy effective from 1 July 1868 and one that has been followed ever since. In fact, from then until 1890, the Legislature confined its direct support of higher education to two schools which the Government itself established through the Provincial Departments of Education and Agriculture: the School of Practical Science at Toronto (in 1873) and the Ontario College of Agriculture at Guelph (in 1874).

Despite their difficulties, all the institutions survived the 1870s. The denominational colleges benefitted from increased support from their adherents. The University of Toronto benefitted from the location on its campus of the School of Practical Science, some of whose laboratory facilities the University's science students were allowed to use. But there remained limitations to the University's capacity for teaching the sciences, and this led to a request to the Government for direct assistance in 1882. Although the request was turned down, it prompted a renewed attempt to restructure the Provincial University so that the other colleges could be associated with it in a functional way rather than a nominal way. The result was the University of Toronto Federation Act of 1887 which, in addition to continuing the

Robert Lansdale

University College, University of Toronto, 1969

affiliation arrangement, reestablished the University as a teaching institution and provided for denominationally controlled universities to enter into federation with it as follows: the denominational universities would continue their independent work as theological colleges and, as federated arts colleges in the University of Toronto, would provide instruction in the relatively inexpensive disciplines of classics, English, French, German, Oriental languages, and ethics; likewise, University College would confine itself to instruction in these disciplines; and all other instruction in arts and science would be provided free to federated college students by the University itself. This solution appeared to resolve the 19th century University Question. The Toronto School of Medicine was absorbed as the University's faculty of medicine; a faculty of law was established; both the School of Practical Science and the College of Agriculture became affiliates, preparing their students for degree programs which the University had authorized; and two more professional schools in Toronto – the Royal College of Dental Surgeons (1875) and the Ontario College of Pharmacy (1882) – were also affiliated to the University. Furthermore, in 1889, Victoria College (with which Albert College had merged in 1884) accepted the terms of federation and, in 1892, moved from Cobourg to the University campus. Trinity made the same decision in 1903.

However, the other universities in the Province decided against federation – Queen's remained at Kingston, Western at London, Ottawa at Ottawa, and McMaster at the fringe of the University campus. (Ironically, McMaster was granted a charter by the Legislature at the same session at which the Federation Act was passed and promptly located itself beside the University of Toronto.) Furthermore, the Legislature did not, as had been assumed by the proponents of federation, provide the University of Toronto with additional funds to carry out its expanded role. It did make a special grant of $160,000 in 1890 for the restoration of the University's main building, which had been partially destroyed by fire, and in 1897, it began to make annual grants for the support of the University's science departments. It had also, in 1893, provided a grant in support of the Kingston School of Mines, a newly established non-denominational affiliate of Queen's, but discontinued this grant in 1912 when, Queen's having divested itself of its ties with the Presbyterian Church, the School of Mines became Queen's faculty of applied science.

The actual solution to the 19th century University Question was attained in 1906 with the passage of the University of Toronto Act of that year. This Act retained the federation and affiliation arrangements but removed the possibility of Government interference in the internal affairs of the University and provided the Provincial University with an assured and adequate income – namely, 50 percent of the Province's annual revenue from death duties, a source of income which could be expected to increase (or decrease) in rough proportion to the total income of the Province itself. The Act also provided for the absorption of the School of Practical Science as the University's faculty of applied science and engineering. However, the Ontario Agricultural College remained an affiliate and continued to be supported through the Department of Agriculture until 1964 when, in company with the Ontario Veterinary College (which was purchased by the Government from Andrew Smith in 1909 and placed under the same Department), it became the

"the Ontario Veterinary College"

University of Guelph. The R.C.D.S. and O.C.P. also continued as affiliates until their absorption as integrated University of Toronto faculties of dentistry and pharmacy respectively in 1925 and 1951.

But it was now the 20th century, and in practical and political terms, it was no longer possible for a single university, no matter how adequately funded or how ingeniously associated with other colleges, to meet the provincial needs for higher education. Within six years of the passage of the 1906 Act, two other universities were in receipt of annual grants: Queen's and Western Ontario (as it was renamed in 1924), both of which had become eligible by breaking their ties with their churches. These additional commitments, together with an economic recession and the fact that the University of Toronto's grant from death duties had doubled to $500,000 since 1906, led the Legislature to amend the Act so that the maximum amount receivable by the University of Toronto would be $500,000. This immediately proved to be inadequate for an institution which, since 1906, had doubled its enrolment, established three new faculties (of education, forestry, and household science), and markedly strengthened its faculties of medicine and engineering. Consequently, for the next 50 years, the University of Toronto had to seek each year a supplementary grant from the Legislature. This was always granted, but not in the amount that would have been received had the death duty formula been continued. Furthermore, because it could not securely predict its financial position, the University could no longer properly plan its future development.

The financial problems of Toronto – and also of Queen's and Western – were heightened during World War I by declining enrolments and, hence, reduced income from student fees. To resolve these problems, a royal commission on university finances was appointed in 1920 "to report upon a basis for determining the financial obligations of the Province towards the University of Toronto and the financial aid which the Province may give to Queen's and Western" and to recommend "a permanent plan of public aid to the said universities." The commissioners were impressed by the work at Queen's and Western; they recommended that both continue to receive annual operating grants and that they be given immediate capital grants in the amounts of $340,000 and $800,000 respectively for urgently needed buildings. These recommendations were accepted, enabling Western to establish itself on its present campus.

The commissioners' main concern, however, was that there be adequate support for the Provincial University, particularly so that it could develop and maintain "a strong centre of well-organized post-graduate work" – in contrast to Queen's and Western which they saw as primarily undergraduate institutions. They envisaged the need for "Higher Education in the Arts Departments" in other parts of the Province, and when that day came, they believed that "new Universities should not be established, but that colleges, located in convenient centres, should be linked up with existing Universities." But with post-graduate work, "especially on its scientific side, there must be practical centralization of effort," and this should be at the Provincial University. To enable the University of Toronto to carry out its provincial responsibilities, the commissioners recommended that the death duties formula be reinstituted. This was not done, and the University continued to go to the Government each year for a supplementary grant. Nonetheless, a school of graduate studies was established in 1922, and enrolment for the Ph.D., which had been offered since 1897, increased substantially. This development was accompanied, and to some extent explained, by a serious concern for research which began to evidence itself, particularly in the medical faculty, in the years immediately preceding the First World War. The movement was enormously stimulated by the discovery of insulin by Frederick Banting and Charles Best in 1921, attracting world-wide attention to the University of Toronto.

Following the federation of Trinity with the University

of Toronto in 1904, the number of independent universities in Ontario was reduced to five – Toronto, Queen's, Western, McMaster, and Ottawa – and this remained the number until 1946 when a non-denominational college in Ottawa, established during the Second World War for part-time students in the civil service, was accorded degree-granting powers as Carleton College. From the 1890s on, however, access to the first year of a B.A. course was available in many of the secondary schools of the Province by way of the senior matriculation year, which allowed the student to enter the second year of the four-year B.A. courses offered at the five universities. The availability of senior matriculation (Grade 13 as it was eventually called) in the high schools of many Ontario communities is one reason why Ontario did not follow the example of many American states in establishing two-year junior colleges offering the first two years of an arts course; in practical terms, Ontario already had a network of one-year junior colleges. It is also one of two reasons why Ontario failed to establish any institutes of technology or community colleges prior to the Second World War. The other reason was the development during the 1920s of vocationally oriented programs in the secondary schools; such programs were available to adults through evening classes, and they reduced the need for separate institutions to provide technical training.

In 1944-45, the five Ontario universities had an enrolment of about 13,000 students – a normal increase in relation to that of the population as a whole from the 9,000 students of 1920. Three-quarters of these were at the University of Toronto, a multiversity (to use a term which had not yet been coined) with a wide range of professional faculties (some as affiliates), a respectable graduate school offering the Ph.D. in most disciplines, and a strong liberal arts reputation based on its over 30 separate honours courses in which more than half of its B.A. students were enrolled. Queen's, with 1,600 students, concentrated on arts and science, public administration, engineering, and medicine.

Western, with 1,700 students (including a number at affiliated arts colleges in Waterloo and Windsor), concentrated on arts and science, business administration, and medicine. McMaster, which in 1930 had moved to Hamilton, had 650 students and Ottawa had 1,000 – in both cases confined to arts and theology. This – and the barely established Carleton College – was the institutional base when the Second World War ended and returning veterans began to enrol at Ontario universities.

They did so in very large numbers, enrolment increasing to over 20,000 in 1945-46 and to nearly 30,000 in 1947-48. In financial terms, this remarkable expansion was made possible through funds provided by the Federal Government; the provincial grants to Toronto, Queen's, and Western were not substantially increased, and Carleton was not added to the list of assisted universities until 1949. Some assistance was, however, provided to McMaster by way of an affiliate, Hamilton College (established in 1948 to teach science courses) and to Ottawa for support of a medical school which, with the encouragement of the Government, it had agreed to establish in 1947, the argument for support being that medicine was a non-denominational subject.

Most of the veterans had completed their courses by 1951, but enrolment did not revert to the prewar level; it remained at just over 20,000 from 1952 to 1955, after which it steadily rose. The explanation for this was not only the overall growth in the population of the Province, mainly from immigration, but also from an increase among high school students who were choosing to continue their education. By 1955, it had become apparent that when this rising percentage was projected forward to the number of children born in the post-war years and by this time enrolled in the elementary schools, the number of university places required in Ontario in the 1960s would be up to 100,000.

This projection proved accurate: by 1969 there were 92,000 full-time students in Ontario universities and 40,000 in part-time attendance. These were enrolled in the six

Royal Military College, Kingston, c. 1900

universities discussed previously and in ten new universities, all but two of which were supported by public funds authorized by the Legislature.

Only three of the new institutions were new foundations: York University at Toronto – founded in 1959 and functioning for its first four years as an affiliate of the University of Toronto; Brock University at St. Catharines – founded in 1964; and Trent University at Peterborough – also founded in 1964. Three of them were 19th century foundations: the University of Guelph – founded in 1964 and based on the Ontario Agricultural College and the Ontario Veterinary College; the University of Windsor – founded in 1964 out of Assumption College, which had been an affiliate of Western from 1919 to 1953 and been given degree-granting status as Assumption University in 1953; and the Royal Military College at Kingston – founded as a university in 1959 but established by the Federal Government in 1876 and maintained by it ever since. Waterloo College, established by the Lutherans in 1913, was an affiliate of Western from 1923 to 1956 and was the forerunner of both the University of Waterloo, founded in 1957, and Wilfrid Laurier University, founded in 1959. (Wilfrid Laurier retained its connection with the Lutheran church until 1973, since when it too has become a provincially supported university.) Laurentian University at Sudbury, founded in 1960, developed in part from a Roman Catholic college established in 1913 which, at one stage, was an affiliate of the University of Ottawa. Ontario's other two independent universities – Lakehead at Thunder Bay, founded in 1962, and Ryerson Polytechnic Institute at Toronto, founded in 1970 – were initially institutes of technology established by the Government in 1948.

During the 1950s, the expansion of the number of universities in Ontario from 6 to 12 and of the amount of the Government grants from $9 million to $36 million was achieved not in accordance with any master plan but through a series of independent steps taken by the Government after negotiation with individual institutions or with groups of individuals keen to establish a university in their community. From 1951 to 1956, the Government had a part-time consultant on university affairs (initially the retired principal of Queen's University, then the senior official in the Department of Education, then a cabinet minister). From 1956 to 1961, it had a committee of four senior civil servants who met each year to coordinate requests for funds from the various institutions; but the arrangement was neither statutory nor even widely known. It became both on 21 April 1961 when an Advisory Committee on University Affairs was named "to study all matters concerning the establishment, development, operation, expansion and financing of universities in Ontario and to make recommendations thereon for the information and advice of the Government."

One of the first actions of this Committee was to commission a study of projected university enrolment by Professor R.W.B. Jackson of the Ontario College of Education. The Jackson study indicated that enrolment would triple from the current figure to about 100,000 in 1970, and this led the Advisory Committee to summon to a meeting on 21 March 1962 the presidents of those universities receiving public assistance, who had never previously met together as a group. They were asked to examine the validity of the Jackson projections and, in the likely case that the projections were correct, to indicate the extent to which the existing institutions could provide the student places and what additional measures should be taken.

"... the expansion of the number of universities from 6 to 12. ..."

These tasks were delegated by the presidents to a committee of academics and administrators, whose report, produced in six weeks, did constitute something closely resembling a master plan for university development in Ontario. Its essential conclusions were that the numbers were valid and that the places could be provided by the expansion of the existing institutions and the establishment of four liberal arts colleges – two in Toronto and one each in the Niagara Peninsula and at Peterborough. As we have seen, the places were provided on schedule: Brock and Trent Universities at

Trent University at Peterborough — founded in 1964

St. Catharines and Peterborough respectively, as well as Scarborough and Erindale Colleges as liberal arts colleges of the University of Toronto. This report could also be described as a master plan for the development of post-secondary education in Ontario since it identified the need for community colleges throughout the Province and, along with many similar proposals over the next few years, led to the establishment of the colleges of applied arts and technology in 1965.

Implementation of the plan necessitated dramatic increases in the funds provided by the Legislature and, understandably, increased organization on the part of both Government and the universities as to how the funds should be deployed. The Committee of Presidents became an elaborate organization: by 1970, it had a full-time executive director and professional staff, a half-million dollar budget, an annual report, and over 20 subcommittees composed of academics and administrators in the member institutions; as spokesman for the university community, it was joined by other lobby groups – the Ontario Confederation of University Faculty Associations and the Ontario Federation of Students. On the Government side, the membership of what was now called the Committee on University Affairs was extended in 1965 to include some academics and its responsibilities were increased; in the same year, a Department of University Affairs under a cabinet minister was established to administer the grants and to carry out studies related to the operation and development of the emerging system.

That system, which had certainly emerged by 1970, has continued to operate essentially in the same form ever since. The Committee of Presidents was renamed the Council of Ontario Universities in 1971, the Committee on University Affairs was renamed the Ontario Council on University Affairs in 1974, and the Department of University Affairs became the Ministry of Colleges and Universities in 1971; but their functions and interactions, while rendered more complex by student numbers and increasing costs, have not fundamentally changed. Whether they should is one of the two basic questions that the newly formed Commission on the Future of the Universities of Ontario has been asked to examine.

In particular, the Commission has been directed "to develop an operational plan which without reducing the number of universities provides more clearly defined, different and distinctive roles for the universities of Ontario in order to maintain and enhance the quality of university education by ensuring the appropriate concentration of academic strengths in areas of intellectual and social

---

T he years from 1958 to 1967 were the final period of the old feudalistic university that was based upon certain rigid assumptions that went unquestioned. The first of these assumptions was that the universities were separate, self-contained entities that existed outside of the political process. They were wards of the prime minister's office, and not subject to any direct interference by government. The second assumption was that the university existed as both financial corporation and academic process, and that the two must be kept rigidly separate. The former was the responsibility of laymen who knew at first hand about the mysteries of finance, and the latter was the responsibility of the teaching staff; but ultimate power on any question must lie with the lay board. The third assumption was that students were not active participants in the running of the university; it was their happy lot to receive and to enjoy what had been decided for their benefit.

CLAUDE BISSELL
(FROM *HALFWAY UP PARNASSUS*,
© UNIVERSITY OF TORONTO PRESS 1974)

importance." This latter – the provision of academic strength in areas of importance to the Province's development – has always been the objective of Ontario's publicly supported universities. This was the case in the 19th century when what was considered of intellectual and social importance was essentially confined to undergraduate education in the liberal arts and in a small number of professions. It has remained the objective in the 20th century as the functions of Governor Simcoe's "college of a higher class" have been extended.

Throughout the 200 years, these functions have been defined by the universities themselves, whose autonomy with respect to admissions, the curriculum, and academic freedom have never been seriously questioned. They are being questioned now – not in the absolute sense (with respect to the collectivity of Ontario universities) but in terms of the individual institutions. The number of institutions is not to be reduced, but "more clearly defined, different and distinctive roles" are to be assigned to each. The key word here is *defined*. The current roles of Toronto and York, of Queen's and Wilfrid Laurier, of Guelph, Laurentian, and Ryerson are different and distinct. The Commission's second basic question is not what their functions should be but to what extent these functions should be pursued at particular institutions.

ROBIN S. HARRIS has been with the University of Toronto since 1952, initially as a member of the Department of English of University College and, since 1964, as professor of higher education, the first Canadian appointment in this field. The founder with Edward F. Sheffield of the Higher Education Group, he has been associated with OISE since 1969 on a cross-appointment basis. Prior to 1952, he taught at the University of Michigan, where he obtained his doctorate, and at the University of Western Ontario, which awarded him the degree of Doctor of Letters in 1982. He is the author of *The Undergraduate Essay* (with R. L. McDougall), *Quiet Evolution: A Study of the Ontario Educational System*, and *A History of Higher Education in Canada, 1663-1960*.

Universities abjure
Knowledge they regard impure,
So some people, without apology,
Enrol in colleges of applied arts and technology.

Unemployment has these days
Many openings for B.A.s.
Consequently it may be more prudent
To become a blue-collar post-secondary student.

THE GRADUAL EMERGENCE OF ONTARIO'S COMMUNITY COLLEGES

DELMAR McCORMACK SMYTH

The establishment of Ontario's system of colleges of applied arts and technology in the late 1960s was one of the most remarkable developments in the history of Canadian education. Twenty (and ultimately 22) separate colleges, each with its own board of governors, faculty, and staff, were brought into being within two years.

In their second year (1967-68), after the transfer to them of the responsibilities of existing technical institutes and vocational centres, the new colleges had nearly 14,000 full-time student members. In their fifth year (1970-71), full-time student membership had risen to over 50,000. For such rapid growth to occur and for it to be sustained, the ground had to have been well prepared.

Ontario's new colleges were not spontaneously generated. The ideas and arrangements they embodied evolved slowly over more than a century. The aim of the Government of Ontario in the organization of the new colleges – as explained by the Minister of Education, the Hon. William G. Davis on 21 May 1965 – was not to impose an alien institution on the existing system of education in Ontario. That system already included a number of post-secondary technical institutes and vocational centres. These formed the nucleus from which the new system of colleges grew.

Before the new community college system emerged in the late 1960s, technical education in Ontario went through several stages. In this essay, attention is directed to these stages and to some of those early developments (especially those related to technical education) which shaped, and continue to shape, the character and functioning of Ontario's colleges of applied arts and technology.

* * *

In 1784, when the Loyalists came to what is now southern Ontario, it was almost entirely wilderness. Decades of hard work with hand tools, axes, and saws were necessary to clear the land. Technical training was provided on the job. It was not until 1830, with the establishment in York (now Toronto) of Upper Canada's first Mechanics' Institute, that the first modest efforts began to be made for the education of working people.

During the political tensions in Upper Canada in the 1830s, the Toronto Mechanics' Institute was caught up in the controversy between the reformers and members of the "Family Compact," the ruling elite. After the abortive Rebellion of 1837, the membership of the Institute fell by almost 50 percent. From that time onward, a more conservative group gained control, and the Mechanics' Institute in Toronto, and in other communities throughout Upper Canada, provided educational and other services which were attractive to members of the middle class and not to the working men for whom the Institutes were originally created.

By the late 1850s, there were over 60 Mechanics' Institutes in Ontario; by 1895, there were over 300. They conducted lecture series on popular subjects related to new developments in the arts, sciences, and technology. They also offered evening classes for adults through which basic skills might be secured in reading, writing, and arithmetic. In addition, they provided library services which would not otherwise have been available.

In 1835, after earlier requests had been refused, the Legislature of Upper Canada granted £200 to the Toronto Mechanics' Institute and £100 to the Institute in Kingston. Until 1850 requests for government support were considered individually. On 30 August 1851, however, the Legislature passed "An Act to Provide for the Incorporation and Better Management of Library Associations and Mechanics' Institutes." The passage of that Act marked the beginning of more or less continuous grants by the Legislature to the Institutes.

". . . southern Ontario was almost entirely wilderness."

> Whereas the early leaders saw the (Mechanics') Institute as a way of liberating the working man from the bonds of ignorance, the new directors came to look upon it as the means whereby they might control him by moulding him into a hardworking, docile, and obedient citizen who would accept his subservient role as God-given and never think to question it.
>
> FOSTER VERNON
> (FROM HIS 1969 DOCTORAL THESIS, THE DEVELOPMENT OF ADULT EDUCATION IN ONTARIO 1790-1900)

Toronto Mechanics Institute Board of Management, 1882 and 1883

The prosperity of the Mechanics' Institutes stemmed, in part, from the support they received from prominent individuals. But despite such backing, the ability of the Institutes to make major contributions to the advancement of scientific and technical education was limited. The slow industrial development of Ontario in the early 19th century coupled with the well-entrenched academic tradition in Ontario education resulted in little widespread interest in technical studies. This lack of interest was reflected in a report prepared in 1881 by Dr. S. P. May, Superintendent of Mechanics' Institutes in the Provincial Department of Education, in which he criticized the limited educational activities of the Institutes. In 1886, the Association of Mechanics' Institutes in Ontario came to an end, but Institutes continued in many places in the Province until 1895 when they were converted by Provincial Government action into free public libraries.

* * *

The Great Exhibition held in Hyde Park, London, England, in 1851 and the Paris Exhibition of 1867 stimulated widespread interest in the advancement of scientific and technical education throughout the Western world. These exhibitions were the 19th century counterparts of the launching of "Sputnik" in 1957 which made political and scientific leaders in the West dramatically aware of the need to improve their systems of scientific education.

When he delivered the Speech from the Throne at the opening of the Legislature of Ontario on 7 December 1870, Lieutenant-Governor Howland said that while it was the Government's intention:

> to render Common School Education accessible and free to every Child . . . and to provide more effectually for giving a higher English and Commercial Education in the Superior Schools, . . . (special) attention will be invited to . . . making that Education more practical, and directly instrumental in promoting the interest of Agriculture and Manufacturers.

That statement was the first formal indication that the Government of Ontario had decided on a new initiative for the advancement of technical education. On 12 January 1871, the Ontario Government commissioned Dr. J. George Hodgins, a Deputy Superintendent of Education for Ontario, and Dr. Alexander T. Machattie, a medical doctor, to visit the United States and to report on the buildings, departments of study, and equipment of the technical or science schools or colleges they visited.

On the basis of their study, the Commissioners strongly recommended that a School of Technology be established and that it be kept entirely distinct from any other institution. The Government of Ontario acted on this recommendation and included in the estimates for 1871 an item of 50,000 dollars for a "College of Technology or School of Industrial Science." Speaking in support of this proposal, the Hon. John Sandfield Macdonald, Premier and Attorney General, put forward arguments that echoed observations made 22 years earlier by Egerton Ryerson in an address to the Toronto Mechanics' Institute. The Premier emphasized that lack of adequate facilities for technological training had been most costly to the inhabitants of the Province.

While Edward Blake, Leader of the Liberal Opposition, agreed that increased attention should be devoted to the study of subjects outlined by the Commission, he argued that it would be extravagant to duplicate the work of the University of Toronto which was already offering the subjects which the Commission had recommended (see Footnote). But despite his objections, the Government was convinced that the School of Technology should be established as a separate institution, and arrangements were made to purchase the

---

Footnote: Ontario's first non-degree diploma in a technical field (civil engineering) was offered by Toronto's University College in the late 1850s. None of the College faculty was qualified to give such instruction, and therefore students were forced to rely on prescribed texts and any instruction that they could find outside. In the 26 years this diploma was offered, only seven students received it.

building of the Toronto Mechanics' Institute for the new school. On 18 December 1871, however, the Conservative Government of Ontario was defeated, and the following day Liberal Leader Edward Blake was invited to form a ministry. Since the building had been purchased and equipped in anticipation of the opening of the new School, the new Government proceeded in a limited manner with the plans for the School by starting evening classes.

By the end of 1872, the Government decided that the School of Technology should continue but under a new name. On 21 January 1873, "an Act to Establish a School of Practical Science" (S.P.S.) was introduced in the Ontario Legislature and received final assent on 29 March of that year. The Act provided that S.P.S., the successor of the School of Technology, would be completely under the control of the Government and would offer instruction in mining, engineering, and the mechanical and manufacturing arts. Provision was made for the School and the University of Toronto to reach an agreement regarding the sharing of library and other facilities. A basis was also established for the affiliation of the School with the University.

On 30 January 1877, a proposal was made to the Ontario Cabinet that S.P.S. should have four specific functions: the encouragement of more practical study of the physical sciences; professional training for such persons as desired to become engineers (civil, mining, or mechanical) after a regular course of instruction; the improvement of the knowledge of artisans by means of evening classes; and the diffusion of physical and scientific information through popular lectures.

In supporting these general purposes, the Minister of Education, Adam Crooks, claimed there was insufficient demand in Ontario to justify the establishment of a distinct and separate professional school for engineers. Finally, on 22 February 1877, the Government's proposals for the development of S.P.S. as a professional institution were approved by the Ontario Legislature.

In 1889, the University Federation Act came into force, and the School of Practical Science was formally affiliated to the University of Toronto. A fourth year was added to the existing three-year diploma program, and in 1898, the Senate of the University of Toronto passed a statute establishing the degree of Bachelor of Applied Science, open to students of the School who successfully completed the four-year course. With the passage of the University of Toronto Act of 1906, S.P.S. was officially incorporated into the University of Toronto as the Faculty of Applied Science.

The idea that S.P.S. should become affiliated with the University of Toronto had been steadfastly opposed by at least one person. W. R. Meredith, Member of the Ontario Legislature for London, and later Chief Justice of Ontario and Chancellor of the University of Toronto, argued in 1877 that it would be unjust and absurd to expect young men to come all the way from London to Toronto to be educated in the School of Practical Science. Meredith's view was that primary emphasis should have been placed on evening classes for working men and that classes should be started in London and elsewhere.

If the arguments Meredith made had been accepted and acted upon, the Mechanics' Institutes throughout Ontario might have been revitalized and provided the bases for the much earlier emergence of a system of community colleges. That did not occur for at least one very good reason. Before a comprehensive system of post-secondary technical education could be considered realistically, such education had to be well established at the secondary level.

A first step in that direction was taken in 1871 when an "Act to Improve the Common and Grammar Schools of Ontario" was introduced in and subsequently approved by the Ontario Legislature. There were two reasons for this Act. The first was to make a clear division between the Common Schools and the Grammar Schools: henceforth the Common Schools were to be called Public Schools and were to be responsible for elementary education; the Grammar Schools were to be known as High Schools. The second reason for the Act was to provide:

> in one institution a programme of studies to prepare for admission to a university or to a learned profession the relatively small number in the age groups who at any given time are likely to benefit from such a programme and, as well, programmes of study which are designed to provide a sound general education, with some vocational elements for the much larger number of students for whom a university-type course is inappropriate.

The solution proposed in the 1871 Act involved the creation of two types of secondary school. These were the High Schools, which would concentrate upon general education, and the Collegiate Institutes, which would concentrate upon university preparation.

These changes in the organization of secondary school programs in the early 1870s did not stimulate immediate interest in technical education at the secondary level. A few new subjects of value to those students not planning to go on to university were added, however, to the Ontario secondary school course of study in the 1880s and the 1890s. Among these were certain commercial and science subjects that some parents believed might place their children "in a better position to earn a livelihood." Similar language was used later when the reorganized secondary school program, or "Robarts Plan," was introduced in the early 1960s. When Ontario's colleges of applied arts and technology emerged in the late 1960s, they were likewise regarded as centres in which students would prepare for employment.

By 1882, interest in business studies was rising. That year about half the students in the lower grades of Ontario's high schools studied bookkeeping as one of their subjects. Later, in 1896, a two-year commercial course, which led to a terminal diploma rather than university matriculation, was introduced. The primary commitment in the Ontario secondary schools, however, continued to be traditional academic studies leading either to university or to traditional professional careers.

Given the continuing loyalty to historic academic traditions in Ontario secondary schools, it is not surprising that technical education, at the secondary school level, received its major impetus initially through the efforts of a group of businessmen and labor leaders in Toronto.

* * *

In 1891, the Council of the City of Toronto approved a report which recommended that technical courses be offered for artisans under the direction of a board of technical education. This board, which was separate from the Public School Board and the High School Board, established Toronto's first technical school.

The Toronto Technical School opened on 7 December 1891 as an adjunct to, not an integral part of, the Toronto or Ontario school systems. It pioneered the development of technical education in a remarkable way. Classes were offered in the evenings. There were no day classes. The Toronto City Council made annual grants of from $8,000 to $10,000. There were no provincial grants.

During its first year, student enrolment stood at 299. When William Packenham became Principal in 1902, there were about 1,800 students, and the School was brought under the Toronto Board of Education, which assumed responsibility for all of Toronto's publicly supported elementary and secondary schools.

The Toronto Technical School demonstrated, during its decade of operation outside the public system, what could be accomplished when local labor leaders, businessmen, and public officials decided to co-operate in the field of education. Through their co-operation, technical education and manual training gradually became accepted as integral aspects of the public education system in Ontario.

After the assumption of responsibility for the Toronto Technical School by the Toronto Board of Education, and its redesignation as the Toronto Technical High School, counterparts to that school were soon created in other centres throughout Ontario. In 1909, John Seath was appointed to undertake a comprehensive study and to prepare a plan for the development and establishment of a system of technical education in Ontario. Dr. Seath's report, *Education for Industrial Purposes*, led to the introduction of the Industrial Education Act of 1911.

The Industrial Education Act authorized educational authorities throughout Ontario to establish, with the approval of the Minister of Education, six distinctive types of school: General Industrial Schools offering basic education for the trades and similar manual occupations not classified as trades; Special Industrial Schools offering instruction in the theoretical and practical aspects of particular trades, and when desirable, in the essential subjects of a good general education; Technical High Schools and Technical Departments in existing high schools; Co-operative Industrial Classes as agreed upon by Board of Education and employers for (a) apprentices employed in workshops who might receive trades training in day schools and (b) pupils in day schools who might receive practical instruction in workshops; Schools for Instruction in the Fine and Applied Arts; and Industrial Technical and Arts Schools in which people employed during the day might receive instruction in their trades during the evenings.

This Act resulted in more advances being made in the establishment of industrial and technical education programs at the secondary level in Ontario than had been made in all the preceding years. By the time Dr. F. W. Merchant assumed his responsibilities as Ontario's first Director of Industrial Technical Education, in September 1914, the work of the General Industrial Schools in Brantford, Hamilton, London, and Toronto and in the Technical High Schools in Haileybury, Hamilton, Sault Ste Marie, Sudbury, and

"Special Industrial Schools offering instruction in the theoretical and practical aspects of particular trades. . . ."

Toronto had already begun to expand. It was hoped that the Government of Canada would provide a major portion of the funds for the expansion of industrial and technical education. This did not occur until after the First World War.

Mackenzie King, who had served prior to the election of 1911 in Prime Minister Laurier's Cabinet as Minister of Labour, had noted that all over the world there was a growing struggle for industrial supremacy. In this struggle, King argued that the slightest difference in processes or technical devices and advantage in knowledge or adaptability might have far-reaching effects. As far as individuals were concerned, he said:

Society does owe something to the great body of working people who are obliged to begin their working lives early, to toil before their education is completed; we owe something to them in the way of conferring upon each an opportunity, at least, to realize capacities of which his nature may be capable.

The Report of the Royal Commission on Industrial Training and Technical Education was published in 1913. In their Report, the Commissioners noted the backward state of technical education in Canada, and urged Dodminion-Provincial co-operation to improve it. The Report listed types of programs which would be implemented. Since he had been the Minister responsible when the Royal Commission was appointed, Mackenzie King had an understandable interest in action taken on the Report.

Sixteen technical and commercial high schools, with nearly 7,000 full-time students, were operating throughout Ontario by 1919. Instruction was being provided in a variety of trades and occupations. In 1920 the Technical Education Act came into force. Funds made available through this Act made possible the rapid expansion of facilities for technical education in Ontario and the other provinces of Canada. The Act provided financial assistance not only for secondary technical schools but also for special agricultural schools which had been developed in Ontario as well as for mining schools at Haileybury and Sudbury and navigation schools at Kingston, Midland, and Collingwood. Although the Federal subsidy was withdrawn in 1928, the beginnings of a good foundation had been established for technical education at the secondary level. In 1928 there were 42 day vocational schools with an enrolment of 21,604 students. A decade later there were 62 vocational schools with 36,481 students (see Footnote).

* * *

During the Second World War, the Canadian Parliament approved the Dominion-Provincial Vocational Training Co-ordination Act in which provision was made for the financing of technical education in the provinces on a shared basis with the Federal Government. The passing of this legislation facilitated the development of new technical education programs which were to be established in Ontario following the end of the War.

As Allied Forces fought their way across the Rhine in Germany in March 1945, the Government of Ontario appointed a group of distinguished citizens "to enquire into and report upon the Provincial educational system." In their report, members of the Commission recommended that a new structure of public education be established in Ontario involving six years of elementary education, four years of secondary education, and three years of publicly supported junior college education.

While many of the recommendations of the Royal Commission were gradually implemented, none of the recommendations which would have involved fundamental alteration of the basic structure of public education in Ontario (such as the proposed creation of junior colleges) was adopted.

* * *

More than two decades before the Royal Commission reported in 1950, a special program of technical studies, related to the mining industry, had been developed in the

---

Footnote: While these advances were being made in the establishment of technical and vocational education at the secondary level, valuable steps had been taken to provide educational opportunities for those employed in the primary industries. Thus, in 1899, Frontier College was established – with its headquarters in Toronto and with the aim of ensuring that education would be provided "not only in schools and universities, but in the shops, in the works, in the camps and fields and settlements of the frontier." The work of the College involved studies at both pre-university and university levels, and from 1922 to 1932 it enjoyed degree-granting status. The College still functions to this day.

Established in 1899, Frontier College continues to bring education to workers in remote areas

Haileybury High School. Prior to the end of the Second World War, this program was established on a more permanent basis and organized as the Provincial Institute of Mining.

This was the first of a series of institutes which emerged at that time. In 1946, a Provincial Institute of Textiles was organized in Hamilton. The same year, Lakehead Technical Institute at Port Arthur was established by an Order-in-Council of the Ontario Government, and two years later Ryerson Institute of Technology was established in Toronto.

Ryerson Institute, which was opened officially on 22 September 1948, was described in the Report of the Ontario

Minister of Education of Ontario in 1949 as "a Polytechnical type of institution offering instruction on the Junior College level." At that time, there was continuing need to provide specialized training for veterans preparing to return to civilian employment. Therefore, in contradiction to some suggestions that Ryerson should endeavor to become the "M.I.T." of Canada, the Institute's curriculum emphasized practical rather than theoretical studies and did not develop comprehensive arrangements whereby its graduates might proceed to universities to complete more advanced studies.

Rapid growth in enrolment compared to other institutions established in the post-war period contributed to the central role Ryerson was to play in later years. The Institute began to flourish for two major reasons: first, it was established in the centre of Toronto, a large city with an expanding demand for technically trained people of the type graduating from Ryerson; and second, the Principal of Ryerson, Howard H. Kerr, was determined that his Institute should develop as a pioneering centre of technological education in Ontario.

After enrolment in Ryerson began to burgeon, it was decided to establish a separate institute to handle apprenticeship and artisan training. In 1952, the Provincial Institute of Trades was established with responsibilities in these areas. From that time, the emphasis at Ryerson was on the offering of programs for engineering technologists and technicians and of programs of equivalent level for various types of business and service functions.

Along the Queen Elizabeth Way, the Provincial Institute of Textiles in Hamilton became, in 1956, the Hamilton Institute of Technology. Originally, the Provincial Institute of Textiles had been established as a result of representations made by textile manufacturers in the Hamilton area. Enrolment in the special textile programs increased from 14 students in 1947/48 to a high of 42 students in 1951/52. Thereafter, there was a decline until 1955/56 when only 21 students enrolled. At this point, the decision was taken in the Ontario Department of Education to broaden the base of the Hamilton institution.

When the Hamilton Institute of Technology was established, the immediate task was to expand the offerings in technology and other vocational fields. Courses were inaugurated in electrical, electronic, and mechanical technologies, identical to those offered at Ryerson. At that time, students from many Ontario centres were seeking admission to Ryerson, which was unable to accommodate all who wished to enrol.

Fifty-five years before the establishment of the Lakehead Technical Institute in Port Arthur in 1946, the Ontario Legislature had passed an Act in which provision was made for mining schools in several Ontario centres. A grant was set up for such a school in Port Arthur. It was not until 1948, however, that the first post-secondary program in mining technology was offered through the Lakehead Institute. Programs in Forestry, Arts, and Applied Science, at levels equivalent to first year of recognized university programs, were also introduced.

During the session 1950/51, steps were taken to expand the work at the Lakehead Institute with the addition of university transfer courses and the development of research interests. In 1956, the Ontario Legislature passed an Act transforming Lakehead Technical Institute into the Lakehead College of Arts, Science and Technology, and in 1965, Lakehead College became Lakehead University.

The academic development at Lakehead was unique among the new institutes. None of the others offered university transfer courses as such; nor did they place emphasis on relationships with universities to the extent that they were developed by Lakehead.

By 1962, there were five Ontario Institutes of Technology: Ryerson, Hamilton Institute, the Eastern Ontario Institute, the Western Ontario Institute, and the Northern Ontario Institute of Technology (established that year in Kirkland Lake). Their curricula for business and industrial occupations were largely identical. They also offered evening courses for employed persons who wished to continue their education. It was sometimes necessary for students from the other institutes to transfer to Ryerson to complete the second or third years of certain courses.

Continuing growth in enrolment at the Provincial Institute of Trades in Toronto led to a decision that it should be divided into three units: the Provincial Institute of Trades, the Provincial Institute of Automotive and Allied Trades, and the Provincial Institute of Trades and Occupations. These three Institutes, which came into being in 1962, were all located in Toronto.

Plans were also made for the opening in 1964 of institutes of trade in Ottawa and London. They were called "Ontario Vocational Centres." This new name was selected to provide a better indication of the scope of the vocational courses they offered. Along with the three Institutes of Trades in Toronto, the new Vocational Centres offered technical courses for apprentices in certified trades; pre-employment courses in non-certified trades and trades approved for vocational training under the Dominion-Provincial Training Agreement; two-year engineering-technical courses for secondary-school graduates; and post-secondary business and commercial courses.

In 1965, a third Vocational Centre was opened in Sault Ste Marie, and a year later another was opened in Hamilton. The Hamilton Vocational Centre was on the same site as the Hamilton Institute of Technology – physically joined to the Institute and administered by the same senior officers.

After the Government of Ontario announced its plans for colleges of applied arts and technology in May 1965, a Board of Governors was appointed to develop a college for Hamilton and nearby counties. This Board was given responsibility for the Hamilton Institute of Technology and for the planning of the new Vocational Centre. The combined enterprise was given the name Mohawk College of Applied Arts and Technology.

Following the Second World War, officers of some industrial organizations – first in St. Catharines and later in Peterborough – discussed with school boards in their areas possibilities for employed persons to complete advanced technical studies on part-time bases, to a level equivalent to Ontario Grade 13. They requested their school boards to establish advanced technical courses at matriculation levels for people who wanted something other than regular academic courses at the Grade 13 level or those offered through University Extension programs.

Through action of the Department of Education, Advanced Technical Evening Classes (A.T.E.C.) were established on a provincial basis. Arrangements were made whereby individuals completing nine subjects through such classes would be granted certificates issued by the Minister of Education. Such certificates gradually became recognized for academic and professional purposes.

The program of Advanced Technical Evening Classes came into operation formally in 1952. By 1965, the A.T.E.C. program was in operation at four Institutes of Technology, two Ontario Vocational Centres, the Provincial Institutes of Trades, and at 24 secondary schools across the Province. Enrolment of adult students in September 1965 exceeded 5,000. Courses were being offered in more than 55 different technological subjects.

Interest in the A.T.E.C. program had quickened after new professional certification arrangements, first proposed in the late fall of 1956, were approved in 1957 by the Association of Professional Engineers of Ontario (A.P.E.O.). A committee of the A.P.E.O., after considering various alternatives, had proposed that there should be two levels of technician in addition to a single category for technologists. The most senior category was that of "Engineering Technologist." To qualify for this, a candidate had to complete successfully three years of technical education beyond high school graduation and two years of acceptable experience in industry. Next to the "Engineering

Technologist" in seniority was the "Senior Engineering Technician," requiring completion of at least two years of satisfactory experience in industry. The third designation was "Engineering Technician," which required successful completion of one year of technical education beyond high school graduation and two years of practical experience in industry. A.P.E.O. set up a Certification Board to establish and monitor the basis on which certificates were granted to Engineering Technicians and Technologists.

Gradually these certification arrangements gained widespread support. Just as university graduates in engineering usually feel it is desirable to become registered as Professional Engineers, so increasing numbers of technicians and technologists began to request status as Certified Engineering Technicians or Technologists. During the first decade, approximately 500 individuals applied for such certification each year.

The certification program gained support since it was recognized by industry, Government, and educational institutions. Officers of institutes of technology (and later, colleges of applied arts and technology) recognized the value of their curricula being accredited by a professional body.

As these new arrangements were being completed and implemented for the education and certification of technicians and technologists, new bases were being established for the finance of technical and vocational training by the Government of Canada. After the passing of the Technical and Vocational Training Assistance Act by the Federal Parliament in December 1960, agreements were reached with the Canadian provinces whereby the Federal Government shared in the financial cost of providing adequate facilities for vocational training. The general purpose of the legislation was to provide the assistance required by the provinces to train personnel for industry, to reduce the number of unemployed, and to ensure that the employment potential of Canadians was developed efficiently.

The Federal/Provincial agreements in vocational education resulted in the establishment of a variety of programs. These programs did not include university-level studies but they did include technical and vocational high school training, technical training, trade and other occupational training, training in co-operation with industry, training of the unemployed and the physically and mentally disabled, training of technical and vocational teachers, training for federal departments and agencies, and student aid and research.

Certain provisions were also made for capital expenditures, for the support of apprenticeship training programs, and for the building and equipping of vocational centres. The Government of Canada agreed when the Technical and Vocational Training Act was passed to provide over a six year period between 50 and 100 percent of the provincial operating costs for vocational education at the various levels, excluding vocational high schools. Federal grants for these purposes made possible the major expansion of technical and vocational training facilities in Ontario and the other provinces during the years 1961 to 1967.

The introduction in 1962 of the "Robarts Plan" into Ontario secondary schools was based on the need to encourage non-academically-oriented students to continue in the formal educational system. The objective of the Plan was to provide courses which would be attractive and challenging to students who would not otherwise continue in secondary school. The "Robarts Plan" involved three major streams – Science, Technology and Trades; Business and Commerce; and Arts and Science – each including four- and five-year programs. The four-year programs were for students planning to proceed to institutes of technology or vocational centres, to enter apprenticeships, or to seek immediate employment. For students who encountered difficulty in the four- or five-year programs, special one- and two-year programs would be offered in various occupational subjects. Students might move from one type of program to another.

The general aim of the "Robarts Plan" was to increase

the prestige of non-academic educational programs. It was hoped that improved public regard for such programs would moderate the traditional over-emphasis in Ontario on academic programs at the secondary level and the resultant university aspirations, which operated to the detriment of non-university programs.

While the Select Committee on Manpower Training was in general agreement with the changes resulting from the introduction of the "Robarts Plan," members of the Committee did have certain reservations. They were concerned about the "stigma" which continued to adversely affect vocational education in Ontario. In various communities, the negative attitude towards technical education resulted in its being used "as a form of dumping ground for poor students, discipline problems and others unwanted by academic teachers." The Committee was anxious for the Government to take appropriate steps to foster the successful operation of the new system and the development of appropriate status and prestige of the non-academic streams.

To the degree that the "Robarts Plan" was successful in occupying non-academic students through a full program of four years, it increased the demand for post-secondary education of an occupationally-oriented kind – because enrolment of students in four-year non-academic programs disqualified them for admission to university studies without preparing them fully for employment.

From this point of view, the implementation of the "Robarts Plan" was in essence a promise to provide for the expansion of the institutes of technology and vocational centres or the establishment of new colleges in time to meet the needs of the first graduates of the four-year stream. That the Government of Ontario intended to honor that promise was clear when legislation for the Ontario colleges of applied arts and technology was introduced in the Ontario Legislature.

On 21 May 1965, the Minister of Education, the Hon. William G. Davis, outlined to the Ontario Legislature the policies the Government proposed for the establishment and operation of a system of colleges of applied arts and technology. In introducing the legislation, the Minister reviewed the general social and economic background against which the proposed Act had been developed, and stated that what the Government had in mind was not "the imposition of an imported or alien institution on our education system." The Government, he emphasized, was not planning to import and implant unchanged in Ontario the system of junior colleges or community colleges that had developed in the United States, although the new type of colleges being established in Ontario would resemble some of their United States counterparts in many respects. The Minister made it clear that the Government had "deliberately sought to learn from others and to select the features which strengthened our own proposals."

The Government had in mind composite or comprehensive institutions, preferably with several buildings on the same campus, providing a wide variety of programs of varying lengths, "including work-experience programs, by day and in the evening, for adults as well as for youth, and for probably more part-time than full-time students." The new colleges would be "occupation-oriented" and would be "commuter" colleges. Housing accommodation for students would not be provided except possibly in some areas of northern Ontario.

Each college would have three major responsibilities: to provide courses of types and levels beyond, or not suited to, the secondary school setting; to meet the needs of graduates from any secondary school program, apart from those wishing to attend university; and to meet the educational needs of adults and out-of-school youth, whether or not they were secondary school graduates.

The Minister anticipated that the range of courses offered, in most if not all of the colleges, would include the following:

- Engineering technicians' and technologists' programs below the university level.
- Semi-professional non-engineering type programs (e.g., in the para-medical field).
- High level programs in office and distributive occupations, specifically of junior and middle management level and including courses for small business.
- Agricultural and agricultural-related programs, at least in rural areas, in co-operation with the Department of Agriculture.
- General adult education programs, including cultural and leisure time activities.
- Programs of recreation, including physical education.
- General or liberal education courses, including remedial courses in basic subjects, and often incorporated as part of the other programs (e.g., English, Mathematics, Science).
- Retraining, upgrading, and updating courses.
- Trade skills, pre-apprenticeship, and apprenticeship training.
- Service industry courses, (e.g., for tourist industry).
- Commercial courses (e.g., cost accounting, junior accounting, data processing, computer programming).
- Other courses to meet local needs.

The general or liberal education courses and the general adult education programs to be offered by the new colleges were not thought of as university level courses. "Nevertheless," the Minister emphasized, "no able and qualified student should be prevented from going on from a college of applied arts and technology to a university." Indeed, he said, such a pattern existed for able graduates of the institutes of technology. On the subject of transfers to universities, he stated:

> The university doors should always be open to capable and ambitious young men and women. We will set up a committee of representatives of my Department and of the universities to determine . . . the conditions and procedures under which universities may grant admission to outstanding students who have completed successfully an appropriate program at one of our colleges of applied arts and technology and who have demonstrated that they are prepared to undertake university work.

The new institutions were to be financed by the Province without local taxation. "For the present at least," said the Minister, the colleges would commence operations under the Department of Education, even though they would be post-secondary institutions. He indicated that the Technological and Trades Training Branch of the Department of Education might be re-constituted and expanded to fulfill the necessary functions of overseeing and helping to co-ordinate the work of the new colleges.

The Act approved by the Ontario Legislature for the establishment of the new colleges stated unequivocally that "Subject to the approval of the Lieutenant Governor in Council (The Cabinet), the Minister may establish, name, maintain, conduct and govern colleges of applied arts and technology." Thus the Ontario Minister of Education, assuming he had the approval of his Cabinet colleagues, was completely in control of the new system of colleges. Whether or not they emerged as creative centres for human and social development would be dependent initially on the action he took on the responsibilities and opportunities which had been entrusted to him.

* * *

In February 1966, the thirteen men and one woman, appointed by the Minister of Education to the Ontario Council of Regents for Colleges of Applied Arts and Technology to assist him "in the planning, establishment, and co-ordination of programs of instruction and services for such colleges," met for their first formal session. Considerable preparatory work for that meeting had been completed by the Technological and Trades Training Branch (later renamed the Applied Arts and Technology Branch) of the Department of Education. That branch served as the administrative arm of the Minister for the new colleges.

The statement made to the Ontario Legislature by the Minister of Education on 21 May 1965 clearly indicated that the colleges would not be modelled on the unitary pattern of American community colleges, with their university transfer arrangements. Rather, the Ontario Government (unconsciously it seems) had chosen to develop its system on the binary model of Great Britain, with its universities and colleges of advanced technology on the one hand and its colleges of technology and arts and regional colleges on the other.

What precise form the new colleges would take and where they would be located was a matter of great interest, especially for the original members of the Council of Regents. I was one of those original members, and I recall that a colleague on the Council made it clear that he wanted to return home with one of the new colleges "in his pocket." That statement indicated clearly that the creation of the new colleges would be devoid neither of human interest nor of the political dimension.

At its meetings in early February 1966, the Council of Regents recommended to the Minister that the ten regions of Ontario which had been used as the bases for economic planning be used also for the development of plans for the new colleges. It was recognized that, in each region, there might be one or more colleges. The Council also recommended that all the existing post-secondary technical institutes and vocational centres operated by the Technological and Trades Training Branch be integrated and reorganized into colleges of applied arts and technology and that a board of governors be appointed to operate each college. These recommendations were approved by the Minister and implemented.

In 1966, Boards of Governors were appointed for two colleges, and on their respective recommendations, the colleges were named Centennial (Scarborough) and Lambton (Sarnia). The following year, Boards were appointed for colleges which, on their recommendations, were named Algonquin (Ottawa), George Brown (Toronto), Cambrian (Sudbury), Confederation (Thunder Bay), Durham (Oshawa), Fanshawe (London), Georgian (Barrie), Humber (Etobicoke and York), Loyalist (Belleville), Mohawk (Hamilton), Niagara (Welland), Northern (Haileybury, Kirkland Lake, and Timmins), Seneca (North York), Sheridan (Peel and Halton Counties), Sir Sandford Fleming (Peterborough), St. Clair (Windsor), and St. Lawrence (Kingston, Brockville, and Cornwall). In 1968, a Board of Governors was appointed for a college in the Kitchener area which was named Conestoga. Later, Canadore College (North Bay) and Sault College (Sault Ste Marie) were established.

These new colleges emerged in the midst of an unprecedented demand for post-secondary education in Ontario occasioned by "the baby boom" and the pervasive technological and social changes which followed the Second World War. The success of the colleges, in terms of the measure of public funding they have enjoyed and the numbers of students who have registered, is reflected graphically in the following table.

Confederation College, Thunder Bay — founded in 1967

Year	Full-time Student Enrolment	Operating funds
1967-68	13,969	$ 19.5 million
1970-71	53,372	68.9 million
1980-81	100,638	312.8 million
1983-84	117,984	433. million

If the colleges had had the facilities and staff, the levels of enrolment could have been appreciably higher. In the early years of the work of the Council of Regents, however, we were determined to ensure that there would not be a surplus of community college graduates. The Government of Ontario had decided that a primary role of the new colleges would be to offer courses which would prepare people directly for employment. If the colleges failed to do this, if there were substantial numbers of unemployed graduates of the colleges, their credibility would have been threatened. This had to be avoided.

When officers of the colleges presented proposals for their educational programs and course offerings to the Council of Regents, they were required to submit data concerning employment prospects for graduates of such programs. By taking such precautions, we were able to avoid unnecessary duplication of programs and courses and to help graduates of the colleges, in the midst of high levels of unemployed youth, to become almost as successful as university graduates in gaining employment in fields related to their training.

The record of rapid development of the colleges and the success their graduates have enjoyed in finding employment are highly gratifying to those who contributed to their establishment and early development. But the world in which the new colleges now find themselves is not nearly as sunny as the one in which they emerged. There are clouds in the sky. Some are exceedingly dark. No account, however brief, of how these new centres for learning emerged would be complete without a fleeting glance at what lies ahead.

The future of the new colleges is clouded to some degree by the prevailing philosophy which, in overall terms, governs college and university affairs in Ontario. The systems of post-secondary education are based on a separatist, rather than an integrationist, philosophy of higher education. Universities in Ontario are separate from the new colleges. Ryerson Polytechnical Institute lies in between but is organically separate from both these systems. The regional

---

It was my first day at college, all alone in a new city. It seemed as though I was the only person who was alone; everyone else had friends that they could turn to. But there I was, Kim Gelineau, a girl who never before had done anything without someone by her side to guide and reassure her.

But college, I discovered, is definitely the place to find all that you are looking for. The instructors treat you as adults, and they let you make your own decisions. You are free to come and go as you please, and the new friends that you meet are fantastic.

It is now only February; the second semester isn't half over, and I feel that if I had to go anywhere to do anything on my own that I couldn't have done before, I most certainly could do it now.

Going to college was the best decision that I ever made. It gave me confidence I never knew that I had, and I will have an excellent education when I'm through.

KIM GELINEAU,
STUDENT AT CANADORE COLLEGE OF APPLIED ARTS & TECHNOLOGY

agricultural colleges function under the Ontario Ministry of Agriculture and are not related directly to either the college system or that of the universities.

There were reasons for this when the community colleges came into being – the abundance of money, the lack of qualified faculty members, and the lack of library resources – but times and circumstances have changed. The abundance of money was more apparent than real (as we became painfully aware), and now there are many young teachers well qualified to offer degree-level courses in the colleges. The time has therefore come to examine in depth the strengths and weaknesses of the prevailing separateness of Ontario's universities and community colleges. Thoughtful, decisive action must be taken on the basis of such an examination.

Just as the articulation between the community college and the university systems must be improved (in the interests of students who wish to transfer from one system to another and of the taxpayers of Ontario who foot a large part of the bill), so the relationship between vocational education at the secondary level and that provided in the new colleges must also be examined. The preoccupation of the Ontario Government during recent decades with vocational education in the new colleges while it has languished at the secondary level may be a significant, though rarely discussed, source of Ontario's economic problems.

The dark cloud in the sky for the colleges has been generated by the changing status of work. During the last 200 years in the industrialized world, society has been organized in highly significant ways around work. Training for work became increasingly important. Ontario's community colleges emerged to provide such training. But the colleges came into being just as the industrial work-oriented society began to disintegrate. In the increasingly "workless" world of the late 20th century, many traditional work systems are handled by machines and not by human beings. There is a growing need, therefore, to train young people in the

---

In today's complex and pressure-ridden society, to fulfill its role an educational institution must base its philosophic aims on the innate, but paramount needs of the individual. To enjoy happy and productive lives people must be accepted for the kind of human beings they are as well as for what they are capable of doing.

The students' program of studies at Seneca College must consequently be designed to help them learn more about themselves, their fellows and their environment, as well as to prepare them to earn a living. This establishes the responsibility of the College — in order of priority, to each individual student first, and then to the community of which that student is a part.

A community college must offer programs of relevance, programs which are close to life and living, programs based on realism and practicality in concert with those which reflect the human need for the cultural, the aesthetic, the beautiful. Accordingly, not only does Seneca College stress through its offerings broad and varied programs and subjects in the technical and vocational areas, it also offers through its English and Communications, Liberal Studies and Visual Arts, subjects designed to prepare its students for the full, rich enjoyment of their post-college lives. They are designed to equip the student to think critically, to write effectively and to understand the Canadian milieu in the last quarter of the twentieth century.

(FROM A STATEMENT ABOUT GENERAL STUDIES
AT SENECA COLLEGE, 1978)

analysis, development, refinement, and thoughtful application of information in the many new forms which such machines need and which millions of human beings in the new world of leisure, both enforced and voluntary, will also urgently require.

If Ontario's new colleges are able to provide the essential forms of education for this new world of information and leisure, they will merit continuing high levels of support both from students and from the taxpayers of Ontario. The extent of this support will depend on the quality of the colleges' response to the complex challenges which lie before them.

In company with Ontario's other institutions of post-secondary education, the colleges of applied arts and technology must demonstrate that they can satisfy four conditions. First, they must maintain the support of knowledgeable and influential authorities in the public and private sectors. Second, they must develop a sense of internal cohesion by creating effective systems for the resolution of their own internal problems and the enhancement of their community life. Third, they must demonstrate that they are helping society to deal with its current and emerging problems. Finally, and perhaps most important of all, they must help their individual students and faculty members to develop their own abilities, skills, and sensitivities to the highest possible levels.

In our age of increasingly sophisticated technologies (both human and machine), the need to ensure that each student and each faculty member develops a sound, natural, and harmonious balance between rational and technical capacities on the one hand and intuitive and imaginative capacities on the other grows more urgent. The extent to which Ontario's new colleges are able to provide such a balance will determine in considerable measure whether or not their members and those with whom they live and work will be victims of the technical anesthesia and accompanying uncaringness which are so pervasive in the late 20th century.

Shortly after he graduated from Victoria College, **DELMAR McCORMACK SMYTH** established a successful electrical manufacturing business. After selling this enterprise, he spent five years in international trade development for the Government of Canada, served as director of admissions at the University of Toronto, and was the first Canadian to be appointed a senior member of Churchill College, Cambridge. He moved to York University in 1962, first as assistant to the president, then as dean of Atkinson College. He was also the first director of York's Centre for Continuing Education. Since 1970, he has taught full-time in the Social Science Department at Atkinson College. He is currently completing a two-volume history of the university as an intellectual and social institution in the Western world.

Regarding Ryerson through our backward prism
We find no madness in his Methodism,
But see in all those works he left behind
The logic of his energetic mind.
The House he built remains — though renovated
By many hands, as previously related;
Some minister, concerned to waterproof,
Deciding that he needs to raise the roof
Whereafter his successor with disdain
Decides she ought to lower it again.
Yet still there stands the ever open door
And cross the threshold still the children pour.
The teachers still their expertise bestow
And still the generations come and go.
And on foundations that still stand secure
The House that Ryerson built will long endure.

THE FUTURE OF THE HOUSE THAT RYERSON BUILT: ONTARIO EDUCATION IN THE 21ST CENTURY

IAN WINCHESTER

There are very few people of whom one can say that they influenced their age both widely and deeply. There are far fewer of whom one could say that they influenced the education of their age in this fashion. Perhaps the most striking example in modern times is Karl Wilhelm von Humbolt, who became the Prussian Minister of Public Instruction and Religion in 1808. Von Humbolt (a home educated polymath like his even more famous brother Alexander) was given free rein to completely restructure Prussian education from kindergarten through to university, and in a couple of years he practically invented an educational system which, when copied throughout the German princedoms, would reshape the face of the modern world. The scientific research university (initially the University of Berlin) tethered to the nation state was its pinnacle and chief result; and the two world wars with Germany were its chief 20th century manifestation, which, in its turn, has led to the universal spread of the scientific research university as the educational summit.

Ryerson's place in the history of education is not as grand as that of Von Humbolt. Rather, he is to be ranked with, perhaps, Horace Mann in Massachusetts and probably a notch above Kay Shuttleworth in England. But in many respects Ryerson, although located in the much humbler setting of 19th century Upper Canada, is a Humboltian figure. Like Von Humbolt, he shaped the face of Canadian universities (and not just Ontario ones) by being in at the creation of the University of Toronto as a non-sectarian, state-funded institution. Indeed, his contribution to its creation was decisive in that not only did he prevent, by argument and action, the provincial university becoming an Anglican foundation but also he managed to establish his own university, independently and before the University of Toronto was founded, thereby having something to donate (namely Victoria College) to the University when the time came for a federated university.

The school system which he founded and maintained between 1846 and 1876 was his chief ornament and his major legacy to our own age. In building it, he had looked at Horace Mann's Massachusetts and at Von Humbolt's Prussian school systems. He was influenced by both of these, and to some degree there are elements of them, borrowed by Ryerson, in the system which came to be Ontario's. But his work was for another place and a slightly different time, and Ryerson was a pragmatic man. He did not build on pedagogical principles or educational theory or even on

> **D**r. Ryerson's great success lay in his infinite ability to find practical ways to implement wonderful ideals.
>
> J. BASCOM ST. JOHN,
> (FROM *150 YEARS OF EDUCATIONAL PROGRESS, ONTARIO EDUCATION*, Vol. 1, No. 1, 1966)

curriculum content. Rather, he built on principles for the organization and maintenance of a vast, state-supported and state-guided educational system, which could be expected to work in Upper Canada and subsequently in Ontario. If Ryerson had been asked to talk about the future of education in Ontario, I think that he would have said that the future of education has nothing to do with *predictions* as to what will or is likely to happen. Rather, it has to do with the values which one chooses and with the will with which one holds to these. What is needed for the discussion of the future of an educational system is a striking picture of what is valuable and a discussion of how to sustain those things of value.

Ryerson's biographer, Nathaniel Burwash, who followed him as the Principal of Victoria College and was no mean educational figure himself, said this of the success of Ryerson's educational system:

> The simplicity, unity, and efficiency of this system are its highest praise. It was built upon no theory of education. It involved no complicated machinery. It was not unduly centralized. It involved the intelligent cooperation of the people of the whole country, and of all the bodies responsible for executive government and legislation. It thus made the schools at once the schools of the people, of the counties and of the province, almost compelling an interest in them at every point. But beyond this, its grand success – for its success everyone must acknowledge – depended in no small measure upon the energy, the wisdom, the administrative ability and the tireless energy of the grand personality who stood at its head as chief superintendent. (*Egerton Ryerson*, 1903)

What was it that Ryerson thought so valuable? And does that which he thought valuable remain so today? Is there any sense to the notion that the House that Ryerson built can, in the future, be rebuilt on the same foundations, the same values, which he and the majority of his generation held dear?

The principles to which I think he held are these: (1) the public educational system, from beginning to end, ought to be available to the whole people and be free; (2) the system should be centralized only insofar as is necessary to maintain high general standards of teacher preparation, textbook selection, curriculum content, and school organization – otherwise it should be locally controlled and popular; (3) the public educational system should be better in all respects than any rival system of private or religious schools – better facilities, better teachers, more up-to-date, and with higher standards; (4) the public educational system should be non-denominational, but should encourage generally subscribed-to Christian moral principles; and (5) the public school system should not discourage, but rather should directly encourage, patriotism.

In light of these principles, I think that one can make sense of many of Ryerson's otherwise apparently contradictory acts of educational diplomacy. For example, although he was a Methodist minister, he was among the first to encourage the Methodist university, which he had been instrumental in founding, to move to Toronto and to affiliate with the provincial, non-denominational university, the University of Toronto. As Chief Superintendent of Education, he constantly aided and abetted French- and German-speaking schools to maintain their status, in spite of his strongly avowed belief in the superiority of British traditions.

Similarly, he always tried to maintain a Roman Catholic bishop as a member of the Council of Public Instruction, which directed curricular and teaching standards for the public schools, even though he also aided the Roman Catholic party to set up separate schools and to gain tax concessions.

These apparently contradictory acts are, I think, all explicable in terms of Ryerson's attempt to maintain each of these principles to the highest degree possible. Thus centralized control and popularity can only be met when minority groups – French, German, and Roman Catholic in his day – are encouraged to maintain their own language or their own religious education in schools in which the general public standards are nonetheless maintained. Similarly, if the educational system is to be for all of the people, then the higher educational part of it cannot be splintered along denominational lines – Anglican, Presbyterian, Methodist, or Roman Catholic, to name the major denominational splits in his own day.

But can such principles – and I think it is reasonably clear that they are still the principles that we actually operate under today – continue to be maintained as embodying the genuinely valuable both for the present and for the long-term future? Let us take them one by one.

* * *

The Educational System Should Be Available to the Whole People and Be Free — In Ryerson's day, the notion that education provided by a public system should be available to the whole people and be free was a revolutionary notion which was sweeping Europe and North America. It is true that, for religious reasons, Scotland had a compulsory school system earlier than 1840; and in Sweden, there was a 200-year-old tradition of universal literacy by that time, also connected with the Protestant requirement that everyone should be able to read God's word for him- or herself. But with these exceptions, Ryerson's Upper Canada and Ontario were in at the beginning.

The notion of an educational system available to the whole people and free was not understood in 1840 (or, for that matter, in 1960) as meaning that everyone, regardless of age and means, should be able to go to school for as long as they liked or to study anything they liked. Simply, it meant that children six and over should be in school so many days each year in order that they should learn the rudiments of reading, of writing, of arithmetic, and of certain habits of conduct, these latter understood as being Christian habits. "The whole people" did not include the sick, the lame, the blind, or the deaf. Nor did it include adults who had happened to miss their elementary education. Also it was free

". . . *minority groups are encouraged to maintain their own language.* . . ."

> On the importance of education generally, we may remark it is as necessary as the light — it should be as common as water, and as free as air.... Education among the people is the best security of a good government and constitutional liberty; it yields a steady, unbending support to the former, and effectually protects the latter. An educated people are always a loyal people to good government; and the first object of a wise government should be the education of the people.
>
> EGERTON RYERSON
> (FROM AN EDITORIAL IN *THE CHRISTIAN GUARDIAN*, APRIL 1831)

only up to the grammar school level, and that only latterly. Initially, the local school boards were able to set a local fee schedule or to waive the fee in certain circumstances.

Does such a principle, suitably extended, serve for our own day? It seems to me that as an ideal it certainly does, and although there are some challenges to it at the moment, it is the principle which is and should be basic to the whole public educational system in Ontario. School in Ontario is still mainly for kids; and even the universities and community colleges are still mainly for kids – at least if one includes those between 18 and 21 or so within the meaning of the term. But the whole people – namely, people of all ages and with various abilities and disabilities – are increasingly able to find a place *in* the system rather than outside it.

In Ryerson's day one justified the tremendous public organization and expense of a public education system as necessary for the growth and maintenance of a democratic society – the whole people (in particular, the next generation) must be able to vote intelligently and to act in a publicly beneficial manner (get, keep, or create jobs; stay out of jail). The critics of such a system argued that educating the whole people was a great danger to public order – because educated people were a potentially revolutionary people. All the older hierarchies which were necessary for peace, order, and good government would be threatened by democratizing education. Also, inevitably, standards had to be lower in a public educational system than in a smaller more locally dedicated system based on class or religion or language or ethnic origin or the like.

In the event, the first 100 years of Ryerson's system, at least at the points at which the public system could be compared with the other competing arrangements, proved that not only was the public system not a danger to public order but, on the contrary, made an enormous contribution to it. Similarly, whenever the public system could be directly compared with its local competitors – for example, success in Grade 13 examinations when they were universal – it was better in all general respects and usually better individually as well. Even today on the few genuine opportunities for accurate and impartial comparison, such as the Sir Isaac Newton prize competition run by the University of Waterloo Physics Department, the collegiate institutes or high schools in the public system usually win both the team prize and the individual prize.

Thus, as an empirical matter, the free education of the whole people understood in Ryerson's terms is and has been a whopping success. The criticisms against the principle do not appear to have any validity whatsoever.

Can such a principle serve for the future of Ontario education? Understood in Ryerson's fashion, I don't think that it any longer can. In our own day, school, although it is for kids, is not any longer exclusively for kids. This is partly due to the fact of a radical redistribution of the age structure in our society, so that adults can no longer be expected to stay at one main job through their working lives. And it is also due to a change in expectations following a radically altered economic order.

Age structures can change rapidly, or at any rate within a 15-year period or so. But with no baby-boom in sight and a rapidly aging population, the kinds of pressure on adults for further education or for beginning all over again or for deepening the education which they already have seems likely to be a permanent feature of the Ontario scene. This process has, perhaps, gone farthest in our North Atlantic neighbor Iceland, where it is not uncommon for someone to be, say, a baker, a potter, and a city father; or say, a physicist, the head of the computing centre, a demographer, and perhaps a librarian – simultaneously. In Iceland, the pressure for this kind of thing is not only the low birth rate but also the problem of maintaining a highly sophisticated 20th century society with a population of 200,000 people or so – a kind of Greek city-state in the North Atlantic. It is the requirements of sophistication in the workplace which seem to me to be decisive in rejecting the principle of the free education of the whole people in Ryersonian terms for the future. Rather, the principle must be reinterpreted so that it means the free education of the whole people, where *the whole people* precludes sex, health, or age barriers, where *education* includes higher and advanced education, and where *free* means, at these higher levels, not only free but, perhaps, salaried as well.

In the first instance, this new or reinterpreted principle will remain an ideal. It will be some time before we are able, or feel ourselves able, to afford it. It will also be some time before we can conceptually grasp the notion of an education with no age, sex, or health barriers, since the notion of a public education being "for kids" is presently so deeply ingrained. And the notion of augmenting one's education as an adult as being of *public* benefit (an idea we have no difficulty with as regards schooling between 4 and 18) is, I suspect, not one that will be easily taken for granted.

*   *   *

The System Should Be Centralized Only as far as Is Necessary – Should "the free education of the whole people" in the sense I am advocating come about, it seems to me that it necessarily must put strain on Ryerson's second great principle. In Ryerson's day, distances were great, communications slow, and local communities strong and often very determined. For Ryerson, the only way (so he believed) that a strong public educational system with vigorous public support could come into being and remain in being was if local communities had a great deal of autonomy in making local arrangements for education. Thus the design of the school house, the particular teachers hired (or fired), the level of local taxation for the maintenance of the school and the like seemed to him to be essentially matters to be left up to local decision through duly elected representatives of the local population. At the same time, he believed that such local autonomy (not least because of the general poverty of the times and in some places) must be augmented by central and system-wide control on a few crucial matters. Thus in matters of standards and in the provisions for teacher preparation, for the selection of textbooks, and for the standard organization of the schools and school boards, central control was necessary. Also, because of the variability of local conditions and the capacity to tax, central funds would be necessary to bring all schools up to the same standard.

Again, I think, in all these matters Ryerson was right about the needs of his time. Had he attempted to impose a Prussian or French centralized system in Ontario, he would have been met by local revolt, not local cooperation. And had he not imposed system-wide standards for the training of teachers, for the selection of textbooks, for the inspection of schools (including the private ones), and the organization and operation of the local boards, there would have been a danger of anarchy or of extreme local incompetence or lack of interest.

But need we assent to such a principle of limited

centralization in our own day or for the foreseeable future? Were Ontario to become a homogeneous society of overwhelmingly similar language, ethnic origin, religion, and economic and class structure, there might be little harm in, or at any rate little grass-roots objection to, a highly centralized education system. Where presuppositions are shared, such things are possible. Continuous history or decisive revolution are helpful in leading to shared presuppositions. Russia after Lenin, France after Napoleon, Prussia probably both before and after Bismarck, and Cuba after Castro were places where the conditions for centralization were in place. But Ontario is not as Anglo-Saxon or as Protestant or as democratic or as economically egalitarian as it was in Ryerson's time. Revolution seems unlikely. *A fortiori*, limited centralization seems as imperative now as it was then, although the details have changed.

No one could have predicted in 1840 that Toronto would become a vast cosmopolitan city-state, a kind of fourth-century Athens of one hundred times greater extent and diversity transplanted to the late 20th century. Such a teeming metropolis is a babble of tongues each wishing to be maintained. Not so Pembroke or Arnprior or even Ottawa. Supposing a centralizing power were to impose a half-hour each day for the maintenance of the ancestral tongues in each and every school in the Province: in Toronto, the program might be a stunning success, whereas in many areas the ancestral tongue would have to be mediaeval Latin or Old Norse or Chaucerian English or Languedoc – which would not be the intent of such a dictate. Even in Toronto, such matters are intensely local – even block by block. But no central rule could cover the detailed local needs or do justice to them. The solution in France was to deny officially that anything but French was ever spoken in France – although in the south, in the Pyrenees, near the German border, and in the north west, indigenous tongues still struggle against central pressures to this day.

But if over-centralization has its present dangers, so too does complete local autonomy. On the one hand, one might suppose that schooling could be left to local block-by-block authority in a large city – for example, the autonomous neighborhood school. But in cities like Toronto, neighborhoods change composition rapidly. Not only do the number of children fluctuate wildly over a 10- or 20-year period but also the ethnic and religious compositions oscillate, shift, and whirl with every economic, political, or social change in the world at large or in the Ontario arena. Thus if block-by-block authority were the norm, educational practices, contents, standards, and aims could just as easily vary wildly block by block. On the other hand, while diversity has

". . . *whereas in many areas the ancestral tongue would have to be medieval Latin or Old Norse or Chaucerian English or Languedoc.*"

many merits, a democratic society requires some measure of standardization in its education if that democracy is to be maintained. Just as education is too important to be left to the individual teacher, so it is too important to be left to the individual neighborhood. Ryerson's compromise of variably-sized school districts as being the unit of local standardization is probably as good as any.

Ryerson's second great principle – that the public educational system of Ontario should be centralized only so far as is necessary to maintain high general standards of teacher preparation, textbook selection, curriculum content, and school organization – seems therefore, at least as regards the school system, to require no qualification whatsoever for the present and future age. There is, however, one feature of present circumstances which Ryerson's intentions did not cover.

The universities of Ontario, not just the provincial university, the University of Toronto, are now part of the publicly funded educational system of Ontario, as are the colleges of applied arts and technology. To what extent, if at all, ought Ryerson's principle be extended to apply to these institutions of the post-secondary educational system? Traditionally, universities have enjoyed an arms-length relationship with Government precisely because any form of centralized control has been seen as inimical to the proper functions of advanced teaching and research in the disciplines and professions. Universities only transmit definite curriculum content as a byproduct, so the argument goes. Their real function is to encourage thinking at the borderlines of human thought; and this is stifled by any kind of control which does not come from within.

In fact, although the universities are still remarkably autonomous, a certain amount of centralized control has begun to creep in. This is not as yet exercised by direct Government intervention. Rather, a buffer body (the Ontario Council of University Affairs) functions as an intermediary between the Government and the universities. This body tries to regulate such things as the size and shape of university funding formulae, the introduction of new programs at the graduate level, and the future specialization of various institutions in the "system."

There is little likelihood in the foreseeable future that any source other than Government-appropriated funds will be available for the running of the universities and colleges of Ontario. As a consequence, there will be continuing pressure on the universities and colleges to "serve the public" according to lights not necessarily those of the universities and colleges themselves. A university's prestige is, in part, connected with its having the capacity to teach in all subjects and disciplines and to do this through to the doctoral level. As a consequence, the natural tendency of any well-funded university is to expand both the number of its programs and the number of degree offerings in the programs which it has. Were each university run by funding from an enormously successful lottery, there would probably be no harm in this tendency. But given that funds are limited and the claimants many, some means of control over the unjustified proliferation of programs has probably to be exercised. Consequently, it does look as if Ryerson's second principle – that the public educational system should be centralized, but only as far as is necessary to maintain standards – must for the future be extended to include the universities and the colleges as well. Guidelines for legitimate central control, leaving all the remaining activities to the universities and the colleges, are urgently needed.

* * *

The Public Educational System Should Be Better in All Respects than Its Rivals – Perhaps the most remarkable accomplishment of public education in Ontario (and, for that matter, in Canada) is that, by and large, it has been superior to all its rivals. There may be reasons why a boy or girl might be sent to a private school – for linguistic, ethnic, social, or other reasons. But in Ontario, it would be hard to argue that

MTL T11671

A monument to Egerton Ryerson stands outside the Ryerson Polytechnical Institute, formally the Toronto Normal School

the best teachers, the best facilities, and the highest standards were not to be found in the public system during the great majority of the years from 1840 to the present day. To a considerable extent, this is due to the successful application of Ryerson's first two principles. The public system has been available to the whole people and free. And it has been centrally guided but locally controlled. The vigor of the popular interest in the schools which these two principles helped to engender meant that it was relatively easy to raise the taxes to build and maintain splendid schools, to train and hire increasingly well qualified teachers, and to equip the schools with increasingly better laboratories, shops, libraries, auditoria and music rooms, playing fields, gymnasia, and swimming pools.

Is there any reason now to discourage the principle of the clear superiority of the public system? In Britain and the United States, where private schools maintain higher prestige than the public schools and where the facilities which have accumulated over the centuries are often better than any publicly funded school can match, no principle like Ryerson's could be implemented save by a revolution. In Ontario, the private schools tend to be associated with special purposes – perhaps music or dance (as at the National Ballet School) – or discipline is strict or the sciences are emphasized. Some, like Upper Canada College, enjoy fine facilities, a good teaching staff, and a connection with the economic elite of Canada. Others, like the Toronto French School, emphasize a bilingual French and English education and offer preparation for a variety of high school graduation possibilities – Ontario Grade 13, the English A-Levels, the International Baccalaureate.

Such schools are often as good as, and in some respects better than, their public school counterparts in various specialized ways. But even if all such schools were better than their public school counterparts, this would be no reason to abandon the principle that the public schools should *aim* to be better than any possible rivals. And Ontario is certainly one of the few places in the English-speaking world where this has usually been true and always has been feasible.

At the level of the colleges and universities of Ontario, there are no alternatives to the publicly funded institutions. But it is not so long ago that, with the exception of the University of Toronto, all of the universities of Ontario were privately funded by religious bodies and by the collection of fees from their students. During the earlier period, Ryerson's principle certainly held with respect to the publicly funded University; it was in all respects clearly superior to its rivals across the board. If that is not so today, it is probably due to public funds as much as to anything else.

As regards the future, even were that future to hold privately endowed universities in its shadowy mists, there is no reason to think that one should not abide by the principle that the publicly funded universities ought to be superior to any such private rivals. So I think that there is no reason to weaken in any way Ryerson's third great principle. The public educational system should be better in all respects than any rival system both now and in the future.

* * *

The Public Educational System Should Be Non-Denominational – For Ryerson, this principle was a corollary of the first three principles. No denominational system could be for the whole people. Nor would it be possible to exert that minimum of central control which would see it as better than its rivals – presumably non-denominational private schools. In his own day, the various Protestant sects were warring with one another and with the Roman Catholics. There were virtually no other sects to consider. Consequently, he conceived of the public system as founded on non-denominational yet Christian principles. In the event, this proved to be a successful formula. Even the Roman Catholic population has heavily supported the public system over the century and more in which Ryerson's system has been in place, although a certain Catholic element has continued to press for stronger parochial schools. To some extent, success has been due to the actual legislation, which made better financial provisions available to the public system than any of its potential religious rivals could muster. But mainly, I think, it has been due to the genuine insight that a public system could not be established on denominational principles without internecine strife and highly variable standards of instruction. The history of such systems in Newfoundland and Quebec tends to bear out this observation.

In his own day, Ryerson also extended this principle to the university. Even when Victoria College was not a part of the University of Toronto, Ryerson believed that admission should in no way be based on membership in the Methodist church. And as regards the provincial University, the history of strife between his own denomination and the Anglicans over the educational land reserves had convinced him of the destructiveness of any denominational principle in higher educational organization as well. Universities, too, must be for the education of the whole people.

Can one give any plausible reasons for abandoning the non-denominational principle in public education today? Today there is much more religious and sectarian diversity in Ontario than in Ryerson's day, reflecting the varied ethnic mix in the Province and the mushrooming of sects within specific religions. Certainly Ontario could have a denominational system of schools, but it would hardly be a public one in any significant sense of that term. It would be a system of bitter little solitudes rather than an education for the whole people. Obviously then, great religious diversity is no argument for abandoning the non-denominational principle in public education. On the contrary, it is probably one of the strongest reasons for maintaining it.

* * *

The Public School System Should Directly Encourage Patriotism – In Ryerson's day, a significant problem in perpetuating Canada's existence – whether West or East, whether Upper or Lower, whether Confederated or not – was the tremendous draw of the United States, both its principles and its form of government. Ryerson thus saw the public school system as the main vehicle for fostering that healthy patriotism which would maintain Canada as an independent entity – much the same vision which René Lévesque has today for the role of the Quebec school system, albeit to serve another purpose. If there has been any lapsing since Ryerson's day, it has probably been with respect to the direct fostering of patriotism. Our textbooks have only nominal Canadian content and our British historical past has been nearly lost via the choice of textbooks. Commissions and surveys and doctoral theses continue to show how badly we perform in this regard. Yet it seems clear that a country cannot be maintained without "love of country" on the part of

---

My book *The Schools of Ontario 1876-1976* had been published by the University of Toronto Press in the spring of 1982, and the reviews were starting to appear in the journals and magazines. Most of the reviews were quite thorough and contained a good mix of praise and criticism. But the most unusual review appeared in an Ontario teachers' newsletter. This particular reviewer had nothing but criticism. His sharp barbs came in machine gun-like order. The book was too long. Didn't I know that teachers were too busy to read 300 pages of text? The book did not contain enough pictures. Didn't I know that teachers were visually oriented? The book was too expensive. Why was I charging $29.95 and not even providing a dust jacket? Worst of all, the book did not focus on Egerton Ryerson. Didn't I know that everything in Ontario education had been determined by Ryerson? For all time!

ROBERT M. STAMP,
WRITER AND BOOKSELLER

the population. Patriotism in the schools probably reached its peak during and shortly after the Second World War. But heavy post-war immigration from all over the world has tended to weaken the short-lived picture of a remarkably homogeneous country – British in origin and principles – and replaced it with a strictly cosmopolitan, North American agglomeration of city-states north of the undefended border. In such conditions, while healthy patriotism is probably more important than ever to foster, it is also exceedingly difficult to bring off without resentment. Not everyone who came to Canada came for love of Canada. Many were displaced; and justifiably, such people long for their homeland. Yet Canada as a nation, and Ontario as a province, cannot in the long run be composed of people longing for their homelands. Its youth and, just as important, its elderly should love Canada as no other. As Ryerson realized, the schools have a role to play here; although if it is to be a successful role, it must not be a crude or blatant one.

Must the universities, too, directly encourage patriotism? I think not. Universities are essentially international vehicles for scholarship and research which happen to be funded for our age by nation-states. They should, perhaps, not be subversive, but they cannot be directly patriotic. It is therefore only the last of Ryerson's principles which cannot be extended to include the universities.

In sum, then, Ryerson's five great principles are not only very successful principles for the past and of considerable use in the present but also, when suitably modified, they are sound principles for the future. For it seems clear that our public educational system should, in the future, be freely available to the whole people; be centralized only where necessary; be better than any rival system in every respect; be non-denominational; and, where it can, encourage a healthy patriotism. If we could ensure the observance of these principles, Ontario's educational system would enjoy a promising future.

IAN WINCHESTER was born in 1940 in a Hudson's Bay trading post in northern Alberta. He spent much of his early childhood in Newfoundland, where he remembers the foghorns and a hospital run by nuns in which he almost succumbed to pneumonia. After the war, he moved back to northern Alberta, where he went to a variety of one and two room schools. He has worked as a surveyor, swimming instructor, control laboratory chemist, and physicist; but having been converted to philosophy and not having anything else to do with a couple of degrees in the subject from Oxford, he now teaches at OISE.

Key to Credits
AO   Archives of Ontario
MTL   Metropolitan Toronto Library
PAC   Public Archives Canada